CliffsNotes®
Geometry
Common Core
Quick Review

CliffsNotes®
Geometry
Common Core
Quick Review

By M. Sunil R. Koswatta, Ph.D.

Houghton Mifflin Harcourt
Boston • New York

About the Author

M. Sunil R. Koswatta, Ph.D., Mathematics, has been an educator for 25 years. Dr. Koswatta was a member of the EngageNY Common Core curriculum writing team. He is currently a professor of Mathematics at Harper College in Illinois.

Acknowledgments

I would like to thank the author of *CliffsNotes Geometry Quick Review* (1st edition), Ed Kohn, MS, for his invaluable contributions to this project.

Dedication

I would like to dedicate this book to Professor Hung-Hsi Wu of the University of California, Berkeley. The definition of the slope of a line in this book is an invention of Professor Wu.

Editorial

Executive Editor: Greg Tubach
Senior Editor: Christina Stambaugh
Production Editor: Erika West
Copy Editor: Lynn Northrup
Technical Editors: Mary Jane Sterling and Tom Page
Proofreader: Pamela Weber-Leaf
Indexer: Potomac Indexing, LLC

CliffsNotes® Geometry Common Core Quick Review

Library of Congress Control Number: 2017934409
ISBN: 978-0-544-78508-3 (pbk)

Printed in the United States of America
DOC 10 9 8 7 6 5 4 3 2 1

For information about permission to reproduce selections from this book, write to trade.permissions@hmhco.com or to Permissions, Houghton Mifflin Harcourt Publishing Company, 3 Park Avenue, 19th Floor, New York, New York 10016.

www.hmhco.com

Table of Contents

Introduction..1
   Common Core State Standards for Mathematics (CCSSM) 1
   Connecting to Common Core Mathematics 2
   Why You Need This Book.....................................3
   How to Use This Book 3
   Hundreds of Practice Questions Online!.........................4

Chapter 1: Fundamental Ideas 5
   Points, Lines, and Planes....................................6
      Point 6
      Line 6
      Plane 7
      Set 7
   Postulates and Theorems 7
   Segments, Midpoints, and Rays...............................9
      Line segment 9
      Midpoint 10
      Ray..11
   Angles 11
      Adjacent angles....................................13
   Circles...13
      Central angles, sectors, and arcs 13
   Special Angles 15
      Right angle..15
      Acute angle..15
      Obtuse angle.......................................16
      Complementary angles 17
      Supplementary angles..............................18
   Parallel, Intersecting, and Perpendicular Lines.................19
      Parallel lines in a plane 19
      Intersecting lines..................................19
      Perpendicular lines 20
      Angle bisector and perpendicular bisector.............21
   Triangles, Quadrilaterals, and Polygons.......................21
      Special triangles and quadrilaterals 23

Chapter 2: Basic Rigid Motions 25
   Rotations...26
      Counterclockwise rotation ρ of θ degrees around O 26
      Clockwise rotation ρ of θ degrees around O 26
   Transversals...30
   Reflections..36
   Translations...37

Chapter 3: Triangles and Congruence **41**

  Exterior Angle of a Triangle. 42

  Angle Sum of a Triangle 44

  Classifying Triangles by Sides or Angles 44

    Special names for sides and angles. 45

  Altitudes, Medians, and Angle Bisectors 46

    Base and altitude. 46

    Median. 47

    Angle bisector. 48

  Special Features of Isosceles Triangles 48

  Triangle Inequalities Regarding Sides and Angles 51

  The Triangle Inequality Theorem 52

  The Concept of Congruence 53

  Corresponding Parts of Triangles 55

    Congruence theorems of triangles. 55

Chapter 4: Polygons **65**

  Triangulation of a Polygon and the Sum of the Interior Angles 65

  Exterior Angles of a Convex Polygon. 67

  Regular Polygons. 69

  Parallelograms 70

    Rectangles. 72

    Rhombus 72

  Trapezoids. 74

    The Midpoint Theorem 77

  Concurrence Theorems 78

Chapter 5: Similarity. **83**

  Dilation. 84

  The Fundamental Theorem of Similarity 85

  The Definition of Similarity 88

  Similar Triangles 89

  Applications of Similarity 92

  Proportional Parts of Similar Triangles 97

  Pythagorean Theorem 98

Chapter 6: Circles **103**

  Parts of Circles 103

  Arcs. 104

  Arcs and Inscribed Angles 110

  Concyclic Points 117

  Segments of Intersecting Chords and Tangents. 121

Chapter 7: Length and Area. **127**

  Length of a Line Segment 128

  Length of a Polygonal Curve. 129

  Squares and Rectangles 130

Triangles. 134
   Right triangles 134
   Arbitrary triangles. 135
Parallelograms 137
Trapezoids. 138
Regular Polygons. 140
   Parts of a regular polygon 140
   Finding the perimeter. 141
   Finding the area 141
   Effect of a dilation of scale factor r on the area of a polygon 142
Area and Circumference of a Circle. 143
Summary of Perimeter, Circumference, and Area Formulas 148

Chapter 8: Geometric Solids. 151

Prisms. 151
Right Prisms 152
   Lateral area of a right prism 152
   Total surface area of a right prism. 153
   Interior space of a solid. 154
Right Circular Cylinders 156
Pyramids. 158
   Regular pyramids 158
Right Circular Cones. 161
Spheres 164
Summary of Lateral Area, Total Area, and Volume Formulas 165

Chapter 9: Coordinate Geometry 167

One-Dimensional Distance Formula. .171
Two-Dimensional Distance Formula .171
Midpoint Formula for One-Dimensional Space 174
Midpoint Formula for Two-Dimensional Space 174
Equation of a Circle 176
Lines on a Coordinate Plane 178
The Slope Theorem 180
   Slopes of parallel lines. 184
   Slopes of perpendicular lines. 187
Linear Equations in x and y 190
Summary of Coordinate Geometry Formulas 199

Review Questions. 201

Glossary 213

Appendix: Postulates and Theorems 221

Postulates 221
Theorems. 222
   Chapter 1: Fundamental Ideas 222

Chapter 2: Basic Rigid Motions 223
Chapter 3: Triangles and Congruence 224
Chapter 4: Polygons.....................................226
Chapter 5: Similarity 227
Chapter 6: Circles.....................................229
Chapter 7: Length and Area 231
Chapter 8: Geometric Solids.............................232
Chapter 9: Coordinate Geometry........................234

Index..**237**

INTRODUCTION

Teachers and students alike will find *CliffsNotes Geometry Common Core Quick Review* to be a valuable course supplement. Many students planning to take standardized college admission tests or to pursue careers requiring more advanced mathematics and physics overlook the significant role of geometry in these undertakings. Whether you are looking for an in-depth reference or occasional reinforcement of one or more aspects of geometry, it is contained in this book. This book helps you get ready for success on the mathematics portion of standardized tests or in the more advanced mathematics and science courses required for careers in mathematics, the sciences, and engineering.

CliffsNotes Geometry Common Core Quick Review begins with undefined terms, definitions, and assumptions; these lead to theorems and constructions. Geometry is an abstract subject but is easy to visualize, and it has many concrete practical applications. Historically, geometry has long been important for its role in the surveying of land. More recently, our knowledge of geometry has been applied to help build structurally sound bridges, experimental space stations, large athletic and entertainment arenas, and more.

The prerequisites for geometry comprehension include familiarity with basic arithmetic operations and with some topics from introductory algebra. The arithmetic prerequisites include converting fractions to decimals, converting improper fractions to mixed numbers, and calculating square roots. The algebraic prerequisites include adding equations, solving linear equations in two variables for one variable in terms of the other, and factoring quadratic equations.

If you feel that you need additional review in any of these topics, refer to *CliffsNotes Basic Math and Pre-Algebra Quick Review* or *CliffsNotes Algebra I Common Core Quick Review*.

Common Core State Standards for Mathematics (CCSSM)

CliffsNotes Geometry Common Core Quick Review topics are aligned to the Common Core State Standards for Mathematics (CCSSM)—the skills you should know and be able to perform in geometry. The concepts presented in this book are closely interrelated with a broader set of Common Core Mathematics conceptual categories:

- Numbers and quantity
- Algebra
- Functions
- Modeling
- Geometry
- Statistics and probability

The CCSSM define what you should know and what you should be able to execute using an integrated approach from each of these domains that builds upon your strengths to critically think at a higher level of mathematics.

Connecting to Common Core Mathematics

CliffsNotes Geometry Common Core Quick Review gives you conceptual approaches to increase your knowledge, fluency, and skills in higher-level mathematics and real-world geometry applications. The standards of mathematical practices are observed in each chapter. In particular, the following Common Core State Standards math practices, MP3 and MP6, are relevant to geometry.

Construct viable arguments and critique the reasoning of others (MP3). Mathematically proficient students understand and use stated assumptions, definitions, and previously established results in constructing arguments. They make conjectures and build a logical progression of statements to explore the truth of their conjectures. They are able to analyze situations by breaking them into cases and can recognize and use counterexamples. They justify their conclusions, communicate them to others, and respond to the arguments of others. Students in all grades can listen to or read the arguments of others, decide whether they make sense, and ask useful questions to clarify or improve the arguments.

Attend to precision (MP6). Mathematically proficient students try to communicate precisely to others. They try to use clear definitions in discussion with others and in their own reasoning. They state the meaning of the symbols they choose, including using the equal sign consistently and appropriately. They are careful about specifying units of measure and labeling axes to clarify the correspondence with quantities in a problem.

They calculate accurately and efficiently and express numerical answers with a degree of precision appropriate for the problem context. In the elementary grades, students give carefully formulated explanations to each other. By the time they reach high school, they have learned to examine claims and make explicit use of definitions.

Why You Need This Book

Can you answer "yes" to any of the following questions?

- Do you need to review the fundamentals of geometry fast?

- Do you need a course supplement to geometry?

- Do you need to prepare for your geometry test?

- Do you need a concise, comprehensive reference for geometry?

- Do you need practice with real-life applications of geometry topics?

If so, then *CliffsNotes Geometry Common Core Quick Review* is for you!

How to Use This Book

Because mathematics builds on itself, many readers benefit most from studying or reviewing this book from cover to cover. However, you're the boss here, and you may choose to seek only the information you want and then put the book back on the shelf for later use. In that case, here are a few recommended ways to search for geometry topics:

- Look for your topic in the table of contents or use the index to find specific topics.

- Flip through the book, looking for subject areas by headings.

- Get a glimpse of what you'll gain from a chapter by reading through the "Chapter Check-In" and "Common Core Standard" references at the beginning of each chapter.

- Use the "Chapter Check-Out" at the end of each chapter to gauge your grasp of the important information you need to know.

- Test your knowledge more completely in the "Review Questions" (pp. 201–212).

- Look in the glossary (pp. 213–220) for important terms and definitions.

- Review the theorems and postulates in the appendix (pp. 221–235).

Geometry Theorems

There are numerous geometry theorems given in this book. They are numbered for organizational purposes. For example, *Theorem 2.2* is the second theorem given in Chapter 2. Study these theorems by their content, not by their number, as the theorem numbering has no significance outside of this book. As a handy study reference, the theorems are compiled in the appendix (pp. 222–235).

Geometry Postulates

There are several geometry postulates given in this book as well. They are sequentially numbered for organizational purposes. As a handy study reference, the postulates are also compiled in the appendix (pp. 221–222).

Hundreds of Practice Questions Online!

Go to CliffsNotes.com for hundreds of additional Geometry Common Core practice questions to help you prepare for your next quiz or test. The questions are organized by this book's chapter sections, so it is easy to use the book and then quiz yourself online to make sure you know the subject. Visit CliffsNotes.com to test yourself anytime and find other free homework help.

Chapter 1

FUNDAMENTAL IDEAS

Chapter Check-In

❑ Understanding what is meant by point, line, and plane

❑ Knowing the relationship between postulates and theorems

❑ Computing the midpoint of a line segment

❑ Identifying right, acute, obtuse, and straight angles as well as complementary angles, supplementary angles, and vertical angles

❑ Understanding the parts of a circle

❑ Identifying parallel lines and perpendicular lines

❑ Identifying angle bisectors and perpendicular bisectors

❑ Identifying triangles, quadrilaterals, and polygons

Common Core Standard: Congruence, Proof, and Constructions

Know precise definitions of angle, circle, perpendicular lines, parallel lines, and line segment based on the undefined notions of point, line, distance along a line, and distance around a circular arc (G.CO.1).

Geometry was the first system of ideas in which a few simple statements were assumed and then used to derive more complex ones. A system such as this is referred to as a deductive system. Geometry introduces you to the ideas of deduction and logical consequences, ideas you will continue to use throughout your life.

Geometry Theorems

The geometry theorems in this book are numbered for organizational purposes. For example, *Theorem 2.2* is the second theorem given in Chapter 2. Study these theorems by their content, not by their number, as the theorem numbering has no significance outside of this book.

Points, Lines, and Planes

Point, line, plane, and *set* are the undefined terms that provide the starting place for geometry. When words are defined, we ordinarily use simpler words, and these simpler words are in turn defined using yet simpler words. This process must eventually terminate. At some point, the definition must use an acceptable meaning for a word that is intuitively clear. Because that meaning is accepted without definition, we refer to these words as *undefined terms.* The following three undefined terms will be used in defining other terms. Although these terms are not formally defined, a brief intuitive discussion is needed.

Point

A **point** is the most fundamental object in geometry. It is represented by a dot and named by a capital letter. A point represents position only; it has zero size (that is, zero length, zero width, and zero height). The following figure illustrates points C, M, and Q.

$$\bullet \; M$$
$$\bullet \qquad\qquad \bullet \, Q$$
$$C$$

Line

A **line** (*straight line*) can be thought of as a connected set of infinitely many points. It extends infinitely far in two opposite directions. A line has infinite length, zero width, and zero height. Any two points on the line name it. The symbol $\longrightarrow$ written on top of two letters is used to denote that line. A line may also be named by one small letter, as shown below.

$$\xleftarrow{\quad\underset{A}{\bullet}\quad\underset{B}{\bullet}\quad}\longrightarrow$$

This is line AB.
It is written as $\overleftrightarrow{AB}$.

$$\ell \longleftrightarrow$$

This is line ℓ.

Collinear points

Points that lie on the same line are called **collinear points.** If there is no line on which all of the points lie, then they are **noncollinear points.** In the following figures, points M, A, and N are collinear, and points T, I, and C are noncollinear.

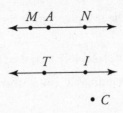

Plane

A **plane** may be considered an infinite set of points forming a connected flat surface extending infinitely far in all directions. A plane has infinite length, infinite width, and zero height (or thickness). It is usually represented in drawings by a four-sided figure. A single capital letter is used to denote a plane. As shown in the figures below, the word *plane* is written with the letter so as not to be confused with a point.

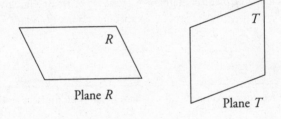

Plane *R*

Plane *T*

Set

A **set** is a collection of points. Examples of sets are line segments, lines, and planes. A *subset* of a set is either the whole set or just a part of it. For example, a line segment on a line is a subset of the line and a line on a plane is a subset of the plane.

Postulates and Theorems

A **postulate** is a statement that is assumed true without proof. A **theorem** is a true statement that can be proven. Listed below are six postulates and the theorems that can be proven from these postulates.

Postulate 1: A line contains at least two points.

Postulate 2: A plane contains at least three noncollinear points.

Postulate 3: Through any two points, there is exactly one line.

Postulate 4: Through any three noncollinear points, there is exactly one plane.

Postulate 5: If two points lie in a plane, then the line joining them lies in that plane.

Postulate 6: If two different planes intersect, then their intersection is a line.

Theorem 1.1: If two different lines intersect, then they intersect in exactly one point.

Theorem 1.2: If a point lies outside a line, then exactly one plane contains both the line and the point.

Theorem 1.3: If two different lines intersect, then exactly one plane contains both lines.

Example 1: State the postulate or theorem you would use to justify the statement made about each figure.

There is exactly one plane containing points *A*, *B*, and *C*.

．*A*   ．*B*

．*C*

(a)

There is exactly one line passing through points *Q* and *T*.

Q．

．*T*

(b)

The line $\overleftrightarrow{KL}$ lies on plane *P*.

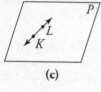

(c)

Planes *G* and *H* intersect along line ℓ.

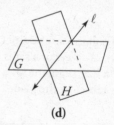

(d)

There is at least one more point on line *m*, besides point *W*.

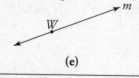

(e)

There is exactly one plane containing lines *n* and ℓ.

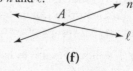

(f)

There is exactly one plane containing line $\overleftrightarrow{AC}$ and point *B*.

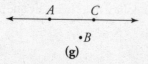

(g)

Lines ℓ and *m* intersect at point *M* and at no other point.

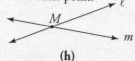

(h)

(a) Through any three noncollinear points, there is exactly one plane (*Postulate 4*).

(b) Through any two points, there is exactly one line (*Postulate 3*).

(c) If two points lie in a plane, then the line joining them lies in that plane (*Postulate 5*).

(d) If two different planes intersect, then their intersection is a line (*Postulate 6*).

(e) A line contains at least two points (*Postulate 1*).

(f) If two different lines intersect, then exactly one plane contains both lines (*Theorem 1.3*).

(g) If a point lies outside a line, then exactly one plane contains both the line and the point (*Theorem 1.2*).

(h) If two lines intersect, then they intersect in exactly one point (*Theorem 1.1*).

Segments, Midpoints, and Rays

The concept of lines has already been introduced, but much of geometry is concerned with portions of lines. Some of those portions are so special that they have their own names and symbols.

Line segment

A **line segment** is a connected piece of a line. It has two endpoints and is named by its endpoints. Sometimes, the symbol $\overline{}$ written on top of two letters is used to denote the segment. Line segment CD is shown below.

It is written $\overline{CD}$. (Technically, $\overline{CD}$ refers to the points C and D and all the points between them, and CD without the $\overline{}$ refers to the distance from C to D.) Note that $\overline{CD}$ is a piece of line $\overleftrightarrow{AB}$.

Postulate 7 (Ruler Postulate): Each point on a line can be paired with exactly one real number called its **coordinate.** The distance between two points is the positive difference of their coordinates (see the following figure). ***Note:*** The capital letters are the names of the points, and the lowercase letters are their respective coordinates.

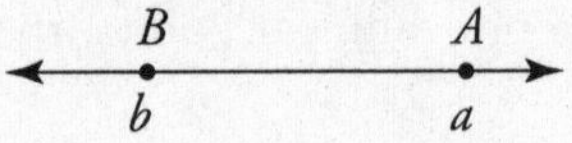

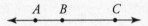

If $a > b$, then $AB = a - b$.

Example 2: Find the length of $\overline{QU}$ in the following figure.

The length of $\overline{QU}$ is 8.

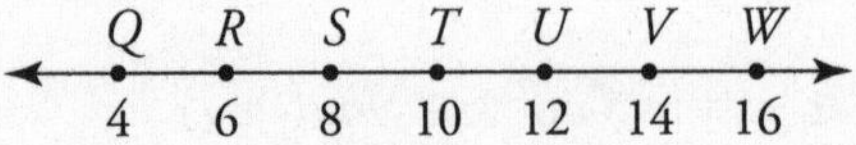

$$QU = 12 - 4$$
$$QU = 8$$

Postulate 8 (Segment Addition Postulate): If B lies between A and C on a line, then $AB + BC = AC$ (see the following figure).

Example 3: In the following figure, point A lies between points C and T. Find the length of $\overline{CT}$ if $CA = 5$ and $AT = 8$.

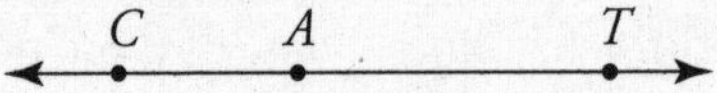

Because A lies between C and T, *Postulate 8* tells you

$$CA + AT = CT$$
$$5 + 8 = 13$$
$$CT = 13$$

Midpoint

A **midpoint of a line segment** is the halfway point, or the point equidistant from the endpoints. In the figure below, R is the midpoint of $\overline{QS}$ because $QR = RS$ or because $QR = \frac{1}{2} QS$ or $RS = \frac{1}{2} QS$.

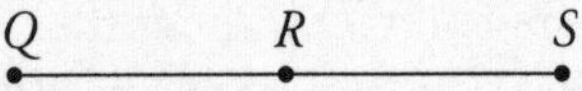

Example 4: In the following figure, find the midpoint of $\overline{KR}$.

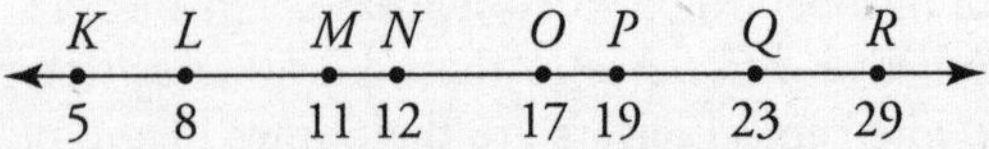

$$KR = 29 - 5 \text{ or } KR = 24$$

The midpoint of $\overline{KR}$ would be $\frac{1}{2}(24)$ or 12 spaces from either K or R. Because the coordinate of K is 5 and it is smaller than the coordinate of R (which is 29), to get the coordinate of the midpoint you could either add 12 to 5 or subtract 12 from 29. In either case, you determine that the coordinate of the midpoint is 17. That means that point O is the midpoint of $\overline{KR}$ because $KO = OR$.

Another way to get the coordinate of the midpoint would be to find the average of the endpoint coordinates. To find the average of two numbers, you find their sum and divide by 2: $(5 + 29) \div 2 = 17$. The coordinate of the midpoint is 17, so the midpoint is point O.

Theorem 1.4: A line segment has exactly one midpoint.

Ray

A **ray** is also a piece of a line, except that it has only one endpoint and continues forever in one direction. It could be thought of as a half-line with an endpoint. The endpoint of a ray is called its **vertex.** A ray is named by using letters to identify the vertex and any other point on the ray. The symbol $\longrightarrow$ written on top of the two letters is used to denote that ray, and the endpoint is always listed first. The following is ray AB. It is written as $\overrightarrow{AB}$.

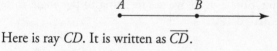

Here is ray CD. It is written as $\overrightarrow{CD}$.

Angles

Easily as significant as rays and line segments are the angles that they form. Without them, there would be none of the geometric figures that you know (with the possible exception of the circle).

A subset, R, of a plane is called *convex* if the given two points A and B in R, the line segment $\overline{AB}$, lies completely in R.

Two rays that have the same vertex form an **angle.** That common vertex of the two rays is called the **vertex** of the angle and the rays are called **sides of the angle.** The angle formed by two rays $\overrightarrow{OA}$ and $\overrightarrow{OB}$ is denoted by $\angle AOB$. If the points A, O, and B are collinear, then the angle is a **straight angle,** as shown in the following figure. If rays $\overrightarrow{OA}$ and $\overrightarrow{OB}$ coincide, then the angle is a *zero angle.*

The symbol ∠ is used to denote an angle. An angle can be named in various ways. For example, in the following figures, there are three different methods for naming the angle.

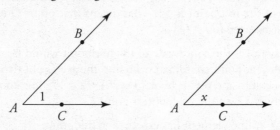

- By the letter of the vertex: ∠A.

- By the number (or small letter) in its interior: ∠1 or ∠x.

- By the letters of three points that form it: ∠BAC or ∠CAB. *Note:* The center letter is always the letter of the vertex.

Consider the angles ∠AOB in the following figures. Two angles can be located in the given shaded areas. The angle in the figure on the left is at most 180°, while the angle in the figure on the right is at least 180°. It is possible that both angles are 180°. In order to avoid ambiguity, from now on when we use the notation ∠AOB, we are referring to the angle with measure less than or equal to 180°.

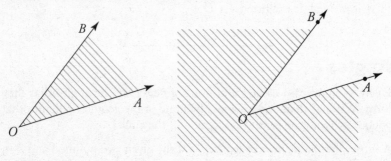

Convex region of ∠AOB
(at most 180°)

Nonconvex region of ∠AOB
(at least 180°)

Example 5: For the following figure,

(a) use three letters to rename ∠3

(b) use one number to rename ∠KMJ

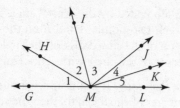

(a) ∠3 is the same as ∠IMJ or ∠JMI.

(b) ∠KMJ is the same as ∠4.

Adjacent angles

Adjacent angles are any two angles that share a common side separating the two angles and that share a common vertex. In the following figure, ∠1 and ∠2 are adjacent angles.

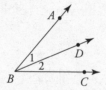

Circles

The collection of all points in a plane (with a fixed distance *r* from a fixed point *O* in the plane) is called the **circle** with **center** *O* and **radius** *r*. A circle with radius 1 is called a **unit circle.** Any line segment whose endpoints lie on a circle is called a **chord.** Any chord that passes through the center of the circle is called the **diameter** of the circle. The region within the circle together with the circle is called the *closed disk of the given circle*. In this guide, however, we will refer to the closed disk of a circle as "circle" when there is no confusion by doing so.

Central angles, sectors, and arcs

Central angles are angles formed by any two radii in a circle. The vertex of the central angle is the center of the circle. In the following figure, ∠AOB is a central angle.

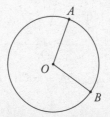

The **arc** *AB* of a circle subtended by the central angle $\angle AOB$ is the portion of the circle between two points *A* and *B* on the circle, within the angle $\angle AOB$. The region of the closed disk of the circle within the angle $\angle AOB$ is called the **sector** of the circle with central angle $\angle AOB$.

Postulate 9 (Protractor Postulate): If the distance around a unit circle is made into 360 adjacent arcs of equal length, then the central angle whose rays pass through the ends of any one of these arcs will have a measure of one **degree.** The symbol for degree is °. The measure of an angle is often denoted by $m\angle$. The measure of the zero angle is 0°, and the measure of the straight angle is 180°. If $\angle AOC$ and $\angle COB$ are adjacent angles, then $m\angle AOC + m\angle COB = m\angle AOB$.

A *protractor* is a geometrical instrument that represents half of a circle, where the semicircular arc is calibrated to show the degrees from 0 to 180. Using the Protractor Postulate, place the protractor so that the center of the protractor coincides with the vertex *O* of the angle $\angle AOB$, as shown in the following figure.

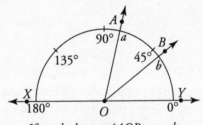

If $a < b$, then $m\angle AOB = a - b$.

Example 6: In the figure below, find the following:

(a) $m\angle SON$

(b) $m\angle ROT$

(c) $m\angle MOE$

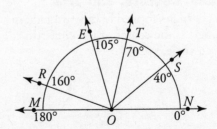

(a) $m\angle SON = 40° - 0°$ or $m\angle SON = 40°$

(b) $m\angle ROT = 160° - 70°$ or $m\angle ROT = 90°$

(c) $m\angle MOE = 180° - 105°$ or $m\angle MOE = 75°$

Example 7: In the following figure, if $m\angle 1 = 32°$ and $m\angle 2 = 45°$, find $m\angle NEC$.

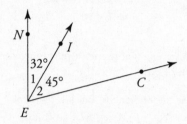

Because ray $\overrightarrow{EI}$ is between rays $\overrightarrow{EN}$ and $\overrightarrow{EC}$, angles 1 and 2 are adjacent angles.

$$m\angle 1 + m\angle 2 = m\angle NEC$$
$$32° + 45° = m\angle NEC$$
$$m\angle NEC = 77°$$

Special Angles

Certain angles are given special names based on their measures.

Right angle

A **right angle** has a measure of 90°. The symbol ⌐ in the interior of an angle designates the fact that a right angle is formed. In the following figure, $\angle ABC$ is a right angle.

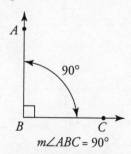

$m\angle ABC = 90°$

Acute angle

An **acute angle** is any angle whose measure is positive and less than 90°. In the following figure, $\angle b$ is acute.

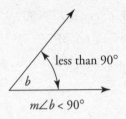

$$m\angle b < 90°$$

Obtuse angle

An **obtuse angle** is an angle whose measure is more than 90° but less than 180°. In the following figure, ∠4 is obtuse.

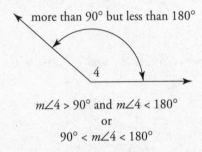

$$m\angle 4 > 90° \text{ and } m\angle 4 < 180°$$
$$\text{or}$$
$$90° < m\angle 4 < 180°$$

Example 8: In the following figure, identify each named angle as acute, right, obtuse, or straight:

(a) ∠BFD

(b) ∠AFE

(c) ∠BFC

(d) ∠DFA

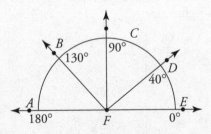

(a) $m\angle BFD = 90°$ (130° − 40° = 90°), so ∠BFD is a right angle.

(b) $m\angle AFE = 180°$, so ∠AFE is a straight angle.

(c) $m\angle BFC = 40°$ (130° − 90° = 40°), so ∠BFC is an acute angle.

(d) $m\angle DFA = 140°$ (180° − 40° = 140°), so ∠DFA is an obtuse angle.

Certain angle pairs are given special names based on their relative position to one another or based on the sum of their respective measures.

Complementary angles

Complementary angles are any two positive angles whose sum is 90°. In the following figure, because ∠*ABC* is a right angle, $m\angle 1 + m\angle 2 = 90°$, ∠1 and ∠2 are complementary.

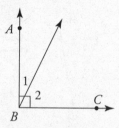

Complementary angles do not need to be adjacent. In the following figure, because $m\angle 3 + m\angle 4 = 90°$, ∠3 and ∠4 are complementary.

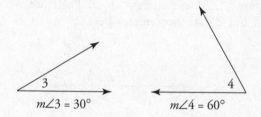

$m\angle 3 = 30°$ $m\angle 4 = 60°$

Example 9: If ∠5 and ∠6 are complementary and $m\angle 5 = 15°$, find $m\angle 6$.

Because ∠5 and ∠6 are complementary,

$$m\angle 5 + m\angle 6 = 90°$$
$$15° + m\angle 6 = 90°$$
$$m\angle 6 = 90° - 15°$$
$$m\angle 6 = 75°$$

Theorem 1.5: If two angles are complementary to the same angle, or to equal angles, then they are equal to each other.

In the top row of the following figure, ∠*A* and ∠*B* are complementary. Also, ∠*C* and ∠*B* are complementary. *Theorem 1.5* tells you that $m\angle A = m\angle C$. In the bottom row, ∠*A* and ∠*B* are complementary. Also, ∠*C* and

∠D are complementary, and $m\angle B = m\angle D$. *Theorem 1.5* now tells you that $m\angle A = m\angle C$.

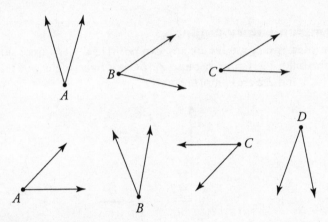

Supplementary angles

Supplementary angles are two positive angles whose sum is 180°. In the following figure, ∠ABC is a straight angle. Therefore, $m\angle 6 + m\angle 7 = 180°$, and ∠6 and ∠7 are supplementary.

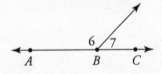

Supplementary angles do not need to be adjacent, as illustrated in the following figure.

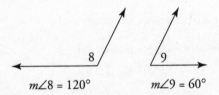

$m\angle 8 = 120°$ $m\angle 9 = 60°$

Because $m\angle 8 + m\angle 9 = 180°$, ∠8 and ∠9 are supplementary.

Theorem 1.6: If two angles are supplementary to the same angle, or to equal angles, then they are equal to each other.

Parallel, Intersecting, and Perpendicular Lines

In geometry, there are three types of lines that you should understand: parallel, intersecting, and perpendicular.

Parallel lines in a plane

Two lines, both in the same plane, that never intersect are called **parallel lines.** The symbol ∥ is used to denote parallel lines. In the figure that follows, $\ell \parallel m$.

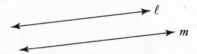

Theorem 1.7: Given two distinct lines in a plane, either they are parallel or they intersect at exactly one point.

Postulate 10 (Parallel Postulate): Given a line ℓ and a point P not on ℓ, there is exactly one line in the plane passing through P parallel to ℓ, in the plane containing ℓ and P.

Theorem 1.8: Let ℓ, m, and n be three distinct lines in a plane. If $\ell \parallel m$ and $m \parallel n$, then $\ell \parallel n$.

Intersecting lines

Two or more lines that meet at a single point are called **intersecting lines.** That point would be on each of these lines. In the figure that follows, lines ℓ and m intersect at point Q.

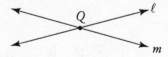

Vertical angles

Vertical angles are formed when two lines intersect and form four angles. Any two of these angles that are *not* adjacent angles are called vertical angles. In the following figure, line ℓ and line m intersect at point Q, forming two pairs of vertical angles and four pairs of adjacent angles.

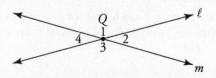

■ Vertical angles:

∠1 and ∠3

∠2 and ∠4

■ Adjacent angles:

∠1 and ∠2

∠2 and ∠3

∠3 and ∠4

∠4 and ∠1

Angles ∠1 and ∠2 are supplementary angles, as are angles ∠2 and ∠3. Therefore, by *Theorem 1.6*, angles ∠1 and ∠3 are equal in measure.

Theorem 1.9: Vertical angles are equal in measure.

Perpendicular lines

If two lines intersect at a point and one of the four angles is a right angle, then the remaining angles are right angles, by the definition of supplementary angles. Two lines that intersect and form right angles are called **perpendicular lines.** The symbol ⊥ is used to denote perpendicular lines. In the following figure, line ℓ ⊥ line m.

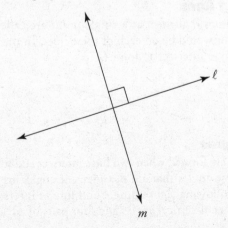

Theorem 1.10: In a plane, if ℓ is a line and P is a point on ℓ, then there is exactly one line passing through P and perpendicular to ℓ.

Angle bisector and perpendicular bisector

An **angle bisector** is a ray that divides an angle into two angles of equal measure. Two angles are equal if they have the same measure.

In the figure below, ray $\overrightarrow{OY}$ is the angle bisector of $\angle XOZ$ because $m\angle XOY = m\angle YOZ$.

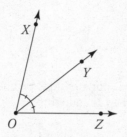

Theorem 1.11: A nonzero angle has exactly one bisector.

The **perpendicular bisector of a line segment** $\overline{AB}$ is the line passing through the midpoint of $\overline{AB}$ and is perpendicular to line $\overline{AB}$.

In the following figure, the line ℓ is the perpendicular bisector of the segment $\overline{AB}$, intersecting at point C.

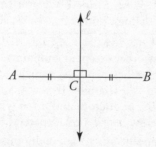

Theorem 1.12: A line segment has exactly one perpendicular bisector.

Triangles, Quadrilaterals, and Polygons

A **triangle** is a geometrical figure on a plane consisting of three points A, B, C and three segments $\overline{AB}$, $\overline{BC}$, $\overline{CA}$ so that none of the three segments intersect (except at endpoints). The three points are called the *vertices* of the triangle and the three segments are called the *sides, legs,* or *edges* of the triangle. (***Note:*** The term *legs* is typically used for either right or isosceles triangles.) We will use the notation $\triangle ABC$ to denote "triangle ABC."

The letters chosen to identify the points are completely arbitrary in this definition, as the figure below shows. It is standard practice in mathematics to use the same letter with different subscripts to represent a set of points or a set of lines, as in the right-most triangle below. This convention is especially useful when there are more than a few points in the set.

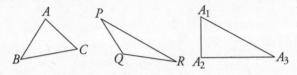

Notice the figure below is not a triangle because the segments $\overline{AB}$, $\overline{BC}$, and $\overline{CA}$ intersect more than at endpoints.

In the left-most triangle above, the angle with sides $\overline{AB}$, $\overline{AC}$, and vertex A is called $\angle A$ of $\triangle ABC$. Similarly, the angle with sides $\overline{BA}$, $\overline{BC}$, and vertex B is called $\angle B$, and the angle with sides $\overline{CA}$, $\overline{CB}$, and vertex C is called $\angle C$.

Let n be an integer ≥ 3. An n-sided polygon (**n-gon**) is a geometric figure consisting of n distinct points A_1, A_2, $\cdots$, A_n in a plane, together with the n segments $\overline{A_1 A_2}$, $\overline{A_2 A_3}$, $\overline{A_{n-1} A_n}$, and $\overline{A_n A_1}$ so that none of these segments intersects any other except at endpoints. The n-gon is denoted by $A_1 A_2 \cdots A_n$. An n-gon has n angles; namely, $\angle A_1$, $\angle A_2 \cdots$, $\angle A_n$. If $n = 3$, then the n-gon is a triangle. If $n = 4$, the polygon is called a **quadrilateral;** $n = 5$ is a **pentagon;** and $n = 6$ is a **hexagon.** By definition, figure $ABCD$ below is not a quadrilateral because segments $\overline{BC}$ and $\overline{DA}$ intersect at a point other than endpoints.

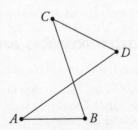

A **diagonal of a polygon** is any segment that joins two nonconsecutive vertices. **Consecutive sides of a polygon** are two sides that have an endpoint in common. In the figure below, the dashed line segments are the diagonals of the pentagon $RSTUQ$.

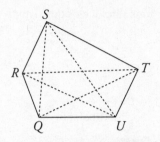

Special triangles and quadrilaterals

An **equilateral triangle** is a triangle whose three sides have the same length. An **isosceles triangle** is a triangle with at least two sides with the same length.

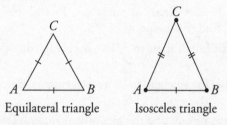

Equilateral triangle   Isosceles triangle

A quadrilateral all of whose angles are right angles is called a **rectangle.** A rectangle all of whose sides have the same length is called a **square.**

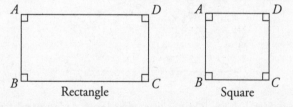

Rectangle   Square

Two sides of a polygon are parallel if the two lines passing through the endpoints of those segments are parallel. A quadrilateral with at least one pair of opposite sides that are parallel is called a **trapezoid.** A quadrilateral with two pairs of parallel opposite sides is called a **parallelogram.** Therefore, a parallelogram is also a trapezoid, but a trapezoid may not be a parallelogram.

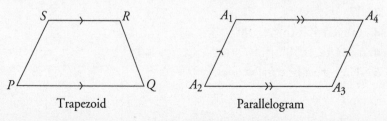

Trapezoid   Parallelogram

A quadrilateral whose four sides have equal length is called a **rhombus.**

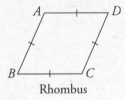

Rhombus

Chapter Check-Out

Questions

1. True or False: A postulate is a mathematical statement that has been proven.

2. On a line, if the coordinate of point A is 11 and the coordinate of point B is 23, find the midpoint of $\overline{AB}$.

3. **(a)** Is it possible for an angle to be its own complement? If so, give an example.

   (b) Is it possible for an angle to be its own supplement? If so, give an example.

4. In the following figure, find the measure of angle $\angle DFC$.

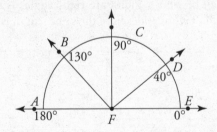

5. If lines ℓ and m are distinct lines that lie in a plane and ℓ and m are both perpendicular to line q, what can be said about the relationship between ℓ and m?

Answers

1. False

2. 17

3. **(a)** yes, 45°; **(b)** yes, 90°

4. $m\angle DFC = 50°$

5. They must be parallel lines.

Chapter 2

BASIC RIGID MOTIONS

Chapter Check-In

❑ Understanding clockwise and counterclockwise rotations

❑ Identifying the angles formed by transversals and their relationship to one another

❑ Understanding reflections

❑ Understanding translations of a point

> **Common Core Standard: Congruence, Proof, and Constructions**
>
> Develop definitions of rotations, reflections, and translations in terms of angles, circles, perpendicular lines, parallel lines, and line segments (G.CO.4). Prove theorems about lines and angles. Theorems include: vertical angles are congruent; when a transversal crosses parallel lines, alternate interior angles are congruent and corresponding angles are congruent; and points on a perpendicular bisector of a line segment are exactly those equidistant from the segment's endpoints (G.CO.9).

A plane transformation is a rule that assigns to each point P of the plane another point P' of the plane. The notation $F(P)$ is sometimes used to identify P' if the transformation F is named. The point $F(P)$ is called the *image of P by F*, or is referred to as *F maps P to F(P)*. If S is a geometric figure on the plane, then $F(S)$ is the collection of all points $F(P)$, where P is a point of S. When identifying $F(S)$ as the image of S by F, it is called *F maps S to F(S)*.

The three plane transformations that we are going to study are known as **basic rigid motions of a plane.** They are simply called **rotations, reflections,** and **translations** on the plane.

Geometry Theorems

The geometry theorems in this book are numbered for organizational purposes. For example, *Theorem 2.2* is the second theorem given in this chapter. Study these theorems by their content, not by their number, as the theorem numbering has no significance outside of this book.

Rotations

As you may have noticed, the words "rotation" and "reflection" both start with the letter *r*. Use the letter *R* for reflections and the Greek letter ρ for rotations. The Greek letters α and θ will be used to represent an angle as well as the measure of the angle.

Counterclockwise rotation ρ of θ degrees around O

Fix a point O on the plane. Let θ be an angle so that $0 \leq \theta \leq 180°$. The counterclockwise rotation ρ of θ degrees around O is defined as follows: Let P be any point on the plane. If P is O, then $\rho(O) = O$. That is, the image of O by ρ is O itself. If P is distinct from O, then $\rho(P) = P'$ is the point on the circle with center O and radius OP so that $\angle POP' = \theta$ and P' is located in the counterclockwise direction of P. The following figure illustrates the image of P by a counterclockwise rotation ρ.

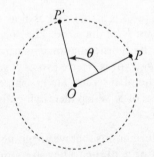

Clockwise rotation ρ of θ degrees around O

The clockwise rotation ρ of θ degrees around O is defined as follows: $\rho(O) = O$ and if P is a point other than O, then $\rho(P) = P'$ is the point on the circle with center O and radius OP so that $\angle POP' = \theta$ and P' is located in the clockwise direction of *P*. The following figure illustrates the image of *P* by a clockwise rotation ρ.

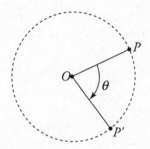

Suppose $\theta = 180°$ and point *P* is a point other than *O*. Then $\rho(P)$ is the same point whether ρ is counterclockwise or clockwise. For this reason, we will refer to a rotation of 180° around *O* without mentioning the direction of the rotation.

Postulate 11 (Line Separation): A point *O* on a line ℓ separates the line into two nonempty subsets called half-lines, so that every point other than *O* in the line belongs on only one of those half-lines, and if two points *A* and *B* belong to different half-lines, then *O* belongs to the segment $\overline{AB}$.

Postulate 12 (Plane Separation): A line ℓ separates the plane into two nonempty convex subsets called *half-planes,* so that every point in the plane belongs on only one of those half-planes or the line ℓ, and if two points *A* and *B* belong to different half-planes, then the line segment $\overline{AB}$ intersects ℓ.

Two points that lie in the same half-plane of ℓ are said to be on the same side of ℓ, and two points that lie in different half-planes of ℓ are said to be on opposite sides of ℓ.

Postulate 13 (Properties of Rotations):
(i) Rotations map lines to lines, rays to rays, and segments to segments.
(ii) Rotations map segments to segments of the same length.
(iii) Rotations map angles to angles of the same degree.

A rotation maps lines to lines, as shown in the following figure.

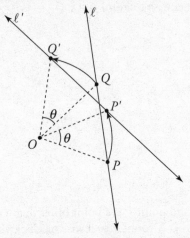

A rotation maps a segment to a segment of the same length, as shown in the following figure.

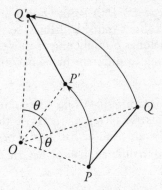

A rotation maps an angle to an angle of the same degree, as shown in the following figure.

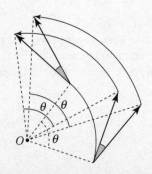

Theorem 2.1: Given a point O and an angle $0 \leq \theta \leq 180°$, there is a clockwise or counterclockwise rotation of θ degrees around O.

Theorem 2.2: Let ρ be the 180° rotation around a given point O and let P be a point other than O. Then P, O, and $\rho(P)$ are collinear and P and $\rho(P)$ lie in different half-lines separated by O.

The following figure shows a 180° rotation.

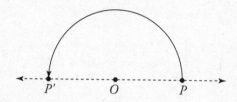

Theorem 2.3: Let ℓ be a line and O be a point not on ℓ. Let ρ be the 180° rotation around O. Then ρ maps ℓ to a line parallel to ℓ.

You can see why *Theorem 2.3* is true by the following argument using proof by contradiction. Suppose ℓ' is $\rho(\ell)$ and suppose contrary to the statement of *Theorem 2.3*, ℓ and ℓ' intersect at the point Q. Specifically, Q is on both ℓ and ℓ'. Since Q is on ℓ', there is a point P on ℓ so that $\rho(P) = Q$. Then by *Theorem 2.2*, P, O, and Q are collinear. However, both P and Q are on ℓ. Hence, O has to be on ℓ. This contradicts that fact that O is not on ℓ. Therefore, $\ell \parallel \ell'$.

An example of a line, and its image by a 180° rotation is given in the following figure.

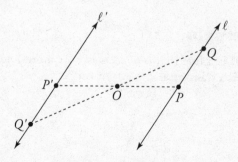

Theorem 2.4: In a plane, two distinct lines perpendicular to the same line are parallel.

Let ℓ_1 and ℓ_2 be the two distinct lines, and on the same plane let both ℓ_1 and ℓ_2 be perpendicular to ℓ. Suppose ℓ_1 and ℓ intersect at P and ℓ_2 and

ℓ intersect at Q. Let M be the midpoint of the segment $\overline{PQ}$, as shown in the following figure. Let ρ be the 180° rotation around M. Then $\rho(P) = Q$ and, therefore, $\rho(\ell_1)$ passes through Q. By *Theorem 2.3*, $\rho(\ell_1)$ is parallel to ℓ_1. Since rotations preserve degrees of angles, $\rho(\ell_1)$ is perpendicular to ℓ. By *Theorem 1.10*, there is only one line perpendicular to a line through a point on that line. Hence, $\rho(\ell_1) = \ell_2$. That is, ℓ_1 is parallel to ℓ_2.

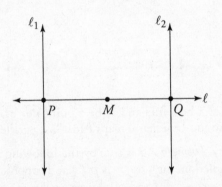

Theorem 2.5: Given a line ℓ and a point P not on line ℓ, there is exactly one line passing through P and perpendicular to ℓ.

Proof of this theorem follows easily from the previous theorem by using proof by contradiction. Suppose there are two distinct lines passing through P perpendicular to ℓ. Then by *Theorem 2.5*, those two lines have to be parallel to each other. In other words, they cannot both pass through P.

Transversals

A **transversal** is a line that intersects two or more lines. In the figure below, line t is a transversal.

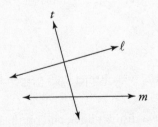

A transversal that intersects two lines forms eight angles; certain pairs of these angles are given special names. They are as follows:

- **Corresponding angles** are the angles that occur in the same relative position in each group of four angles. In the figure below, $\angle 1$ and $\angle 5$ are corresponding angles. Other pairs of corresponding angles in the figure are $\angle 4$ and $\angle 8$, $\angle 2$ and $\angle 6$, and $\angle 3$ and $\angle 7$.

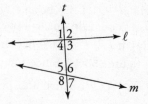

- **Alternate interior angles** are angles inside the two lines being intersected, on opposite sides of the transversal; they are not adjacent. In the figure above, $\angle 4$ and $\angle 6$ are alternate interior angles, as are $\angle 3$ and $\angle 5$.

- **Alternate exterior angles** are angles outside the lines being intersected, on opposite sides of the transversal; they are not adjacent. In the figure above, $\angle 1$ and $\angle 7$ are alternate exterior angles, as are $\angle 2$ and $\angle 8$.

- **Consecutive interior angles** (same-side interior angles) are interior angles on the same side of the transversal. In the figure above, $\angle 4$ and $\angle 5$ are consecutive interior angles, as are $\angle 3$ and $\angle 6$.

- **Consecutive exterior angles** (same-side exterior angles) are exterior angles on the same side of the transversal. In the figure above, $\angle 1$ and $\angle 8$ are consecutive exterior angles, as are $\angle 2$ and $\angle 7$.

Theorem 2.6: Suppose ℓ_1 and ℓ_2 are two parallel lines and ℓ is a transversal intersecting ℓ_1 and ℓ_2. Then alternate interior angles are equal.

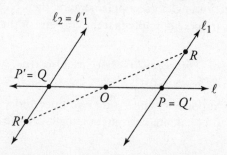

Suppose ℓ_1 and ℓ intersect at P, ℓ_2 and ℓ intersect at Q, and O is the midpoint of the segment $\overline{PQ}$, as shown in the figure above. Let ρ be the 180° rotation around O. Then $P' = Q$, $Q' = P$, and ℓ'_1 is a line parallel to ℓ_1 passing through Q. By the Parallel Postulate (*Postulate 10*), $\ell'_1 = \ell_2$.

We will use the figure as a guide to prove the theorem; however, the proof is valid for any pair of alternate interior angles. The point P separates ℓ_1 into two half lines (*Postulate 11*). Let R be an arbitrary point on one half of ℓ_1 (see figure above). Then it is in one half of the plane separated by ℓ (*Postulate 12*). By Theorem 2.2, $R' = \rho(R)$ lies on the other half plane of ℓ and on $\ell'_1 = \ell_2$ (see figure above). Since rotations map rays to rays, $\rho(\overline{PR}) = \overline{QR'}$, and $\rho(\overline{PQ}) = \overline{QP}$. Therefore, $\rho(\angle RPQ) = \angle PQR'$.

Theorem 2.7: Suppose ℓ_1 and ℓ_2 are two parallel lines and ℓ is a transversal intersecting ℓ_1 and ℓ_2. Then corresponding angles are equal.

Theorem 2.8: Suppose ℓ_1 and ℓ_2 are two parallel lines and ℓ is a transversal intersecting ℓ_1 and ℓ_2. Then alternate exterior angles are equal.

Theorem 2.9: Suppose ℓ_1 and ℓ_2 are two parallel lines and ℓ is a transversal intersecting ℓ_1 and ℓ_2. Then consecutive interior angles are supplementary.

Theorem 2.10: Suppose ℓ_1 and ℓ_2 are two parallel lines and ℓ is a transversal intersecting ℓ_1 and ℓ_2. Then consecutive exterior angles are supplementary.

In the statement of a theorem, there is a hypothesis and a conclusion. For example, in *Theorem 2.10*, "ℓ_1 and ℓ_2 are two parallel lines" is the hypothesis and "consecutive exterior angles are supplementary" is the conclusion. If we name the hypothesis P and the conclusion Q, then the statement of a theorem can be written in a condensed form as "P implies Q."

The converse of the theorem "P implies Q" is the theorem "Q implies P." That is, the converse of *Theorem 2.10* is the following theorem. "Suppose ℓ_1 and ℓ_2 are two lines and ℓ is a transversal intersecting ℓ_1 and ℓ_2. If consecutive exterior angles are supplementary, then $\ell_1 \parallel \ell_2$." **Note:** If a theorem is true, it does not imply that the converse of the theorem is also true.

The converses of *Theorems 2.6–2.10* are also true, and they are in *Theorems 2.11–2.15*, respectively.

Theorem 2.11: Suppose ℓ_1 and ℓ_2 are two lines and ℓ is a transversal intersecting ℓ_1 and ℓ_2. If alternate interior angles are equal, then $\ell_1 \parallel \ell_2$.

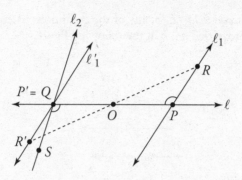

The following is the proof of *Theorem 2.11*. Suppose ℓ_1 intersects ℓ at P, ℓ_2 intersects ℓ at Q, and the alternate interior angles $\angle RPQ$ and $\angle PQS$ are equal as shown in the figure above.

$$\angle RPQ = \angle PQS \qquad (1)$$

Let O be the midpoint of the segment $\overline{PQ}$ tand let ρ be the 180° rotation around O. Let $P' = \rho(P)$, $Q' = \rho(Q)$, $R' = \rho(R)$, and $\ell'_1 = \rho(\ell_1)$. Then $P' = Q$, $Q' = P$, $\ell'_1 \parallel \ell_1$, and ℓ'_1 passes through Q. According to the proof of *Theorem 2.6*,

$$\angle RPQ = \angle PQR' \qquad (2)$$

And R' and S lie on the same half plane of ℓ. By (1) and (2), $\angle PQS = \angle PQR'$.

Since the side $\overrightarrow{OR'}$ is common to both angles, Q is the common vertex, and R' and S lie on the same side of ℓ, $\overrightarrow{QR'}$ and $\overrightarrow{OS}$ must be the same. Then R' lies on ℓ_2. Since there is only one line passing through Q and R', $\ell_2 = \ell'_1$. Since $\ell'_1 \parallel \ell_1$, $\ell_2 \parallel \ell_1$.

Theorem 2.12: Suppose ℓ_1 and ℓ_2 are two lines and ℓ is a transversal intersecting ℓ_1 and ℓ_2. If corresponding angles are equal, then $\ell_1 \parallel \ell_2$.

Theorem 2.13: Suppose ℓ_1 and ℓ_2 are two lines and ℓ is a transversal intersecting ℓ_1 and ℓ_2. If alternate exterior angles are equal, then $\ell_1 \parallel \ell_2$.

Theorem 2.14: Suppose ℓ_1 and ℓ_2 are two lines and ℓ is a transversal intersecting ℓ_1 and ℓ_2. If consecutive interior angles are supplementary, then $\ell_1 \parallel \ell_2$.

Theorem 2.15: Suppose ℓ_1 and ℓ_2 are two lines and ℓ is a transversal intersecting ℓ_1 and ℓ_2. If consecutive exterior angles are supplementary, then $\ell_1 \parallel \ell_2$.

Based on *Theorems 2.11–2.15*, any of the conditions listed below would allow you to prove that *a* || *b* in the following figure.

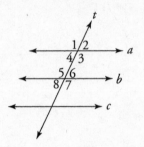

Per *Theorem 2.11*:
$m\angle 4 = m\angle 6$
$m\angle 3 = m\angle 5$

Per *Theorem 2.12*:
$m\angle 1 = m\angle 5$
$m\angle 2 = m\angle 6$
$m\angle 3 = m\angle 7$
$m\angle 4 = m\angle 8$

Per *Theorem 2.13*:
$m\angle 1 = m\angle 7$
$m\angle 2 = m\angle 8$

Per *Theorem 2.14*:
$\angle 4$ and $\angle 5$ are supplementary
$\angle 3$ and $\angle 6$ are supplementary

Per *Theorem 2.15*:
$\angle 1$ and $\angle 8$ are supplementary
$\angle 2$ and $\angle 7$ are supplementary

Example 1: In the figure below, identify the given angle pairs as alternate interior, alternate exterior, consecutive interior, consecutive exterior, corresponding, or none of these: $\angle 1$ and $\angle 7$, $\angle 2$ and $\angle 8$, $\angle 3$ and $\angle 4$, $\angle 4$ and $\angle 8$, $\angle 3$ and $\angle 8$, $\angle 3$ and $\angle 2$, $\angle 5$ and $\angle 7$.

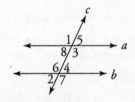

$\angle 1$ and $\angle 7$ are alternate exterior angles.
$\angle 2$ and $\angle 8$ are corresponding angles.
$\angle 3$ and $\angle 4$ are consecutive interior angles.
$\angle 4$ and $\angle 8$ are alternate interior angles.
$\angle 3$ and $\angle 8$ are supplementary angles.
$\angle 3$ and $\angle 2$ are none of these.
$\angle 5$ and $\angle 7$ are consecutive exterior angles.

Example 2: For figures (a), (b), (c), and (d) below, determine which theorem you would use to prove $\ell \parallel m$.

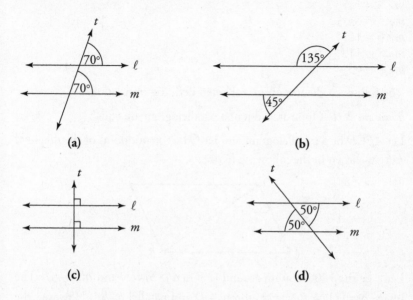

(a): If two lines and a transversal form equal corresponding angles, then the lines are parallel (*Theorem 2.12*).

(b): If two lines and a transversal form consecutive exterior angles that are supplementary, then the lines are parallel (*Theorem 2.15*).

(c): In a plane, if two lines are perpendicular to the same line, then the two lines are parallel (*Theorem 2.4*).

(d): If two lines and a transversal form equal alternate interior angles, then the lines are parallel (*Theorem 2.11*).

Example 3: In the following figure, $a \parallel b$ and $m\angle 1 = 117°$. Find the measure of each of the numbered angles.

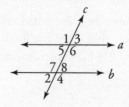

$m\angle 2 = 63°$
$m\angle 3 = 63°$
$m\angle 4 = 117°$
$m\angle 5 = 63°$
$m\angle 6 = 117°$
$m\angle 7 = 117°$
$m\angle 8 = 63°$

The following theorem is useful when defining translations.

Theorem 2.16: Opposite sides of a parallelogram are equal.

Let *ABCD* be a parallelogram and let *O* be the midpoint of the diagonal $\overline{DB}$, as shown in the following figure.

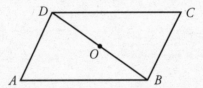

Let ρ be the 180° rotation around *O*. Then $\rho(B) = D$ and $\rho(D) = B$. The image of the line $\overrightarrow{BA}$ passes through *D* and parallel to $\overrightarrow{BA}$. However, the line $\overrightarrow{DC}$ passes through *D* and is parallel to line $\overrightarrow{BA}$. Hence, by the Parallel Postulate (*Postulate 10*), $\rho(\overrightarrow{BA}) = \overrightarrow{DC}$. For similar reasons, $\rho\,(\overrightarrow{DA}) = \overrightarrow{BC}$. The point of intersection of lines $\overrightarrow{BA}$ and $\overrightarrow{DA}$ maps to the point of intersection of $\rho(\overrightarrow{BA})$ and $\rho(\overrightarrow{DA})$, or $\rho(A) = C$. Since rotations preserve lengths of line segments, $BC = DA$ and $BA = DC$.

Theorem 2.17: The angles of a parallelogram at opposite vertices are equal.

Reflections

We say two points *A* and *B* are *symmetric* to each other with respect to a line ℓ if ℓ is the perpendicular bisector of the segment $\overline{AB}$.

As shown in the figure below, the plane transformation reflection *R* across a given line ℓ maps to each point on ℓ the point itself, and to any point *P* not on ℓ, a point $R(P) = P'$ which is symmetric to it with respect to ℓ.

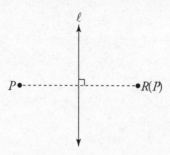

Theorem 2.18: Given a line in the plane, there is a reflection across that line.

Postulate 14 (Properties of Reflections):
(i) Reflections map lines to lines, rays to rays, and segments to segments.
(ii) Reflections map segments to segments of the same length.
(iii) Reflections map angles to angles of the same degree.

Translations

A **vector** is a line segment with one endpoint identified as the *starting point* and the other as the *ending point*. If A is the starting point and B is the ending point, use $\overrightarrow{AB}$ to represent the vector with starting point A and the ending point B. To avoid confusion by using the same notation for the ray passing through A and B, use just one letter with an upper arrow, such as $\overrightarrow{v}$, to denote a vector, as shown in the following figure.

The plane transformation *translation T along a given vector* $\overrightarrow{v}$ maps a given point P to a point $T(P)$ as follows: Let A and B be the starting point and the ending point of $\overrightarrow{v}$. Let ℓ be the line passing through A and B. If P is not on ℓ, then let ℓ_1 be the line passing through P parallel to ℓ. Let ℓ_2 be the line passing through A and P. Suppose the line passing through B and parallel to ℓ_2 intersects ℓ_1 at Q. Then $T(P) = Q$. See the following figure.

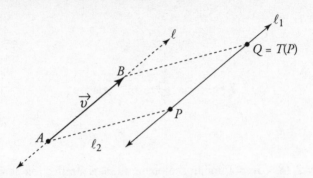

If P lies on ℓ, then $T(P) = P'$ lies on ℓ so that $PP' = AB$ and the vector $\overrightarrow{PP'}$ has the same direction as $\overrightarrow{v}$. See the following figure.

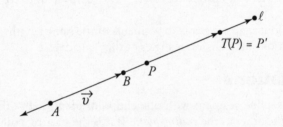

Intuitively, if T is a translation along $\overrightarrow{v}$, then for any point P, the vector with starting point P and ending point $T(P)$ has the same length and direction as $\overrightarrow{v}$.

Postulate 15 (Properties of Translations):
(i) Translations map lines to lines, rays to rays, and segments to segments.
(ii) Translations map segments to segments of the same length.
(iii) Translations map angles to angles of the same degree.

Theorem 2.19: Given any vector, there is a translation along that vector.

Since rotations, reflections, and translations (on a plane) are known as basic rigid motions, *Postulates 13–15* may be combined into one postulate as follows.

Postulate 16 (Properties of Rigid Motions):
(i) Rigid motions map lines to lines, rays to rays, and segments to segments.
(ii) Rigid motions map segments to segments of the same length.
(iii) Rigid motions map angles to angles of the same degree.

Chapter Check-Out

Questions

1. When two parallel lines are cut by a transversal, what is true about corresponding angles?

The following figure should be used for questions 2 and 3.

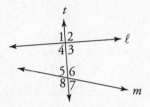

2. In the figure above, if $m\angle 4 + m\angle 5 = 180°$, then what does that guarantee about lines ℓ and m?

3. In the figure above, if $m\angle 1 = m\angle 5$, then what does that guarantee about lines ℓ and m?

4. In the following figure, lines $\overleftrightarrow{AB}$, $\overleftrightarrow{CD}$, and $\overleftrightarrow{EF}$ are parallel to one another, $m\angle A = 39°$, and $m\angle E = 65°$. Find $m\angle ACE$.

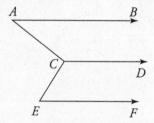

5. True or False: A rigid motion maps line segments to line segments of the same length.

Answers

1. They must be equal.

2. They are parallel.

3. They are parallel.

4. 104°

5. True

Chapter 3

TRIANGLES AND CONGRUENCE

Chapter Check-In

❑ Understanding the concept of exterior angles of a triangle

❑ Computing the measure of the third angle of a triangle, given the measures of the other two angles

❑ Identifying equilateral, isosceles, and scalene triangles

❑ Identifying the hypotenuse of a right triangle as well as the base, altitude, median, and angle bisectors for any triangle

❑ Understanding triangle inequalities

❑ Using the concept of congruence

❑ Using the corresponding parts of two triangles to test for congruence

Common Core Standard: Congruence, Proof, and Constructions

Prove theorems about triangles. Theorems include: measures of interior angles of a triangle sum to 180; base angles of isosceles triangles are congruent; the segment joining midpoints of two sides of a triangle is parallel to the third side and half the length of the third side; and the medians of a triangle meet at a point (G.CO.10).

Use geometric descriptions of rigid motions to transform figures and to predict the effect of a given rigid motion on a given figure; given two figures, use the definition of congruence in terms of rigid motions to decide if they are congruent (G.CO.6).

Use the definition of congruence in terms of rigid motions to show that two triangles are congruent if and only if corresponding pairs of sides and corresponding pairs of angles are congruent (G.CO.7).

Explain how the theorems for triangle congruence (ASA, SAS, and SSS) follow from the definition of congruence in terms of rigid motions (G.CO.8).

> ### Geometry Theorems
> The geometry theorems in this book are numbered for organizational purposes. For example, *Theorem 2.2* is the second theorem given in Chapter 2. Study these theorems by their content, not by their number, as the theorem numbering has no significance outside of this book.

A **triangle** is a three-sided polygon with three angles in its interior. The symbol for triangle is Δ. A triangle is named by the three letters at its vertices (the plural of vertex), a fancy name for corners. The following figure represents Δ*ABC*.

As you can imagine, the measuring of triangles and more complex figures became important long ago because of their role in surveying. Modern science has continued to find more and more practical applications requiring knowledge of triangles.

Note that any closed polygon in a plane with three or more sides can be subdivided into triangles. For example, the figure below shows the triangulation of a pentagon. Consequently, what you learn about triangles can also be useful in studying more complex polygons.

Exterior Angle of a Triangle

An **exterior angle of a triangle** is formed when one side of a triangle is extended. The nonstraight angle (the one that is not just the extension of the side) outside the triangle, but adjacent to an interior angle, is an exterior angle of the triangle; in the following figure, ∠*BCD* is an exterior angle of Δ*ABC*.

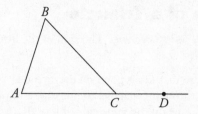

Theorem 3.1 (Exterior Angle Theorem): An exterior angle of a triangle is equal to the sum of the two remote (nonadjacent) interior angles.

Let $\triangle ABC$ be the given triangle.

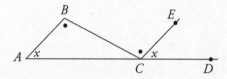

Extend the side $\overline{AC}$ so that D is a point on the extended side and $\overrightarrow{AC} = \overrightarrow{AD}$. Construct the line through C parallel to line $\overleftrightarrow{AB}$ and pick a point E on it so that B and E lie on the same side of $\overleftrightarrow{AC}$. See the figure above. By *Theorem 2.6*, $\angle B$ and $\angle BCE$ are equal, and by *Theorem 2.7*, $\angle A$ and $\angle ECD$ are equal. Hence, the exterior angle $\angle BCD$ is the sum of the remote interior angles $\angle A$ and $\angle B$.

Example 1: In the figure below, if $m\angle 1 = 30°$ and $m\angle 2 = 100°$, find $m\angle 4$.

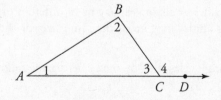

Because $\angle 4$ is an exterior angle of the triangle,

$$m\angle 4 = m\angle 1 + m\angle 2$$
$$m\angle 4 = 30° + 100°$$
$$m\angle 4 = 130°$$

Angle Sum of a Triangle

Theorem 3.2 (Angle Sum Theorem): The sum of the interior angles of any triangle is 180°.

Extend the side *AC* so that *D* is a point on the extended side and $\overline{AC} = \overline{AD}$. Construct the line through *C* parallel to line $\overleftrightarrow{AB}$, and pick a point *E* on it so that both *B* and *E* lie on the same side of line $\overleftrightarrow{AC}$, as shown in the following figure. The angles $\angle BCA$ and $\angle BCD$ are supplementary angles. By the Exterior Angle Theorem (*Theorem 3.1*), $\angle BCD$ is the sum of angles $\angle A$ and $\angle B$. Therefore, the sum of the interior angles of $\triangle ABC$ is 180°.

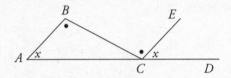

Example 2: In $\triangle ABC$, if $m\angle A = 40°$ and $m\angle B = 60°$, find $m\angle C$.

Because $m\angle A + m\angle B + m\angle C = 180°$, then

$$m\angle C = 180° - (m\angle A + m\angle B)$$
$$m\angle C = 180° - (40° + 60°)$$
$$m\angle C = 80°$$

Classifying Triangles by Sides or Angles

Triangles can be classified either according to their sides or according to their angles. All sides or all angles may be of different or the same sizes; any two sides or angles may be of the same size; or there may be one distinctive angle.

The types of triangles classified by their *sides* are the following:

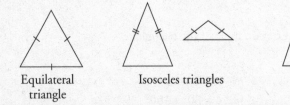

Equilateral triangle   Isosceles triangles   Scalene triangle

- **Equilateral triangle:** A triangle with all three sides equal in measure. The slash marks indicate equal measure.

- **Isosceles triangle:** A triangle in which at least two sides have equal measure.

- **Scalene triangle:** A triangle with all three sides of different measures.

The types of triangles classified by their *angles* includes the following:

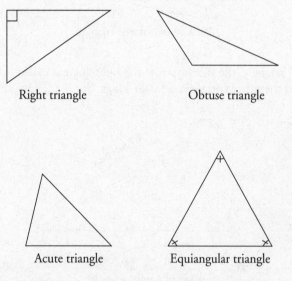

Right triangle   Obtuse triangle

Acute triangle   Equiangular triangle

- **Right triangle:** A triangle that has a right angle in its interior.

- **Obtuse triangle:** A triangle having an obtuse angle in its interior.

- **Acute triangle:** A triangle having all acute angles in its interior.

- **Equiangular triangle:** A triangle having all angles of equal measure.

Because the sum of all the angles of a triangle is 180°, the following theorem is easily shown.

Theorem 3.3: Each angle of an equiangular triangle has a measure of 60°.

Special names for sides and angles

In an isosceles triangle, the two equal sides are called **legs,** and the third side is called the **base.** The angle formed by the two equal sides is called the

vertex angle. The other two angles are called **base angles.** See the following figure.

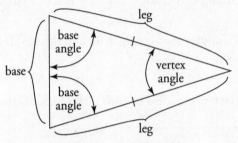

Parts of an isosceles triangle

In a right triangle, the side opposite the right angle is called the **hypotenuse,** and the other two sides are called **legs.** See the following figure.

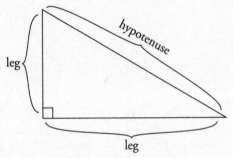

Parts of a right triangle

Altitudes, Medians, and Angle Bisectors

Just as there are special names for special types of triangles, there are also special names for special line segments within triangles.

Base and altitude

Every triangle has three **bases** (any of its sides) and three **altitudes** (heights). Every altitude is the perpendicular segment from a vertex to its opposite side (or the extension of the opposite side), as illustrated in the following figures.

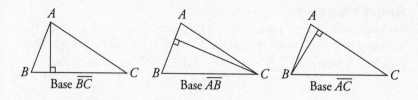

Altitudes can sometimes coincide with a side of the triangle or can sometimes meet an extended base outside the triangle.

In a right triangle, each leg can serve as an altitude. In the following figure, $\overline{AC}$ is an altitude to base $\overline{BC}$, and $\overline{BC}$ is an altitude to base $\overline{AC}$.

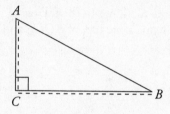

In the obtuse triangle below, $\overline{AM}$ is the altitude to base $\overline{BC}$.

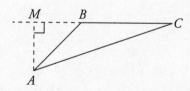

Median

A **median of a triangle** is the line segment drawn from a vertex to the midpoint of its opposite side. Every triangle has three medians. In the figure below, E is the midpoint of $\overline{BC}$. Hence, $BE = EC$ and line $\overleftrightarrow{AE}$ is a median of $\triangle ABC$.

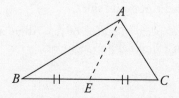

Angle bisector

An **angle bisector** in a triangle is a line passing through a vertex that bisects (cuts in half) that vertex angle. Every triangle has three angle bisectors. In the following figure, line $\overleftrightarrow{BX}$ is an angle bisector in $\triangle ABC$.

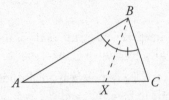

Example 3: Based on the markings in the following figure, **(a)** name an altitude of $\triangle QRS$, **(b)** name a median of $\triangle QRS$, and **(c)** name an angle bisector of $\triangle QRS$.

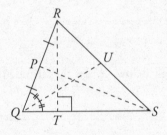

(a) $\overline{RT}$ is an altitude to base $\overline{QS}$ because $\overline{RT} \perp \overline{QS}$.

(b) Line $\overleftrightarrow{SP}$ is a median to base $\overline{QR}$ because P is the midpoint of $\overline{QR}$.

(c) Line $\overleftrightarrow{QU}$ is an angle bisector of $\triangle QRS$ because it bisects $\angle RQS$.

Special Features of Isosceles Triangles

Postulate 17 (Crossbar Postulate): Given a triangle ABC and a point D in the triangle, a ray emanating from any vertex of the triangle and passing through D intersects the opposite side.

Isosceles triangles are special; because of that, there are unique relationships that involve their internal line segments.

Theorem 3.4: The base angles of an isosceles triangle are equal.

Let $\triangle ABC$ be an isosceles triangle with vertex angle $\angle A$ and base $\overline{BC}$, as shown in the following figure. Let line $\overleftrightarrow{AD}$ be the angle bisector of $\angle A$, where D is the point where line $\overleftrightarrow{AD}$ intersects line $\overleftrightarrow{BC}$. By the Crossbar Postulate, D is between B and C.

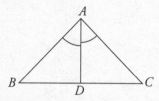

Let R be the reflection across line $\overleftrightarrow{AD}$. Since A and D are on line $\overleftrightarrow{AD}$, $R(A) = A$ and $R(D) = D$. The side $\overline{AD}$ is common to both angles $\angle BAD$ and $\angle CAD$, and $R(\overrightarrow{AB}) = \overrightarrow{AC}$ since reflections preserve degrees of angles. Given that $AB = AC$ and reflections preserve lengths of segments, $R(B) = C$. Hence, $R(\angle ABC) = \angle ACD$.

Theorem 3.5: In an isosceles triangle, the perpendicular bisector of the base, the angle bisector of the vertex angle, the median from the top vertex to the base, and the altitude from the top vertex to the base all coincide.

Theorem 3.5 follows from *Theorem 3.4* after you observe the following. Since $R(A) = A$, $R(D) = D$, and $R(B) = C$, $R(\angle ADB) = \angle ADC$ and $R(BD) = CD$. Since reflections preserve degrees of angles and lengths of segments, $BD = CD$ and $\angle ADB = \angle ADC$.

Theorem 3.6: A point is on the perpendicular bisector of a line segment if and only if it is equidistant from the endpoints of the segment.

Let $\overline{BC}$ be the segment, ℓ be the perpendicular bisector, and A be the point on ℓ. Suppose D is the point of intersection of ℓ and $\overline{BC}$. If $A = D$, then there is nothing to prove. So, assume A is different from D. Let R be the reflection across ℓ. Because $R(A) = A$ and $R(B) = C$, $R(\overline{AB}) = \overline{AC}$. Since reflections preserve lengths of segments, $AB = AC$. The converse of the theorem follows from *Theorem 3.5*.

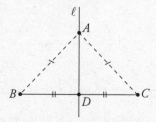

The following theorem follows easily from *Theorems 3.4* and *3.5*.

Theorem 3.7: A triangle is equilateral if and only if the triangle is equiangular.

Example 4: In △*QRS* below, *QR* = *QS*. If *m∠Q* = 50°, find *m∠R* and *m∠S*.

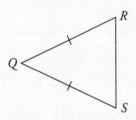

Because *m∠Q* + *m∠R* + *m∠S* = 180°, and because *QR* = *QS* implies that *m∠R* = *m∠S*,

$$m\angle Q + m\angle R + m\angle R = 180°$$
$$50° + 2m\angle R = 180°$$
$$2m\angle R = 130°$$
$$m\angle R = 65° \text{ and } m\angle S = 65°$$

Example 5: In △*ABC* below, *m∠A* = *m∠B* = *m∠C*, and *AB* = 6. Find *BC* and *AC*.

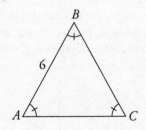

Because the triangle is equiangular, it is also equilateral. Therefore, *BC* = *AC* = 6.

Triangle Inequalities Regarding Sides and Angles

You have just seen that if a triangle has equal sides, the angles opposite these sides are equal, and if a triangle has equal angles, the sides opposite these angles are equal. There are two important theorems involving unequal sides and unequal angles in triangles. They are described in *Theorems 3.8* and *3.9*.

Theorem 3.8: If two sides of a triangle are unequal, then the measures of the angles opposite these sides are unequal, and the greater angle is opposite the greater side.

Let ABC be a triangle so that $BC > AC$, as shown in the following figure. Now show that angle $\angle BAC > \angle B$. Find the point D on $\overline{BC}$ so that $DC = AC$. Then $\triangle ADC$ is isosceles and $\angle CAD = \angle ADC$. Clearly, $\angle BAC > \angle CAD$; therefore, $\angle BAC > \angle ADC$. $\angle ADC$ is an exterior angle of $\triangle ABD$. By the Exterior Angle Theorem (*Theorem 3.1*), $\angle ADC > \angle B$. Therefore, $\angle BAC > \angle B$.

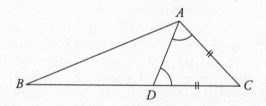

The following theorem then follows from *Theorem 3.8*.

Theorem 3.9: If two angles of a triangle are unequal, then the measures of the sides opposite these angles are also unequal, and the longer side is opposite the greater angle.

Example 6: The figure below shows a triangle with angles of different measures. List the sides of this triangle in order from least to greatest.

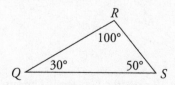

Because $30° < 50° < 100°$, then $RS < QR < QS$.

Example 7: The following figure shows a triangle with sides of different measures. List the angles of this triangle in order from least to greatest.

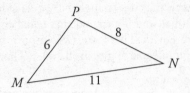

Because $6 < 8 < 11$, then $m\angle N < m\angle M < m\angle P$.

Example 8: The following figure shows right $\triangle ABC$. Which side must be the longest?

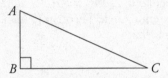

Because $m\angle A + m\angle B + m\angle C = 180°$ by the Angle Sum Theorem (*Theorem 3.2*) and $m\angle B = 90°$, we have $m\angle A + m\angle C = 90°$. Thus, both $m\angle A$ and $m\angle C$ are less than 90°. Therefore, $\angle B$ is the angle of greatest measure in the triangle, meaning its opposite side is the longest. Hence, the hypotenuse, $\overline{AC}$, is the longest side in a right triangle.

The Triangle Inequality Theorem

In $\triangle TAB$ below, if T, A, and B represent three points on a map and you want to go from T to B, going from T to A to B would obviously be longer than going directly from T to B. The following theorem expresses this idea.

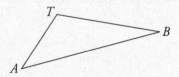

Theorem 3.10 (Triangle Inequality Theorem): The sum of the lengths of any two sides of a triangle is greater than the length of the third side.

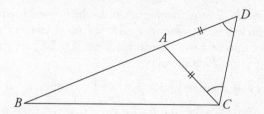

Let $\triangle ABC$ be a triangle with $\overline{BC}$ as its longest side. If we can show that $AB + AC > BC$, then the triangle inequality is true. Extend the side $\overline{BA}$ and locate the point D so that $AD = AC$. Connect D to C with a line segment, as shown in the figure above. Then $\triangle ADC$ is isosceles and $m\angle D = m\angle ACD$. Now consider $\triangle DBC$. Clearly, $m\angle BCD > m\angle ACD$; therefore, $\angle BCD > \angle D$. Then, by *Theorem 3.8*, $BD > BC$. But $BD = BA + AC$. Therefore, $BA + AC > BC$.

Example 9: In the figure below, the measures of two sides of a triangle are 7 and 12. Find the range of possibilities for the third side, x.

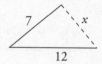

Using the Triangle Inequality Theorem (*Theorem 3.10*), you can write the following:

$$7 + x > 12, \text{ so } x > 5$$
$$7 + 12 > x, \text{ so } 19 > x \text{ (or } x < 19)$$

Hence, the third side must be more than 5 and less than 19.

The Concept of Congruence

Let F and G be two plane transformations so that the composition of F and G is denoted by $G \circ F$. This rule maps each point P of the plane to the point $G(F(P))$. That is, the transformation F maps the point P to the point $F(P)$ and then the transformation G maps the point $F(P)$ to the point $G(F(P))$. If F, G, H, and K are plane transformations, then $F \circ G \circ H \circ K$ is the rule that maps each point P on the plane to a point $F\big(G\big(H\big(K(P)\big)\big)\big)$.

At this point, the *identity transformation I,* which maps any point *P* of the plane to itself, will be introduced, or $I(P) = P$ for all points *P* on the plane. It can also be said that two transformations, *F* and *G,* are equal if $F(P) = G(P)$ for any point *P* on the plane.

Theorem 3.11: If *R* is a reflection across a line ℓ, then $R \circ R = I$.

Theorem 3.12: If ρ_1 is the counterclockwise rotation around a point *O* by an angle θ and if ρ_2 is a clockwise rotation around the same point *O* by the same angle θ, then $\rho_1 \circ \rho_2 = I$.

Theorem 3.13: If T_1 is the translation along the vector $\overrightarrow{AB}$ and T_2 is the translation along the vector $\overrightarrow{BA}$, then $T_1 \circ T_2 = I$.

A **congruence** in the plane is a plane transformation that is equal to the composition of a finite number of basic rigid motions. Let *S* and *R* be two geometric figures on the plane. Then *S* is congruent to *R* if there is a congruence *C* so that $C(S) = R$. This is denoted by the notation $S \cong R$. If $S \cong R$, then you can verify that $R \cong S$. That is, if $S \cong R$, then there is another congruence *D* so that $D(R) = S$.

Theorem 3.14: A congruence:

(i) maps lines to lines, rays to rays, and segments to segments.

(ii) maps line segments to line segments of equal length.

(iii) maps an angle to an angle of the same degree.

Theorem 3.15: A line segment is congruent to a line segment of equal length.

Theorem 3.16: An angle is congruent to an angle of the same degree.

Two triangles are congruent when the three sides and the three angles of one triangle have the same measurements as the three sides and the three angles of another triangle. For example, there is a congruence that maps $\triangle ABC$ to $\triangle DEF$ in the figure below. Therefore, they are congruent triangles.

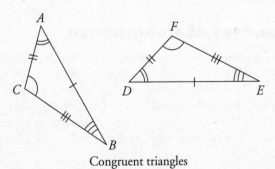

Congruent triangles

Let T be the translation along the vector $\overrightarrow{AD}$. Then $T(A) = D$. Let ρ be the rotation around D, if necessary, so that $\rho(T(B)) = E$. Let R be the reflection around line $\overleftrightarrow{DE}$, if C and F are not on the same half plane of line $\overleftrightarrow{DE}$. Otherwise, let R be the identity transformation. Then by *Theorem 3.14*, $R(\rho(T(C))) = F$. Let K be the congruence $R \circ \rho \circ T$. Then $K(ABC) = DEF$, or $\triangle ABC \cong \triangle DEF$.

Corresponding Parts of Triangles

The parts of the two triangles that have the same measurements are referred to as **corresponding parts of triangles.** This means that *corresponding parts of congruent triangles are congruent* by *Theorem 3.14*. Congruent triangles are named by listing their vertices in corresponding orders. For example, for the congruent triangles shown on p. 54, write $\triangle ABC \cong \triangle DEF$.

Example 10: If $\triangle PQR \cong \triangle STU$, which parts must have equal measurements?

$$m\angle P = m\angle S$$
$$m\angle Q = m\angle T$$
$$m\angle R = m\angle U$$
$$PQ = ST$$
$$QR = TU$$
$$PR = SU$$

These parts are equal because corresponding parts of congruent triangles are congruent by *Theorem 3.14*.

To show that two triangles are congruent, it is not necessary to show that all six pairs of corresponding parts are equal.

Congruence theorems of triangles

If two sides and the angle between those two sides of a triangle are congruent to the corresponding two sides and the angle of another triangle, then those two triangles are congruent. This observation is known as the *SAS Theorem.*

Theorem 3.17 (SAS Theorem): Given two triangles $\triangle ABC$ and $\triangle DEF$ so that $m\angle A = m\angle D$, $AB = DE$, and $AC = DF$, then the triangles are congruent.

Consider $\triangle ABC$ and $\triangle DEF$ shown below.

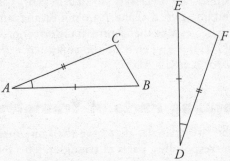

Triangles with SAS properties

Let T be the translation along the vector $\overrightarrow{AD}$. Then $T(A) = D$. The following figure shows $T(ABC)$ and DEF.

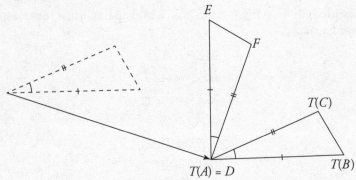

Let ρ be the rotation around D that maps $T(B)$ to E. This is possible because rigid motions preserve lengths of segments since $AB = DE$. Then $\rho(T(A)) = D$ and $\rho(T(B)) = E$. The following figure shows the triangles $\rho(T(ABC))$ and DEF.

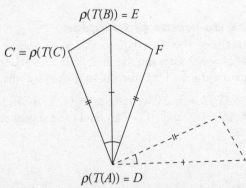

Let R be the reflection across line $\overleftrightarrow{DE}$. Then $R\big(\rho\big(T(A)\big)\big) = D$ and $R\big(\rho\big(T(B)\big)\big) = E$ because the points D and E are on the line of reflection. Let $\rho(T(C)) = C'$. Since rigid motions preserve degrees of angles and since $m\angle A = m\angle D$, ray $\overrightarrow{DC'}$ maps onto ray $\overrightarrow{DF}$. Since rigid motions preserve lengths of segments and since $AC = DF$, $R(C') = F$.

Using L to be the congruence of $L = R \circ \rho \circ T$, $L(ABC) = DEF$. Therefore, $\triangle ABC \cong \triangle DEF$. This is the general case. It is possible that the two points A and D are the same. If this is the case, the translation T is not necessary and $L = \rho \circ R$. It is also possible that the translation T maps both A to D and B to E. In this instance, the rotation is not necessary and $L = T \circ R$. Finally, it is possible that the final reflection may not be necessary. Then, $L = T \circ \rho$.

Theorem 3.18 (ASA Theorem): Given two triangles $\triangle ABC$ and $\triangle DEF$ so that $m\angle A = m\angle D$, $m\angle B = m\angle E$, and $AB = DE$, then the triangles are congruent.

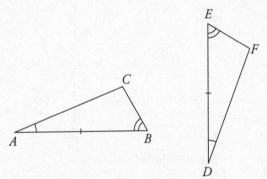

Triangles with ASA properties

Proof of this theorem is similar to the SAS Theorem (*Theorem 3.17*) except for the final argument. Let T be the translation along the vector $\overrightarrow{AD}$ and ρ be the rotation around D that maps $T(B)$ to E. Once again, this is possible because rigid motions preserve lengths of segments and because $AB = DE$. Let $\rho(T(A)) = A'$, $\rho(T(B)) = B'$, and $\rho(T(C)) = C'$. Then $D = A'$ and $E = B'$, as shown in the figure below. Let R be the reflection across line $\overleftrightarrow{DE}$. Since $m\angle B = m\angle E$ and reflections preserve degrees of angles, ray $\overrightarrow{B'C'}$ maps onto ray $\overrightarrow{EF}$. Since $m\angle A = m\angle D$ and reflections preserve degrees of angles, ray $\overrightarrow{A'C'}$ maps onto ray $\overrightarrow{DF}$. Now C' is the intersection of $\overrightarrow{B'C'}$ and $\overrightarrow{A'C'}$, and F is the intersection of $R\big(\overrightarrow{B'C'}\big)$ and $R\big(\overrightarrow{A'C'}\big)$. Therefore, C' maps onto F. Let L be the congruence $L = R \circ \rho \circ T$ so that $L(ABC) = DEF$ and $\triangle ABC \cong \triangle DEF$.

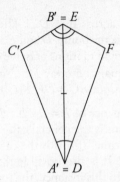

Theorem 3.19 (AAS Theorem): If two angles and a side not between them in one triangle are congruent to the corresponding parts in another triangle, then the triangles are congruent.

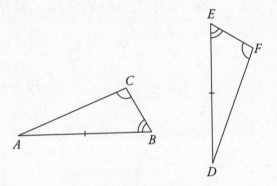

Triangles with AAS properties

Since it can be shown that if two angles of one triangle are equal to two angles of another triangle, the remaining angles are equal to each other, this AAS situation resolves itself to being the ASA situation, which states the triangles will now be congruent.

Theorem 3.20 (HL Theorem): If two right triangles have equal hypotenuses and one pair of equal legs, then the two triangles are congruent.

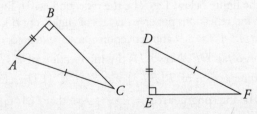

Triangles with equal hypotenuses and one pair of equal legs

Let $\triangle ABC$ and $\triangle DEF$ be the given right triangles so that $\angle B$ and $\angle E$ are right angles, $AB = DE$, and $\overline{AC}$ and $\overline{DF}$ are the equal hypotenuses. As we have seen the previous proofs of ASA and SAS theorems, you can find a composition of rigid motions, say J, to transform that would map $\triangle ABC$ in the figure above to $\triangle A'B'C'$ in the figure below.

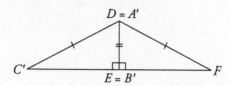

At this point, the proof cannot proceed the same way as in the ASA Theorem or the SAS Theorem because it is not known if $m\angle D = m\angle A$. If they are not equal, then after the reflection R across line $\overleftrightarrow{DE}$, ray $\overrightarrow{A'C'}$ will not coincide with ray $\overrightarrow{DF}$. However, if it can be shown that $\angle C'A'B' = \angle FDE$, then the argument is identical to the proof of the ASA Theorem from this point on.

Since $C'D = FD$, $\triangle C'DF$ is isosceles. The altitude of $\triangle C'DF$ is $\overline{ED}$. By *Theorem 3.5*, line $\overleftrightarrow{ED}$ is the angle bisector of $\angle C'DF$. Therefore, $\angle C'A'B' = \angle FDE$.

Theorem 3.21 (SSS Theorem): Two triangles with three equal sides are congruent.

Let $\triangle ABC$ and $\triangle DEF$ be the given triangles so that $AB = DE$, $BC = EF$, and $CA = FD$.

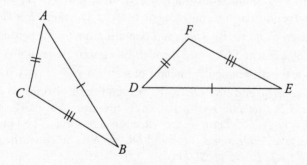

Let J be the composition of rigid motions so that $J(A) = D$ and $J(B) = E$. Once again, this is possible since $AB = DE$. Let $J(A) = A'$, $J(B) = B'$, and $J(C) = C'$. Then $A' = D$ and $B' = E$, as shown in the figure below. Our usual technique at this point is to reflect across line $\overleftrightarrow{DE}$. However, it is not known if $m\angle FDE = m\angle C'DE$ or $m\angle FED = m\angle C'ED$. If at least one of these conditions exists, then reflection across line $\overleftrightarrow{DE}$ will map C' to F.

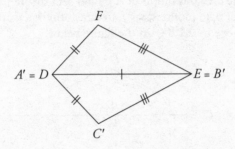

So our goal now is to get at least one of those conditions satisfied. Construct the segment $\overline{FC'}$, as shown in the following figure.

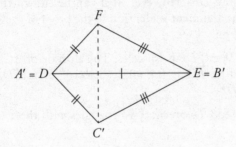

The point D is equidistant from F and C'. By *Theorem 3.6*, point D lies on the perpendicular bisector of segment $\overline{FC'}$. The point E is also equidistant from F and C'. By *Theorem 3.6*, point E lies on the perpendicular bisector of segment $\overline{FC'}$. Since through two points passes only one line, line $\overleftrightarrow{DE}$ is the perpendicular bisector of segment $\overline{FC'}$. Now $\triangle FDC'$ is an isosceles triangle and line $\overleftrightarrow{DE}$ is the perpendicular bisector of $\overline{FC'}$. By *Theorem 3.5*, line $\overleftrightarrow{DE}$ is also the angle bisector of $\angle FDC'$. That is, $m\angle FDE = m\angle C'DE$. Let R be the reflection across line $\overleftrightarrow{DE}$. Then $R(C') = F$ because $m\angle FDE = m\angle C'DE$ and $DC' = DF$. Therefore, the congruence $J \circ R$ maps $\triangle ABC$ to $\triangle DEF$.

Example 11: Decide if the pairs of triangles shown in figures **(a)** through **(i)** below are congruent based on the given information and known theorems. (Do not base your decision just by appearances.) State the theorems that you used to make your decision or note if there is not enough information given to determine the answer.

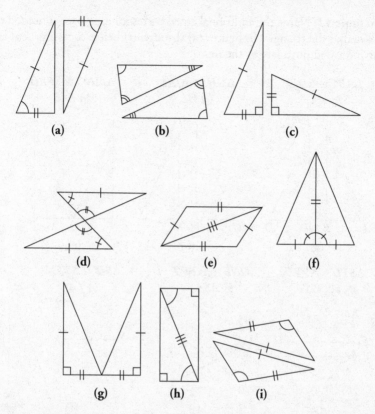

(a) The triangles are congruent by the SAS Theorem.

(b) There is not enough information to decide if these triangles are congruent.

(c) The triangles are congruent by the HL Theorem.

(d) The triangles are congruent by the Angle Sum Theorem, the ASA Theorem, and the AAS Theorem.

(e) The triangles are congruent by the SSS Theorem. The third pair of congruent sides is the side that is shared by the two triangles.

(f) The triangles are congruent by the SAS Theorem.

(g) The triangles are congruent by the SAS Theorem.

(h) The triangles are congruent by the AAS Theorem.

(i) There is not enough information to decide if these triangles are congruent.

Example 12: Name the additional equal corresponding part(s) needed to prove that the triangles in figures **(a)** through **(f)** below are congruent by the indicated postulate or theorem.

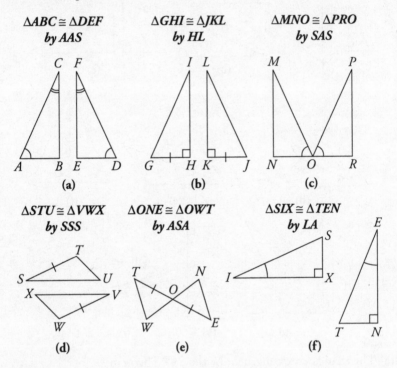

$\triangle ABC \cong \triangle DEF$
by AAS

$\triangle GHI \cong \triangle JKL$
by HL

$\triangle MNO \cong \triangle PRO$
by SAS

(a)

(b)

(c)

$\triangle STU \cong \triangle VWX$
by SSS

$\triangle ONE \cong \triangle OWT$
by ASA

$\triangle SIX \cong \triangle TEN$
by LA

(d)

(e)

(f)

(a) $BC = EF$ or $AB = DE$ (but not $AC = DF$ because these two sides lie between the equal angles)

(b) $GI = JL$

(c) $MO = PO$ and $NO = RO$

(d) $TU = WX$ and $SU = VX$

(e) $m\angle T = m\angle E$ and $m\angle TOW = m\angle EON$

(f) $IX = EN$ or $SX = TN$ (but not $IS = ET$ because they are hypotenuses)

It is important to note that the concept of congruence is not limited to triangles. Take a look at *Theorem 3.22* below.

Theorem 3.22: Two circles of the same radius are congruent. Let C_1 and C_2 be the two circles so that their centers are O_1 and O_2. Let r be the common radius. Let T be the translation along the vector $\overrightarrow{O_2O_1}$. Then $T(C_2) = C_1$, because translation preserves lengths of line segments.

Chapter Check-Out

Questions

1. If a triangle has two angles with degree measures 65° and 75°, what is the degree measure of the third angle?

2. True or False: In a triangle, an angle bisector must also bisect the side opposite the angle that was bisected.

3. True or False: If each angle of a triangle is congruent to the corresponding angle of another triangle, then the two triangles must be congruent.

4. The lengths of two sides of a triangle are 11 and 23. If the third side is x, find the range of possible values for x.

Answers

1. 40°

2. False

3. False

4. $12 < x < 34$

Chapter 4

POLYGONS

Chapter Check-In

❏ Understanding triangulation

❏ Distinguishing between convex and concave polygons

❏ Classifying polygons

❏ Recognizing special quadrilaterals (trapezoids and parallelograms) and special parallelograms (rectangles, rhombuses, and squares)

❏ Understanding concurrence theorems

Common Core Standard: Congruence, Proof, and Constructions

Prove theorems about parallelograms. Theorems include: opposite sides are congruent, opposite angles are congruent, the diagonals of a parallelogram bisect each other, and conversely, rectangles are parallelograms with congruent diagonals (G.CO.11).

Geometry Theorems

The geometry theorems in this book are numbered for organizational purposes. For example, *Theorem 2.2* is the second theorem given in Chapter 2. Study these theorems by their content, not by their number, as the theorem numbering has no significance outside of this book.

Triangulation of a Polygon and the Sum of the Interior Angles

Let *ABCD* be a quadrilateral. Draw the diagonal *AC* as shown in the figure below. The diagonal *AC* separates the quadrilateral into two adjacent triangles with the diagonal as the common side. This is known as

triangulation of the quadrilateral. Using triangulation, you can find the sum of the interior angles of quadrilateral *ABCD*; that is, the sum of ∠*A*, ∠*B*, ∠*C*, and ∠*D*.

Theorem 4.1: The sum of the interior angles of a quadrilateral is 360°.

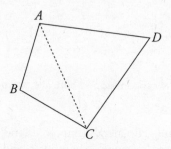

By using the Angle Sum Theorem (*Theorem 3.2*) for Δ*ABC*, you have $m\angle B + m\angle BAC + m\angle BCA = 180°$. By the same theorem, the sum of the angles of Δ*ADC* is $m\angle D + m\angle DAC + m\angle DCA = 180°$. Then, $m\angle B + (m\angle BAC + m\angle DAC) + m\angle D + (m\angle DCA + m\angle BCA) = 360°$. Therefore, $m\angle A + m\angle B + m\angle C + m\angle D = 360°$.

Theorem 4.2: The sum of the angles of a pentagon is 540°.

Let *ABCDE* be the pentagon, as shown below.

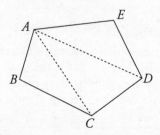

Consider two adjacent sides and draw the diagonal connecting the two noncommon vertices of those two sides. For example, connect *A* and *C* to get the diagonal $\overline{AC}$, as shown in the figure above. Hence, *ACDE* is a quadrilateral and we know how to triangulate it. Draw the diagonal $\overline{AD}$ to complete the triangulation of the pentagon. The proof of the theorem is similar to that of *Theorem 4.1*, and the sum of the interior angles of *ABCDE* is $3(180°) = 540°$.

Theorem 4.3: The sum of the interior angles of a hexagon is four times 180°.

Let *ABCDEF* be the hexagon. Once again, consider two adjacent sides and draw the diagonal connecting the two noncommon vertices of those two sides. For example, connect *A* and *C* to get the diagonal $\overline{AC}$, as shown in the figure below. Then *ACDEF* is a pentagon, and you have previously learned how to triangulate it. The proof of the theorem is similar to the proof of *Theorem 4.2.*

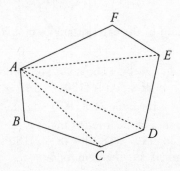

In general, you can triangulate an *n*-gon for any positive integer greater than or equal to 3.

Theorem 4.4: Any *n*-gon can be triangulated.

Theorem 4.5: The sum of the interior angles of an *n*-gon is $(n-2)$ times 180°.

Exterior Angles of a Convex Polygon

Now let's narrow our attention to **convex polygons.**

 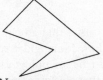

Convex pentagon   Nonconvex pentagon

Consider an interior angle of a convex *n*-gon. Extend one side of that interior angle. The angle formed by the extended side and the other side of the interior angle is called the *exterior angle of that interior angle* of the *n*-gon. Draw only one exterior angle at each vertex of a convex polygon. The exterior angle is supplementary to the associated interior angle.

The following figure shows one exterior angle at each vertex of a convex pentagon.

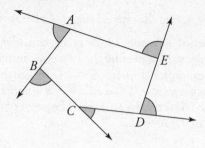

Theorem 4.6: The sum of the exterior angles of a convex *n*-gon, one at each vertex, is 360°.

Let $A_1 A_2 A_3 \cdots A_{n-1} A_n$ be a convex *n*-gon. Then the sum of the *n* exterior angles of a convex *n*-gon is $(180° - \angle A_1) + (180° - \angle A_2) + \cdots + (180° - \angle A_n)$. This is the same as $n(180°) - (\angle A_1 + \angle A_2 + \cdots + \angle A_n)$. By *Theorem 4.5,* the sum of the interior angles is $(n-2)180°$. Hence, the sum of the exterior angles is $n(180°) - (n-2)180°$. By the distributive property of real numbers, the theorem follows.

Example 1: Find the interior angle sum of a 10-gon.

A 10-gon has 10 sides. Using *Theorem 4.5:*

$$S = (10-2) \times 180°$$
$$S = 1,440°$$

Example 2: Find the sum of the exterior angles, one at each vertex, of a nine-sided convex polygon.

By *Theorem 4.6,* the sum of the exterior angles of any convex polygon is 360°.

It was shown earlier that an equilateral triangle is automatically equiangular and that an equiangular triangle is automatically equilateral. This does not hold true for polygons in general. Here are some examples of quadrilaterals that are equiangular but not equilateral, equilateral but not equiangular, and both equiangular and equilateral.

Equiangular but
not equilateral

Equilateral but
not equiangular

Equiangular and
equilateral

Regular Polygons

When a polygon is both equilateral and equiangular, it is referred to as a **regular polygon.** For a polygon to be regular, it must also be convex. Here are some examples of regular polygons.

Regular Polygons

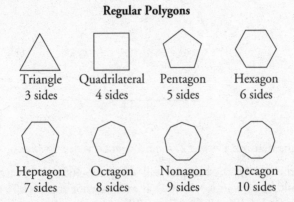

| Triangle | Quadrilateral | Pentagon | Hexagon |
| 3 sides | 4 sides | 5 sides | 6 sides |

| Heptagon | Octagon | Nonagon | Decagon |
| 7 sides | 8 sides | 9 sides | 10 sides |

As mentioned earlier, names for *n*-gons for $n = 3$ to $n = 6$ (triangles, quadrilaterals, pentagons, and hexagons) are in regular use. Even though names of *n*-gons for $n = 7$ to $n = 10$ are given in the figure above, they are usually identified as 7-gon, 8-gon, 9-gon, and 10-gon.

Example 3: Find the measure of each interior angle of a regular hexagon.

Method 1: Because the polygon is regular, all interior angles are equal, so you only need to find the interior angle sum and divide by the number of angles.

$$S = (6 - 2) \times 180°$$
$$S = 720$$

There are six angles, so $720 \div 6 = 120°$.

Each interior angle of a regular hexagon has a measure of 120°, as labeled below.

Regular hexagon
$m\angle 1 = 120°$

Method 2: Because the polygon is regular and all its interior angles are equal, all its exterior angles are also equal. Look at the following figure.

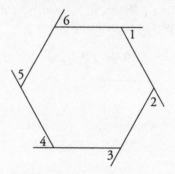

This means that $m\angle 1 = m\angle 2 = m\angle 3 = m\angle 4 = m\angle 5 = m\angle 6$.

Because the sum of these angles will always be 360°, then each exterior angle would be 60°: 360° ÷ 6 = 60°. If each exterior angle is 60°, then each interior angle is 120°: 180° − 60° = 120°.

Parallelograms

Recall that a parallelogram is any quadrilateral with both pairs of opposite sides parallel. Remember that the opposite sides of a parallelogram are equal (*Theorem 2.16*). Now you are ready to prove the converse of *Theorem 2.16*. The converse of *Theorem 2.16* is stated in *Theorem 4.7*.

Theorem 4.7: In a quadrilateral, if a pair of opposite sides are both parallel and equal in length, then the quadrilateral is a parallelogram.

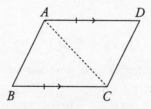

Suppose $ABCD$ is a quadrilateral with $\overrightarrow{AD} \parallel \overrightarrow{BC}$ and $AD = BC$, as shown in the figure above. Construct the segment $\overline{AC}$. Then $\overrightarrow{AD}$ and $\overrightarrow{BC}$ are parallel lines cut by the transversal line $\overleftrightarrow{AC}$. Angles $\angle DAC$ and $\angle BCA$ are alternate interior angles and by *Theorem 2.11*, $m\angle DAC = m\angle BCA$. Consequently, $\triangle ABC$ and $\triangle ADC$ are congruent by the SAS Theorem (*Theorem 3.17*), ($AD = CB$, $m\angle DAC = m\angle BCA$, and $AC = CA$), and

$m\angle DCA = m\angle BAC$. However, $\angle DCA$ and $\angle BAC$ are alternate interior angles of the transversal line $\overleftrightarrow{AC}$ with respect to lines $\overleftrightarrow{AB}$ and $\overleftrightarrow{CD}$. Using *Theorem 2.11*, $\overleftrightarrow{AB} \parallel \overleftrightarrow{CD}$ and *ABCD* is a parallelogram by definition.

The following theorem follows from *Theorem 2.9*.

Theorem 4.8: Consecutive angles of a parallelogram are supplementary.

The following theorem follows from *Theorem 4.8*.

Theorem 4.9: The opposite angles of a parallelogram are equal.

The following theorem follows from *Theorem 2.14*.

Theorem 4.10: If an angle of a quadrilateral is supplementary to both of its consecutive angles, then the quadrilateral is a parallelogram.

The following theorem follows from *Theorem 4.10*.

Theorem 4.11: If both pairs of opposite angles of a quadrilateral are equal, then it is a parallelogram.

Theorem 4.12: The diagonals of a parallelogram bisect each other.

Let *ABCD* be a parallelogram. Construct the diagonal $\overline{AC}$ and let *E* be the midpoint of $\overline{AC}$ (see the figure below). Let ρ be the 180° rotation around *E*. By the proof of *Theorem 2.16*, $\rho(D) = B$ and $DE = EB$. Also, by *Theorem 2.2*, points *D*, *E*, and *B* are collinear, and *E* is the midpoint of the diagonal $\overline{DB}$.

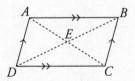

Theorem 4.13: If the diagonals of a quadrilateral bisect each other, then it is a parallelogram.

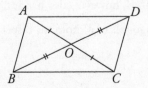

Let $ABCD$ be a quadrilateral with bisecting diagonals, as shown in the figure above, and O is the point of intersection of the diagonals. Let ρ be the $180°$ rotation around O. Then $\rho(C) = A$, $\rho(A) = C$, $\rho(B) = D$, and $\rho(D) = B$ according to *Theorem 2.2*. Therefore, $\rho\left(\overrightarrow{CD}\right) = \overrightarrow{AB}$ and $\rho\left(\overrightarrow{BC}\right) = \overrightarrow{DA}$. Then by *Theorem 2.3*, $\overrightarrow{AD} \parallel \overrightarrow{CB}$ and $\overrightarrow{AB} \parallel \overrightarrow{CD}$; and by definition, $ABCD$ is a parallelogram.

Theorem 4.13 can also be proven using the SAS Theorem (*Theorem 3.17*).

Rectangles

Recall that a rectangle is a quadrilateral with all right angles. Using *Theorem 4.11*, the following theorem follows.

Theorem 4.14: A rectangle is a parallelogram.

As a result of *Theorem 4.14*, rectangles have all the properties found for parallelograms. In addition, a rectangle has the following property.

Theorem 4.15: The diagonals of a rectangle are equal.

Consider a rectangle $ABCD$ as shown below. $AD = BC$ because $ABCD$ is a parallelogram. Then $\triangle ADC$ and $\triangle BCD$ are congruent by the SAS Theorem (*Theorem 3.17*), and $AC = DB$.

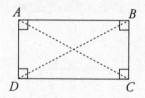

Rhombus

Recall that a rhombus is a quadrilateral with all equal sides.

Theorem 4.16: A rhombus is a parallelogram.

By *Theorem 4.16*, a rhombus has all of the properties associated with a parallelogram. A rhombus, however, also has additional properties.

Theorem 4.17: The diagonals of a rhombus bisect opposite angles.

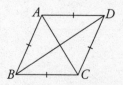

Let *ABCD* be a rhombus. Draw the diagonals $\overline{AC}$ and $\overline{BD}$, as shown in the figure above. Since $AB = AD$, $BC = DC$, and $AC = AC$, $\triangle ABC$ and $\triangle ADC$ are congruent by the SSS Theorem (*Theorem 3.21*). Thus, $\angle BAC \cong \angle DAC$ and $\angle BCA \cong \angle DCA$ because corresponding parts of congruent triangles are congruent.

Hence, the diagonal $\overline{AC}$ bisects $\angle BAD$ and $\angle BCD$. Similarly, it can be proven that the diagonal $\overline{BD}$ bisects $\angle ABC$ and $\angle ADC$.

Theorem 4.18: The diagonals of a rhombus are perpendicular to one another.

Notice that $\triangle ABD$ in the figure above is an isosceles triangle. From *Theorem 4.12*, it is known that $\overline{AC}$ bisects $\overline{BD}$. From *Theorem 4.17*, $\overline{AC}$ is the angle bisector of $\angle A$. Therefore, using *Theorem 3.5*, $\overline{AC}$ is the perpendicular bisector of $\overline{BD}$. Similarly, $\overline{BD}$ is the perpendicular bisector of $\overline{AC}$.

Example 4: In the following figure, find $m\angle A$, $m\angle C$, $m\angle D$, CD, and AD.

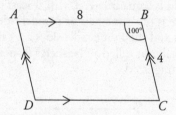

$m\angle A = m\angle C = 80°$ because consecutive angles of a parallelogram are supplementary.

$m\angle D = 100°$ because opposite angles of a parallelogram are equal.

$CD = 8$ and $AD = 4$ because opposite sides of a parallelogram are equal.

Example 5: In the following figure, find TR, QP, PS, TP, and PR.

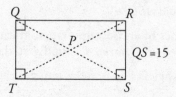

$TR = 15$ because diagonals of a rectangle are equal.

$QP = PS = TP = PR = 7.5$ because diagonals of a rectangle bisect each other.

Example 6: In the following figure, find $m\angle MOE$, $m\angle NOE$, and $m\angle MYO$.

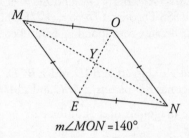

$$m\angle MON = 140°$$

$m\angle MOE = m\angle NOE = 70°$ because diagonals of a rhombus bisect opposite angles.

$m\angle MYO = 90°$ because diagonals of a rhombus are perpendicular.

Trapezoids

Recall that a trapezoid is a quadrilateral with at least one pair of opposite sides parallel. If there is only one pair of parallel sides, then the parallel sides are called **bases** and the nonparallel sides are called **legs.** If the legs of a trapezoid are equal, it is called an **isosceles trapezoid.** The following figure is an isosceles trapezoid.

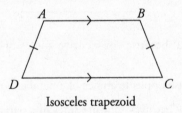

Isosceles trapezoid

A pair of angles that share the same base are called **base angles of a trapezoid.** In the isosceles trapezoid above, $\angle A$ and $\angle B$ or $\angle C$ and $\angle D$ are base angles of trapezoid $ABCD$.

Two special properties of an isosceles trapezoid can be proven. These properties are depicted in *Theorems 4.19* and *4.20* that follow.

Theorem 4.19: Base angles of an isosceles trapezoid are equal.

Let $ABCD$ be an isosceles trapezoid so that $\overleftrightarrow{AD} \parallel \overleftrightarrow{BC}$, $AB = DC$, and $BC > AD$. Construct a line passing through D and parallel to line $\overleftrightarrow{AB}$ that intersects line $\overleftrightarrow{BC}$ at E. Then, by definition, $ABED$ is a parallelogram and

$BE = AD$. This implies that E lies between B and C because $BC > AD$, as shown in the following figure.

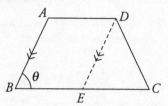

Let $m\angle ABC = \theta$. By *Theorem 2.7*, $m\angle DEC = \theta$, and by *Theorem 2.16*, $AB = DE$. Therefore, ΔDEC is an isosceles triangle, and by *Theorem 3.4* $m\angle DCE = \theta$. This proves that base angles $\angle B$ and $\angle D$ are equal.

Now by using Angle Sum Theorem (*Theorem 3.2*) on ΔDEC, $m\angle EDC = 180 - 2\theta$. Since $ABED$ is a parallelogram and opposite angles of a parallelogram are equal (*Theorem 4.9*), $m\angle ADE = \theta$. Then $m\angle ADC = 180° - \theta$, since $m\angle ADC = m\angle ADE + m\angle EDC$. Now, $\angle A$ and $\angle B$ are consecutive angles of the parallelogram $ABED$, and by *Theorem 4.8*, $m\angle A = 180° - \theta$, and $m\angle A = m\angle ADC$. This proves that base angles $\angle A$ and $\angle D$ are equal.

Theorem 4.20: Diagonals of an isosceles trapezoid are equal.

Let $ABCD$ be an isosceles trapezoid so that $\overrightarrow{AB} \parallel \overrightarrow{DC}$, $AD = BC$, and $DC > AB$, as shown in the following figure.

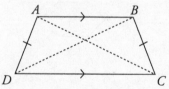

Construct the diagonals $\overline{AC}$ and $\overline{BD}$. Consider ΔADC and ΔBCD. The angles $\angle ADC$ and $\angle BCD$ are equal by *Theorem 4.19*. Therefore, by the SAS Theorem (*Theorem 3.17*), ΔADC and ΔBCD are congruent and as a consequence, $AC = BD$.

Example 7: In the following figure, find $m\angle ABC$ and BD.

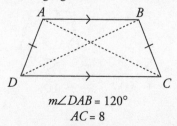

$$m\angle DAB = 120°$$
$$AC = 8$$

$m\angle ABC = 120°$ because the base angles of an isosceles trapezoid are equal.

$BD = 8$ because diagonals of an isosceles trapezoid are equal.

The following diagram summarizes the relationships among various quadrilaterals that we have seen in this chapter.

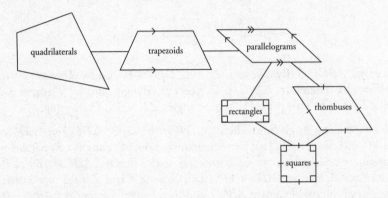

Example 8: Identify the following polygons in figures **(a)** through **(j)**.

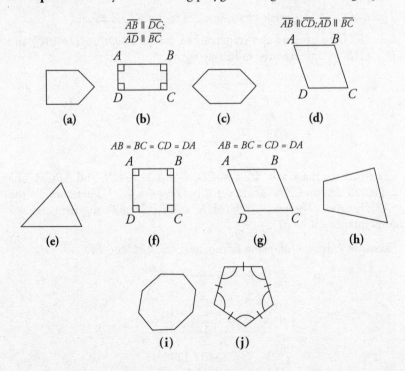

(a) pentagon
(b) rectangle
(c) hexagon
(d) parallelogram
(e) triangle

(f) square
(g) rhombus
(h) quadrilateral
(i) octagon
(j) regular pentagon

The Midpoint Theorem

Theorem 4.21 (Midpoint Theorem): The segment joining the midpoints of two sides of a triangle is parallel to the third side and is half as long as the third side.

Let $\triangle ABC$ be a triangle so that D is the midpoint of $\overline{AB}$ and E is the midpoint of $\overline{AC}$, as shown in the following figure. Now, let's show that $\overline{DE} \parallel \overline{BC}$ and $DE = \dfrac{1}{2} BC$.

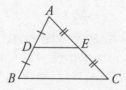

Locate point F on ray $\overrightarrow{DE}$ so that $DE = EF$, as shown in the following figure.

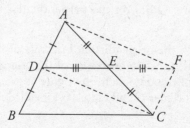

The diagonals bisect in the quadrilateral $ADCF$, and by *Theorem 4.13*, $ADCF$ is a parallelogram, and $AD = FC$ and $\overrightarrow{AD} \parallel \overrightarrow{FC}$. Then $DB = FC$ and $\overrightarrow{DB} \parallel \overrightarrow{FC}$. Therefore, by *Theorem 4.7*, $DBCF$ is a parallelogram, $DF = BC$, $\overrightarrow{DF} \parallel \overrightarrow{BC}$ or $\overrightarrow{DE} \parallel \overrightarrow{BC}$, and $DE = \dfrac{1}{2} BC$.

Concurrence Theorems

If three or more lines meet at the same point, they are **concurrent lines.**

Theorem 4.22: The perpendicular bisectors of the three sides of a triangle are concurrent.

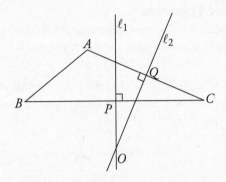

Let $\triangle ABC$ be the given triangle and let ℓ_1 and ℓ_2 be the perpendicular bisectors of $\overline{BC}$ and $\overline{AC}$, respectively. Let O be the point of intersection of ℓ_1 and ℓ_2. Now show that O lies on the perpendicular bisector of $\overline{AB}$ as well. Let the midpoints of $\overline{BC}$ and $\overline{AC}$ be P and Q respectively, as shown in the figure above. Since O is on ℓ_1, O is equidistant from B and C, by *Theorem 3.6.* By the same theorem, O is equidistant from A and C since O is on ℓ_2. That means O is equidistant from A and B. Therefore, O lies on the perpendicular bisector of $\overline{AB}$ by *Theorem 3.6.*

The point at which the perpendicular bisectors of the three sides of a triangle meet is called the **circumcenter of the triangle.** The point O is the circumcenter of the triangle in the figure above. Since $OA = OB = OC$, the circle with center O and radius OA is called the **circumcircle of the triangle** $\triangle ABC$.

Theorem 4.23: There is a unique circle passing through the vertices of a triangle whose center is the circumcenter.

Theorem 4.24: The three altitudes of a triangle are concurrent.

If the triangle is acute, then all three altitudes lie inside the triangle. If one angle of the triangle is obtuse, then two of the altitudes lie outside the triangle, as shown in the following figure.

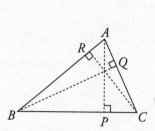
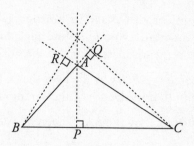

Let the altitudes of $\triangle ABC$ be $\overline{AP}$, $\overline{BQ}$, and $\overline{CR}$. Through each vertex of $\triangle ABC$, draw a line parallel to the opposite side. The intersections of these lines form $\triangle A_1B_1C_1$, as shown in the following figure.

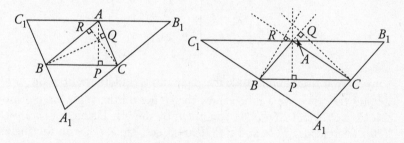

By construction (opposite sides of the quadrilateral are parallel), $ABCB_1$ is a parallelogram, and $BC = AB_1$. By construction, C_1BCA is a parallelogram, and $BC = AC_1$. Therefore, A is the midpoint of $\overline{B_1C_1}$. Lines $\overleftrightarrow{BC}$ and $\overleftrightarrow{B_1C_1}$ are parallel, and line $\overleftrightarrow{AP}$ is perpendicular to line $\overleftrightarrow{BC}$. By the converse of *Theorem 2.4*, line $\overleftrightarrow{AP}$ is perpendicular to line $\overleftrightarrow{B_1C_1}$, and line $\overleftrightarrow{AP}$ is the perpendicular bisector of $\overline{B_1C_1}$. Similarly, line $\overleftrightarrow{CR}$ is the perpendicular bisector of $\overline{A_1B_1}$ and line $\overleftrightarrow{BQ}$ is the perpendicular bisector of $\overline{A_1C_1}$. By *Theorem 4.22*, the three altitudes of $\triangle ABC$ are concurrent.

The point where the three altitudes of a triangle meet is called the **orthocenter of a triangle.**

Given a line ℓ and a point P not on the line, it is known that a line can be drawn through P perpendicular to ℓ by *Theorem 2.5*. Let Q be the point of intersection of ℓ and the perpendicular through P. Then the length PQ is called the *distance between P and ℓ*.

Theorem 4.25: The angle bisector of an angle is the collection of all points equidistant from the two sides of the angle.

Consider $\angle AOB$ and its bisector, as shown in the figure below. Let P be an arbitrary point on the angle bisector. Let A and B be the feet of the perpendiculars from P to the sides of the angle. Show that $PA = PB$.

$\angle AOP = \angle BOP$, by the hypothesis, $\angle OAP = \angle OBP$, by construction, and OP is the length of the common side.

Therefore, by the AAS Theorem, $\triangle OAP \cong \triangle OBP$, and $PA = PB$.

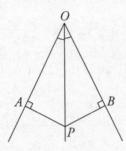

Conversely, if P is a point inside the angle and is equidistant from the rays $\overrightarrow{OA}$ and $\overrightarrow{OB}$, then we want to show that P lies on the angle bisector of $\angle AOB$. $\triangle OPA$ and $\triangle OPB$ are congruent by the HL Theorem (*Theorem 3.20*). Therefore, $\angle POA$ and $\angle POB$ are equal. Thus, P lies on the angle bisector of $\angle AOB$.

Theorem 4.26: The three angle bisectors of a triangle are concurrent.

Suppose the angle bisectors of the angles $\angle B$ and $\angle C$ of $\triangle ABC$ meet at P, as shown in the figure below. By *Theorem 4.25*, P is equidistant from lines $\overrightarrow{BA}$ and $\overrightarrow{BC}$ since P is on the angle bisector of $\angle B$. By the same theorem, P is equidistant from lines $\overrightarrow{CA}$ and $\overrightarrow{BC}$ since P is on the angle bisector of $\angle C$. Hence, P is equidistant from lines $\overrightarrow{BA}$ and $\overrightarrow{CA}$, or P lies on the angle bisector of $\angle A$, by *Theorem 4.25*.

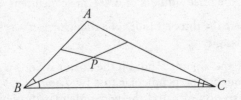

The point where three angle bisectors of a triangle meet is called the **incenter of the triangle.**

The following theorem follows from *Theorems 4.25* and *4.26*.

Theorem 4.27: The incenter of a triangle is equidistant from all three sides of the triangle.

Theorem 4.28: The three medians of a triangle are concurrent. (This theorem will be proven later in Chapter 5 after learning about similarity of triangles; See pp. 99–100.)

The point where three medians of a triangle meet is called the **centroid of a triangle.**

Theorem 4.29: If F is the centroid of a triangle, then on each median, the distance from F to the vertex is twice the distance from F to the opposite side.

Let $\triangle ABC$ be a triangle. Let the median from B to $\overline{AC}$ be $\overline{BE}$, as shown in the figure below. We want to show that $BF = 2FE$.

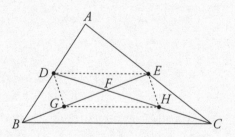

Since the choice of B is arbitrary (that is, we could have carried the following argument by choosing A or C instead of B), when we show $BF = 2FE$, the proof is complete.

Let $\overline{CD}$ be the median from C to $\overline{AB}$, as shown in the figure above. Let G and H be the midpoints of $\overline{BF}$ and $\overline{CF}$.

By applying the Midpoint Theorem (*Theorem 4.21*) to $\triangle ABC$, $\overrightarrow{DE} \parallel \overline{BC}$ and $DE = \dfrac{1}{2}BC$. By applying the Midpoint Theorem to $\triangle BFC$, $\overrightarrow{GH} \parallel \overline{BC}$ and $GH = \dfrac{1}{2}BC$. Hence, by *Theorem 4.7*, $DGHE$ is a parallelogram, and by *Theorem 4.12*, $GF = FE$ or $BF = 2FE$.

Chapter Check-Out

Questions

1. True or False: All triangles are convex.
2. What is the degree measure of the interior angle determined by two adjacent sides of a regular decagon?
3. True or False: A rectangle is a square.
4. True or False: A square is a rectangle.
5. True or False: Diagonals of a parallelogram bisect each other.
6. True or False: Diagonals of a parallelogram have the same length.

Answers

1. True
2. 144°
3. False
4. True
5. True
6. False

Chapter 5
SIMILARITY

Chapter Check-In

☐ Using the concept of dilation

☐ Knowing the Fundamental Theorem of Similarity

☐ Understanding the concept of similarity

☐ Applying the following criteria for similarity: SAS, AA, and SSS

☐ Knowing the Pythagorean Theorem and its converse

Common Core Standard: Similarity, Proof, and Trigonometry

A dilation takes a line not passing through the center of the dilation to a parallel line, and leaves a line passing through the center unchanged (G.SRT.1a). The dilation of a line segment is longer or shorter in the ratio given by the scale factor (G.SRT.1b).

Given two figures, use the definition of similarity in terms of similarity transformations to decide if they are similar; explain using similarity transformations and the meaning of similarity for triangles as the equality of all corresponding pairs of angles and the proportionality of all corresponding pairs of sides (G.SRT.2).

Use the properties of similarity transformations to establish the AA criterion for two triangles to be similar. Prove theorems involving similarity (G.SRT.3). Prove theorems about triangles. Theorems include: a line parallel to one side of a triangle divides the other two proportionally and conversely; the Pythagorean Theorem proved using triangle similarity (G.SRT.4). Use congruence and similarity criteria for triangles to solve problems and to prove relationships in geometric figures (G.SRT.5).

> **Geometry Theorems**
>
> The geometry theorems in this book are numbered for organizational purposes. For example, *Theorem 2.2* is the second theorem given in Chapter 2. Study these theorems by their content, not by their number, as the theorem numbering has no significance outside of this book.

Dilation

You have learned that a rigid motion is a plane transformation that preserves lengths of line segments and degrees of angles, among other things. A composition of rigid motions (called a **congruence**) also preserves triangles that satisfy one of the requirements, known by the abbreviations SAS, ASA, AAS, SSS, and HL.

In this chapter, we will look at a less rigid transformation called a **dilation.** A dilation D with center O and scale factor r, where r is a positive number, maps each point P in the plane to a point $D(P)$ so that:

(1) $D(O) = O$ and

(2) If $P \neq O$, then the point $D(P)$, denoted by P', is the point on ray $\overrightarrow{OP}$ so that $OP' = r \cdot OP$.

A dilation D with center O and scale factor 2 maps points P, Q, and R to points P', Q', and R', as shown in the following figure.

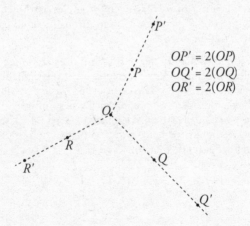

$$OP' = 2(OP)$$
$$OQ' = 2(OQ)$$
$$OR' = 2(OR)$$

A dilation D with center O and scale factor $\dfrac{1}{2}$ maps points P, Q, and R to points P', Q', and R', as shown in the following figure.

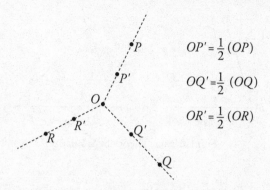

$$OP' = \frac{1}{2}(OP)$$

$$OQ' = \frac{1}{2}(OQ)$$

$$OR' = \frac{1}{2}(OR)$$

Let F be a figure in the plane and let D be a dilation with center O and scale factor r. Then $D(F)$ is the collection of all points $D(P)$, where P is any point on F.

The transformation of a figure by a dilation with center O and scale factor 2 can be seen in the following figure.

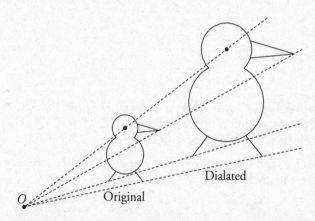

Dilated

Original

The Fundamental Theorem of Similarity

Theorem 5.1 (Fundamental Theorem of Similarity, or FTS): Let D be the dilation with center O and scale factor $r > 0$ and $r \neq 1$. Let P and Q be two points so that O, P, and Q are noncollinear. If $D(P) = P'$ and $D(Q) = Q'$, then $\overleftrightarrow{P'Q'} \parallel \overleftrightarrow{PQ}$ and $P'Q' = r(PQ)$.

We will use the following convention. Let D be a dilation with scale factor $r > 0$, and P and Q be two points on the plane. Then $D(P)$ and $D(Q)$ are the images of the point P and Q, and the length of the segment $\overline{D(P)D(Q)}$ is $D(P)D(Q)$. We will write $D(PQ)$ for $D(P)D(Q)$ for convenience.

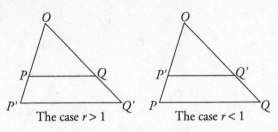

Fundamental Theory of Similarity

The Midpoint Theorem (*Theorem 4.21*) is a special case of the Fundamental Theorem of Similarity (FTS) in the following sense. Take a look at the following figure. Let D be the dilation with center A and scale factor $\frac{1}{2}$. Then $D(B) = P = B'$ and $D(C) = Q = C'$.

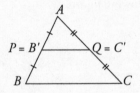

Theorem 5.2: Let D be the dilation with center O and scale factor $r > 0$. If P and Q are two points in the plane, then $D(PQ) = r(PQ)$. That is, the dilation changes distance by a factor of r.

Suppose O, P, and Q are collinear and P and Q lie on the same ray issuing from O (see figure below).

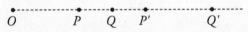

Let us assume that $OQ > PQ$, as shown in the figure. Then $P'Q' = OQ' - OP' = r(OQ) - r(OP) = r(PQ)$.

Now, suppose O, P, and Q are collinear and P and Q lie on the opposite rays issuing from O, as shown in the figure below. Then $P'Q' = P'O + OQ' = r(PO) + r(OQ) = r(PO + OQ) = r(PQ)$.

Finally, assume that O, P, and Q are noncollinear. Then the result follows from FTS.

The following theorem summarizes the basic properties of dilations. You can easily prove these theorems using the definition and FTS.

Theorem 5.3: A dilation
(i) maps lines to lines, rays to rays, and segments to segments.
(ii) maps a line passing through the center O to itself.
(iii) maps a line not passing through O to a line parallel to it.

Theorem 5.4: A dilation preserves degrees of angles.

The following theorem is a reformulation of FTS.

Theorem 5.5 (Fundamental Theorem of Similarity 2): Let $\triangle ABC$ be a triangle and let P be a point on ray $\overrightarrow{AB}$. Suppose a line passing through P and parallel to line $\overleftrightarrow{BC}$ intersects ray $\overrightarrow{AC}$ at Q. Then $\dfrac{AP}{AB} = \dfrac{AQ}{AC} = \dfrac{PQ}{BC}$.

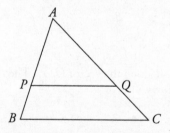

In the figure above, point P is between A and B. The following proof is based on this figure. However, if B lies between A and P, then the proof is similar and is left as an exercise to the reader. Let D be the dilation with center A and scale factor $r = \dfrac{AP}{AB}$. Then, by definition, $D(P) = B$. Suppose $D(Q) = R$ for some point R. By the definition of dilation, R lies on ray $\overrightarrow{AC}$. Then by FTS, line $\overleftrightarrow{PR}$ is parallel to line $\overleftrightarrow{BC}$. However, by hypothesis, line $\overleftrightarrow{PQ}$ is also parallel to line $\overleftrightarrow{BC}$. Then by the Parallel Postulate, $\overleftrightarrow{PR} = \overleftrightarrow{PQ}$. Since two lines intersect at exactly one point, $R = Q$. Now, by the definition of dilation, $\dfrac{AQ}{AC} = r$, and by FTS, $\dfrac{PQ}{BC} = r$.

The Definition of Similarity

Let S and R be two figures in the plane. It is understood that S is similar to R, denoted by $S \sim R$, if there is a dilation D and a congruence F, so that $D(F(S)) = R$. The composition of a congruence F followed by a dilation D, $D \circ F$, is called a **similarity.** Let $S = D \circ F$. Suppose r is the scale factor of the dilation D. Then r is also the scale factor of the similarity S.

Example 1: Let S_1 be the sector of a circle with center O_1, radius r_1, and central angle θ. Let S_2 be the sector of a circle with center O_2, radius r_2, and the same central angle θ, as shown in the following figure. Show that $S_1 \sim S_2$.

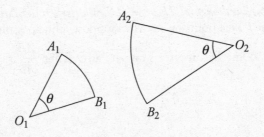

Let T be the translation along the vector $\overrightarrow{O_1 O_2}$. The translated S_1 is shown in the figure that follows.

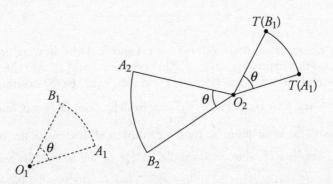

Let R be the counterclockwise rotation around O_2 by $\angle T(A_1)O_2B_2$. Let F be the congruence $R \circ T$. The sector $F(S_1)$ is shown in the following figure.

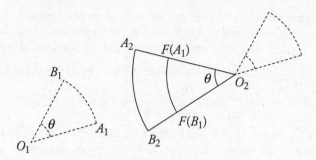

Let D be the dilation with center O_2 and scale factor $r = \dfrac{O_2 A_2}{O_2 F(A_1)}$.
Notice that $r = \dfrac{r_2}{r_1}$. Then it is easy to show that $D(F(S_1)) = S_2$.

Theorem 5.6: Any two circles are similar.

Similar Triangles

The following important theorem from algebra will be used often and, therefore, is included here as a reminder.

Theorem 5.7 (Cross-Multiplication Algorithm): If a, b, c, and d are nonzero real numbers, then $\dfrac{a}{b} = \dfrac{c}{d}$ if and only if $ad = bc$.

If two triangles are similar, then because of *Theorem 3.14* and *Theorem 5.2*, the following theorem can be understood.

Theorem 5.8: Suppose ABC and PQR are two triangles so that $\triangle ABC \sim \triangle PQR$. Then $m\angle A = m\angle P$, $m\angle B = m\angle Q$, $m\angle C = m\angle R$, and
$$\frac{AB}{PQ} = \frac{BC}{QR} = \frac{CA}{RP}.$$

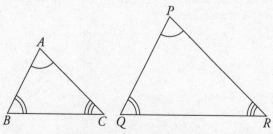

Properties of similar triangles

The converse theorems of *Theorem 5.8* are even more important. To show that two triangles are similar, you do not need all six properties listed in *Theorem 5.8*. The converse theorems (*Theorems 5.9–5.11*) are detailed below.

Theorem 5.9 (SAS Theorem for Similarity): Given two triangles $\triangle ABC$ and $\triangle PQR$, if $m\angle A = m\angle P$ and $\dfrac{AB}{PQ} = \dfrac{AC}{PR}$, then $\triangle ABC \sim \triangle PQR$.

If $AB = PQ$, then $AC = PR$, and by the SAS Theorem (*Theorem 3.17*), the two triangles are congruent. Hence, there is a congruence F so that $F(ABC) = PQR$. Let D be the dilation with center P and scale factor 1; then $D(F(ABC)) = PQR$ and the two triangles are similar. Now, suppose $PQ > AB$, as shown in the figure below. Let F be the congruence so that $F(A) = P$ and $F(\angle A) = \angle P$. Let $F(B) = B'$ and $F(C) = C'$. Two triangles $\triangle F(ABC) = PB'C'$ and $\triangle PQR$ are shown in the following figure.

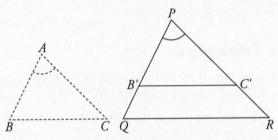

Let $\dfrac{1}{r}$ be the common value of $\dfrac{AB}{PQ}$ and $\dfrac{AC}{PR}$. That is, $\dfrac{AB}{PQ} = \dfrac{1}{r} = \dfrac{AC}{PR}$.

Then, by the Cross-Multiplication Algorithm (*Theorem 5.7*), $PQ = r(AB)$ and $PR = r(AC)$. Since congruences preserve lengths of segments, $AB = PB'$ and $AC = PC'$. Therefore, $PQ = r(PB')$ and $PR = r(PC')$. Let D be the dilation with center P and scale factor r. Then by the definition of dilation, $D(B') = Q$, $D(C') = R$, and $D(A') = P$. Therefore, $\triangle ABC \sim \triangle PQR$.

Theorem 5.10 (AA Theorem for Similarity): Two triangles with two pairs of equal angles are similar.

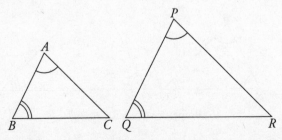

Let $\triangle ABC$ and $\triangle PQR$ be two triangles so that $m\angle A = m\angle P$ and $m\angle B = m\angle Q$, as shown in the figure above. If $PQ = AB$, then by the ASA Theorem for Congruence (*Theorem 3.18*), the two triangles are congruent, and therefore similar. If $PQ > AB$, let F be the congruence that maps $\angle A$ to $\angle P$, B to B', and C to C', as shown in the following figure, where B' lies on the ray $\overrightarrow{PQ}$ and between P and Q, and C' lies on the ray $\overrightarrow{PR}$. Since $m\angle B = m\angle B'$, angles $\angle B'$ and $\angle Q$ are equal. Then by *Theorem 2.12*, line $\overleftrightarrow{B'C'}$ is parallel to line $\overleftrightarrow{QR}$, and C' lies between P and R, as shown in the following figure.

By *Theorem 5.5* (Fundamental Theorem of Similarity 2), $\dfrac{PB'}{PQ} = \dfrac{PC'}{PR}$.

Then by the SAS Theorem for Similarity (*Theorem 5.9*), $\triangle ABC$ and $\triangle PQR$ are similar.

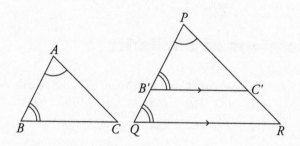

Theorem 5.11 (SSS Theorem for Similarity): If $\triangle ABC$ and $\triangle PQR$ are triangles so that $\dfrac{AB}{PQ} = \dfrac{BC}{QR} = \dfrac{AC}{PR}$, then $\triangle ABC \sim \triangle PQR$.

As you have seen in the proofs of *Theorems 5.9* and *5.10*, let us assume that $AB < PQ$. Let $\dfrac{AB}{PQ} = \dfrac{BC}{QR} = \dfrac{AC}{PR} = \dfrac{1}{r}$. That is, $PQ = r(AB)$, by the Cross-Multiplication Algorithm (*Theorem 5.7*). Because $AB < PQ$, $r < 1$. Choose points B_1 and C_1 on rays $\overrightarrow{PQ}$ and $\overrightarrow{PR}$, respectively, so that $PQ = r(PB_1)$ and $PR = r(PC_1)$, as shown in the following figure.

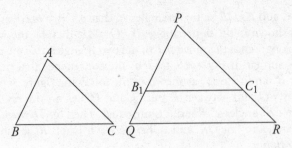

By the hypothesis of the theorem, $AB = PB_1$ and $AC = PC_1$. Let D be the dilation with center P and scale factor r. Then $D(B_1) = Q$ and $D(C_1) = R$. Then by FTS, $r(B_1C_1) = QR$ and $D(PB_1C_1) = PQR$. By the hypothesis, $BC = B_1C_1$, and therefore, by the SSS Theorem (*Theorem 3.21*), $\triangle ABC \cong \triangle PB_1C_1$. That is, there is a congruence F so that $F(ABC) = PB_1C_1$ and $D(F(ABC)) = PQR$. Therefore, $\triangle ABC \sim \triangle PQR$.

Applications of Similarity

Theorem 5.12: Suppose $\triangle ABC$ and $\triangle PQR$ are triangles so that $\triangle ABC \sim \triangle PQR$. Then $\dfrac{AB}{AC} = \dfrac{PQ}{PR}$, $\dfrac{AB}{BC} = \dfrac{PQ}{QR}$, and $\dfrac{AC}{BC} = \dfrac{PR}{QR}$.

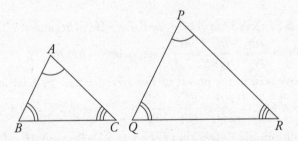

Theorem 5.12 follows from *Theorems 5.7* and *5.11*. It is useful in the following sense.

Consider the dilation of a plane so that we have to change the units of measure of length for convenience. For example, a map of a town is a dilation of the actual town (assuming that the town is on a plane). Then it is convenient to use a smaller unit as the length measure for the map (say, centimeters) rather than the length measure used for the actual town (say, miles). In this case, calculating the scale factor of the dilation requires conversion of centimeters to miles. But with *Theorem 5.12* in place, it is not necessary to make conversions. Since the ratios of lengths in *Theorem 5.12* are all from the same triangle, the ratios have no units.

Example 2: A map is scaled so that 3 cm on the map is equal to 5 actual miles. If two cities on the map are 10 cm apart, what is the actual distance between the cities?

Let x = the actual distance in miles. Let A and B be the two cities on the map. Let C be a point on the map so that line $\overrightarrow{AC}$ is perpendicular to line $\overrightarrow{AB}$ at A and $AC = 3$ cm. Let A' and B' be the actual cities. Consider the point C' in the city so that line $\overleftrightarrow{A'B'}$ is perpendicular to line $\overrightarrow{A'C'}$ at A' and $A'C' = 5$ miles as shown in the figure below.

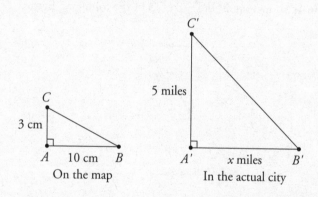

On the map   In the actual city

Now, by the SAS Theorem for Similarity (*Theorem 5.9*), $\triangle ABC$ and $\triangle A'B'C'$ are similar. Then by *Theorem 5.12*, $\dfrac{AB}{AC} = \dfrac{A'B'}{A'C'}$. This is the same as $\dfrac{10}{3} = \dfrac{x}{5}$. Now, using the Cross-Multiplication Algorithm (*Theorem 5.7*), $x = \dfrac{50}{3}$.

Therefore, the cities are $16\dfrac{2}{3}$ miles apart.

Example 3: Show that the following triangles are similar.

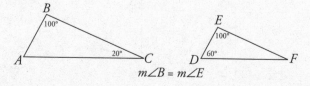

$m\angle B = m\angle E$

In $\triangle ABC$,

$$m\angle A + m\angle B + m\angle C = 180°$$
$$m\angle A + 100° + 20° = 180°$$
$$m\angle A = 60°$$

But in $\triangle DEF$, $m\angle D = 60°$. So, $m\angle A = m\angle D$.

By the AA Theorem for Similarity (*Theorem 5.10*), $\triangle ABC \sim \triangle DEF$. Additionally, because the triangles are now similar, $m\angle D = m\angle F$ and $\dfrac{AB}{DE} = \dfrac{BC}{EF} = \dfrac{AC}{DF}$.

Example 4: Show that $\triangle QRS \sim \triangle UTS$ in the following figure.

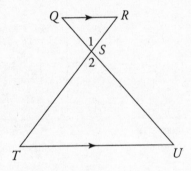

$m\angle 1 = m\angle 2$ because vertical angles are equal.

$m\angle R = m\angle T$ or $m\angle Q = m\angle U$ because if two parallel lines are cut by a transversal, then the alternate interior angles are equal.

So by the AA Theorem for Similarity (*Theorem 5.10*), $\triangle QRS \sim \triangle UTS$.

Example 5: Show that $\triangle MNO \sim \triangle PQR$ in the following figure.

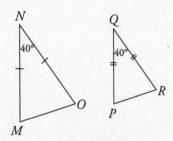

In $\triangle MNO$, $MN = NO$, and in $\triangle PQR$, $PQ = QR$.

$$m\angle M = m\angle O \text{ and } m\angle P = m\angle R$$

By *Theorem 3.4*, if two sides of a triangle are equal, the angles opposite these sides have equal measures.

In $\triangle MNO$, $m\angle M + m\angle N + m\angle O = 180°$.

In $\triangle PQR$, $m\angle P + m\angle Q + m\angle R = 180°$.

Because $m\angle M = m\angle O$ and $m\angle P = m\angle R$,

$$2m\angle M + 40° = 180° \qquad 2m\angle P + 40° = 180°$$
$$2m\angle M = 140° \qquad\qquad 2m\angle P = 140°$$
$$m\angle M = 70° \qquad\qquad\quad m\angle P = 70°$$

So, $m\angle M = m\angle P$, $m\angle O = m\angle R$, and $\triangle MNO \sim \triangle PQR$, by the AA Theorem for Similarity (*Theorem 5.10*).

Example 6: Show that $\triangle ABC \sim \triangle DEF$ in the following figure.

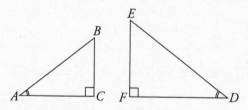

$m\angle C = m\angle F$ (right angles)

$m\angle A = m\angle D$ (They are indicated as equal in the figure.)

$\triangle ABC \sim \triangle DEF$ (by the AA Theorem for Similarity, *Theorem 5.10*)

Example 7: In the following figure, find the value of x.

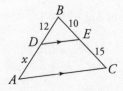

Because $\overline{DE} \parallel \overline{AC}$ in $\triangle ABC$, by *Theorem 5.5* (Fundamental Theorem of Similarity 2), you get

$$\frac{12}{12+x} = \frac{10}{10+15}$$

By the Cross-Multiplication Algorithm (*Theorem 5.7*),

$$12(10+15) = 10(12+x)$$

By using distributive property of real numbers,

$$120 + 180 = 120 + 10x$$

By subtracting 120 from both sides of the equation,

$$180 = 10x$$

Therefore, $x = 18$.

Example 8: In the following figure, find the value of x.

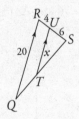

By *Theorem 5.5* (Fundamental Theorem of Similarity 2),

$$\frac{QR}{TU} = \frac{RS}{US} = \frac{QS}{TS}$$

Since $QR = 20$, $TU = x$, $RS = 10$, and $US = 6$, from the first two ratios in the equation,

$$\frac{20}{x} = \frac{10}{6}$$

By the Cross-Multiplication Algorithm (*Theorem 5.7*),

$$10x = 120$$
$$x = 12$$

Proportional Parts of Similar Triangles

The following theorem follows from the SAS Theorem for Similarity (*Theorem 5.9*), the AA Theorem for Similarity (*Theorem 5.10*), and the SSS Theorem for Similarity (*Theorem 5.11*).

Theorem 5.13: If two triangles are similar, then the ratio of any two corresponding segments (such as altitudes, medians, or angle bisectors) equals the ratio of any two corresponding sides.

In the following figure, suppose $\triangle ABC \sim \triangle PQR$.

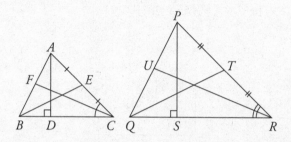

$\overline{AD}$ is the altitude of $\triangle ABC$ to the side $\overline{BC}$, $\overline{PS}$ is the altitude of $\triangle PQR$ to the side $\overline{QR}$, $\overline{BE}$ is the median of $\triangle ABC$ to the side $\overline{AC}$, $\overline{QT}$ is the median of $\triangle PQR$ to the side $\overline{PR}$, $\overline{CF}$ is the angle bisector of $\angle C$ of $\triangle ABC$, and $\overline{RU}$ is the angle bisector of $\angle R$ of $\triangle PQR$.

Then, according to *Theorem 5.13*,

$$\frac{AD}{PS} = \frac{BE}{QT} = \frac{CF}{RU} = \frac{AB}{PQ}$$

Example 9: In the following figure, $\triangle ABC \sim \triangle GHI$. Find the value of x, the length of the altitude $\overline{GY}$.

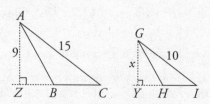

By *Theorem 5.13*, $\dfrac{AZ}{GY} = \dfrac{AC}{GI}$, or $\dfrac{9}{x} = \dfrac{15}{10}$. Using the Cross-Multiplication Algorithm (*Theorem 5.7*),

$$15x = 90$$
$$x = 6$$

Pythagorean Theorem

Theorem 5.14 (Pythagorean Theorem): Let $\triangle ABC$ be a right triangle with $m\angle B = 90°$. Then $AC^2 = AB^2 + BC^2$.

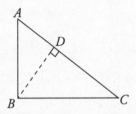

Drop a perpendicular from point B to line $\overline{AC}$. Let the foot of this perpendicular be point D. Then $\triangle ABC$ and $\triangle ADB$, both right triangles, are similar by the AA Theorem for Similarity (*Theorem 5.10*) since the angle $\angle A$ is common to both triangles. Then, by *Theorem 5.12*, $\dfrac{AC}{AB} = \dfrac{AB}{AD}$. By the Cross-Multiplication Algorithm (*Theorem 5.7*), $AB^2 = AC \cdot AD$.

Right triangles $\triangle ABC$ and $\triangle BDC$ are also similar by the AA Theorem for Similarity since $\angle C$ is common to both triangles. Then, by *Theorem 5.12*, $\dfrac{AC}{BC} = \dfrac{BC}{DC}$. By the Cross-Multiplication Algorithm, $BC^2 = AC \cdot DC$. Therefore, $AB^2 + BC^2 = AC \cdot AD + AC \cdot DC$.

By factoring out AC, $AB^2 + BC^2 = AC(AD + DC)$. Since $AD + DC = AC$, $AB^2 + BC^2 = AC^2$.

The converse of the Pythagorean Theorem is also true.

Theorem 5.15 (Converse of the Pythagorean Theorem): Suppose $\triangle ABC$ is a right triangle so that $AB^2 + BC^2 = AC^2$. Then $\triangle ABC$ is a right triangle with $m\angle B = 90°$.

This theorem can be proven using the Pythagorean Theorem. Suppose $\angle B \neq 90°$. Drop a perpendicular from point A to line $\overline{BC}$ and let the foot of the perpendicular be point D.

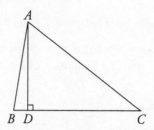

There are two cases: the point D lies between points B and C or the point B lies between points D and C. Proofs of both cases are similar, and we will prove the case where D lies between B and C. $\triangle ADB$ is a right triangle. Then by the Pythagorean Theorem, $AB^2 = AD^2 + BD^2$. Therefore, $AB^2 > AD^2$. Since D is between B and C, $BC > DC$ and $BC^2 > DC^2$.

$\triangle ADC$ is a right triangle. Then by the Pythagorean Theorem, $AC^2 = AD^2 + DC^2$. Then $AC^2 = AD^2 + DC^2 < AB^2 + BC^2$. But by the hypothesis, $AB^2 + BC^2 = AC^2$. Therefore, $AC^2 < AC^2$. This is a contradiction. That is, our assumption that $\angle B \neq 90°$ is false and therefore, $\angle B = 90°$.

Recall that we said we'd prove *Theorem 4.28* (the three medians of a triangle are concurrent) after learning about the similarity of triangles. It's now time to do so. *Theorem 4.28* can be proven by using the Midpoint Theorem (*Theorem 4.21*), the SAS Theorem for Similarity (*Theorem 5.9*), and the following *Theorem 5.16*.

Theorem 5.16: Let $\triangle ABC$ be a triangle so that D and E are the midpoints of the segments $\overline{AC}$ and $\overline{AB}$. Suppose segments $\overline{CD}$ and $\overline{BE}$ meet at F, as shown in the figure below. Then $FE = \dfrac{1}{2} BF$.

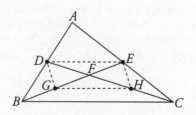

Let G and H be the midpoints of $\overline{BF}$ and $\overline{CF}$, respectively. By applying the Midpoint Theorem (*Theorem 4.21*) to $\triangle ABC$, $\overleftrightarrow{DE} \parallel \overrightarrow{BC}$ and $DE = \dfrac{1}{2}BC$. By applying the Midpoint Theorem to $\triangle BFC$, $\overleftrightarrow{GH} \parallel \overleftrightarrow{BC}$ and $GH = \dfrac{1}{2}BC$. Hence, by *Theorem 4.7* (if in a quadrilateral opposite sides are parallel and equal, then it is a parallelogram), $DGHE$ is a parallelogram, and by *Theorem 4.12* (diagonals of a parallelogram bisect each other), $GF = FE$ or $BF = 2FE$.

Now we will prove *Theorem 4.28*.

Consider $\triangle ABC$. Let D, E, F be the midpoints of the segments $\overline{AC}$, $\overline{AB}$, and $\overline{BC}$, respectively. Suppose $\overline{BD}$ and $\overline{CE}$ meet at G. If we can show that A, G, and F are collinear, then the medians meet at G. Connect A to G, F to G, and D to F by line segments, as shown in the following figure.

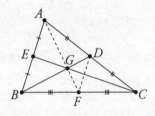

By the Mid-Point Theorem (*Theorem 4.21*), $\overleftrightarrow{DF} \parallel \overleftrightarrow{AB}$ and $DF = \dfrac{1}{2}AB$. Then by the Cross-Multiplication Algorithm, $\dfrac{AB}{DF} = 2$. By *Theorem 5.16*, $GD = \dfrac{1}{2}BG$. By the Cross-Multiplication Algorithm, $\dfrac{BG}{DG} = 2$. Therefore, $\dfrac{BG}{GD} = \dfrac{AB}{DF}$. Since $\overleftrightarrow{DF} \parallel \overleftrightarrow{AB}$, $m\angle ABG = m\angle GDF$ by *Theorem 2.6* (alternate interior angles are equal). Hence, $\triangle ABG$ and $\triangle FDG$ are similar, by the SAS Theorem for Similarity. Therefore, $m\angle AGB = m\angle FGD$. Now, $m\angle AGB + m\angle AGD = 180°$ because $\angle BGD$ is a straight angle. Therefore, $m\angle FGD + m\angle AGD = 180°$ and A, G, and F are collinear.

Chapter Check-Out

Questions

1. In the following figure, $OP = 6$, $OQ = 4$, and $QS = 2$. Find the length of PR.

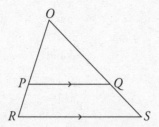

2. Let S be a similarity with scale factor 3. Suppose $S(ABC) = PQR$. Find the ratio $\dfrac{AB}{PQ}$.

3. A map is scaled so that 2 cm on the map is equal to 5 actual miles. If two cities on the map are 8 cm apart, what is the actual distance between the two cities?

Answers

1. $PR = 3$

2. $\dfrac{AB}{PQ} = \dfrac{1}{3}$

3. 20 miles

Chapter 6
CIRCLES

Chapter Check-In

❏ Identifying the parts of a circle

❏ Knowing facts about arcs and inscribed angles

❏ Understanding concyclic points

❏ Applying key facts about chords, secants, and tangents

Common Core Standard: Circles with and without Coordinates

Prove that all circles are similar (G.C.1). Identify and describe relationships among inscribed angles, radii, and chords. *Include the relationship between central, inscribed, and circumscribed angles; inscribed angles on a diameter are right angles; the radius of a circle is perpendicular to the tangent where the radius intersects the circle* (G.C.2). Construct the inscribed and circumscribed circles of a triangle and prove properties of angles for a quadrilateral inscribed in a circle (G.C.3).

Geometry Theorems

The geometry theorems in this book are numbered for organizational purposes. For example, *Theorem 2.2* is the second theorem given in Chapter 2. Study these theorems by their content, not by their number, as the theorem numbering has no significance outside of this book.

Parts of Circles

Recall from Chapter 1 that a **circle** is the collection of all points in the plane equidistant from a fixed point. That fixed point is called the **center** of the circle. A circle is determined by its center and the length of a radius. Any segment with one endpoint at the center of the circle and the other endpoint on the circle is a **radius.** Any segment whose endpoints lie on the circle is a **chord.** Any chord that passes through the center of the circle is a **diameter.**

Arcs

The **arc of a circle** is the intersection of the circle with a central angle of the circle. If the central angle is convex (i.e., the measure is less than or equal 180°), then there are two cases: semicircle or minor arc.

> **Semicircle:** If the measure of the central angle is 180° (a straight angle), then the associated arc is called a semicircle. A semicircle is named by using three points: the two endpoints of the diameter, together with any other point on the arc. For example, in the figure below $\overset{\frown}{ABC}$ is a semicircle.

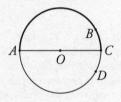

> **Minor arc:** If the measure is less than 180°, then the associated arc is called a minor arc. A minor arc is named by using only the two endpoints of the arc. For example, in the figure below, $\overset{\frown}{ET}$ is a minor arc of circle P.

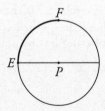

> **Major arc:** If the central angle is not convex (i.e., the measure is more than 180°), then the associated arc is called a **major arc.** A major arc is named by using three points: the two endpoints of the arc together with any other point on the arc. The extra point is placed between the endpoints in naming the arc. For example, in the figure below, $\overset{\frown}{STU}$ is a major arc of circle Q.

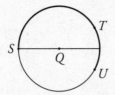

In the circle below, the point M is the center, $\overline{MT}$ is a radius, $\overline{XY}$ is a diameter, and $\overline{QR}$ is a chord. From the definition of radius and diameter, it is clear that all radii of a circle are equal in length and all diameters of a circle are equal in length.

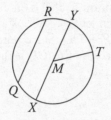

From now on, we simply refer to the length of a radius as the radius and the length of a diameter as the diameter. In this new terminology, a circle is determined by its center and the radius. We will just say "C is a circle with center O" rather than "C is a circle with center O and radius r" if an argument that we make about that circle does not specifically require the exact value of the radius. Sometimes, we will just say "circle C," to name a circle with the letter C.

If ρ is *any* rotation around the center of a given circle C, then $\rho(C) = C$. In this sense, a circle has the maximum rotational symmetry.

Theorem 6.1: In a circle, if two central angles have equal measures, then their corresponding arcs have equal measures.

Theorem 6.2: In a circle, if two arcs have equal measures, then their corresponding central angles have equal measures.

Let O be the center of the given circle. The above two theorems are easy to prove if you consider the appropriate rotation with center O that makes the given sectors congruent.

Theorem 6.3: Let C be a circle with center O and let ℓ be a line passing through O. If R is the reflection across ℓ, then $R(C) = C$. $R(C) = C$ means R maps C to C. We say C is symmetric with respect to ℓ.

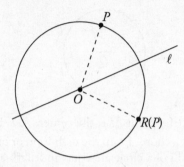

Let P be an arbitrary point on C. If P is on ℓ, then $R(P) = P$ and $R(P)$ is on C. If P is not on ℓ, then let $Q = R(P)$. We want to show that Q is on C. Since $R(O) = O$, $R(OP) = OQ$. Since reflections preserve lengths of segments and OP is the radius of C, OQ is the radius of C. That is, Q is on C.

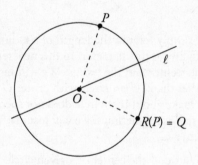

Theorem 6.4: A circle and a line meet at no more than two points.

According to *Theorem 6.4*, a line intersects a circle at no points, at one point, or at two points. It is easy to find a line that intersects a circle at two points. Just pick two points on the circle. Since there is a line passing through those two points, that line intersects the circle at two points. Such a line is known as a **secant** line. A line that meets a circle at exactly one point is known as a **tangent** line. The point where the tangent line and the circle meet is called the **point of tangency**.

Theorem 6.5: Let *C* be a circle with center *O*. If a line ℓ is tangent to *C* at a point *P*, then ℓ is perpendicular to the line $\overleftrightarrow{OP}$.

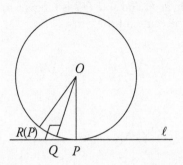

As shown in the figure above, if ℓ is not perpendicular to line $\overleftrightarrow{OP}$, then there is a point *Q* on ℓ so that line $\overleftrightarrow{OQ}$ is perpendicular to ℓ (*Theorem 2.5*). Let *R* be the reflection across line $\overleftrightarrow{OQ}$. Then *R(P)* is on ℓ but on the other half-plane of line $\overleftrightarrow{OQ}$. Hence, *P* is not equal to *R(P)*. The distance from *O* to *R(P)* is the same as *OP*. Hence, *R(P)* is on *C*. This contradicts the fact that ℓ intersects *C* at only one point. Therefore, ℓ is perpendicular to line $\overleftrightarrow{OP}$.

Theorem 6.6: Let *C* be a circle with center *O* and let *P* be a point on *C*. If a line ℓ passing through *P* is perpendicular to the line $\overleftrightarrow{OP}$, then ℓ is tangent to *C*.

Suppose *Q* is *any* arbitrary point on ℓ other than *P*. Then ΔOPQ is a right triangle, and by *Theorem 3.9*, $OQ > OP$. Therefore, *Q* is not on *C*. Since *Q* is arbitrary, the only point of ℓ that is on *C* is *P*. Hence, ℓ is tangent to *C*, as shown in the following figure.

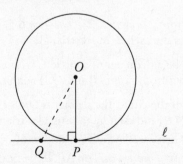

Loosely state *Theorem 6.5* as follows: "A line tangent to a circle at a point *P* is perpendicular to the radius at *P*."

Example 1: Use *Theorem 6.5* to find the center of a circle when two tangents of the circle are known. In the following figure, line $\overleftrightarrow{MN}$ is tangent to the circle at P, and line $\overleftrightarrow{QR}$ is tangent to the circle at S. Use these facts to find the center of the circle.

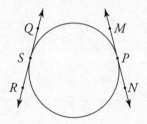

According to *Theorem 6.5*, if a line is drawn perpendicular to line $\overleftrightarrow{MN}$ at P, then it passes through the center of the circle.

Similarly, if a line is drawn perpendicular to line $\overleftrightarrow{QR}$ at S, it too would pass through the center of the circle. The point where these two chords intersect would then be the center of the circle. See the figure below.

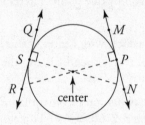

Theorem 6.7: There is exactly one circle tangent to all three sides of a triangle.

Theorem 6.7 follows from *Theorem 4.27*, *Theorem 6.5*, and *Theorem 6.6*. This circle is known as the *incircle* of the triangle.

Theorem 6.8: Let $\overline{PQ}$ be a diameter of a circle C with center O and let R be a point on C distinct from points P and Q. Then $m\angle PRQ = 90°$.

Since O is the center of the circle, the segments $\overline{OR}$, $\overline{OP}$, and $\overline{OQ}$ are all radii of C. Hence, $\triangle POR$ and $\triangle QOR$ are isosceles triangles, as shown in the following figure. Then $m\angle P = m\angle PRO$ and $m\angle Q = m\angle QRO$. By the Exterior Angle Theorem (*Theorem 3.1*) on $\triangle POR$, $m\angle ROQ = 2(m\angle PRO)$. Therefore, $m\angle PRQ = m\angle PRO + m\angle QRO = m\angle P + m\angle Q$. In the triangle $\triangle PRQ$, $m\angle P + m\angle Q + m\angle PRQ = 180°$, by the Angle Sum Theorem (*Theorem 3.2*). Therefore, $2(m\angle PRQ) = 180°$ and $m\angle PRQ = 90°$.

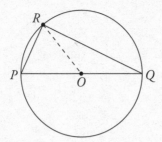

Theorem 6.9: Let $\overline{PQ}$ be a chord of C and let R be a point on C distinct from points P and Q. If the $m\angle PRQ = 90°$, then $\overline{PQ}$ is a diameter.

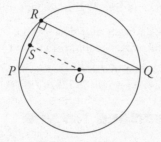

As shown in the figure above, let O be the midpoint of $\overline{PQ}$ and let S be the midpoint of $\overline{PR}$. Then by the Fundamental Theorem of Similarity (*Theorem 5.1*), line $\overleftrightarrow{OS}$ is parallel to line $\overleftrightarrow{QR}$. Line $\overleftrightarrow{PR}$ is perpendicular to one of the parallel lines by the hypothesis. Hence, line $\overleftrightarrow{PR}$ is perpendicular to line $\overleftrightarrow{OS}$ and $m\angle OSP = 90°$. That means line $\overleftrightarrow{OS}$ is the perpendicular bisector of the segment $\overline{PR}$ and O lies on the perpendicular bisector of the segment $\overline{PR}$. Similarly, you can show that O lies on the perpendicular bisector of $\overline{QR}$ and $OQ = OR$. Since $PO = OQ$, O lies on the perpendicular bisector of $\overline{PQ}$. Hence, O is the circumcenter of ΔPQR. Since O is now the center of the circle and lies on $\overline{PQ}$, $\overline{PQ}$ is a diameter of the circle. That is, O is the center of C and $\overline{PQ}$ is the diameter of C.

Theorem 6.10: From a point P outside a given circle C, there are exactly two lines tangent to C.

Let O be the center of the circle C. Suppose a circle with a diameter $\overline{OP}$ intersects C at the point Q, as shown in the following figure. By *Theorem 6.8*, $\angle OQP$ is a right angle. Then by *Theorem 6.6*, line $\overleftrightarrow{PQ}$ is tangent to C.

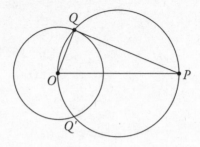

Let *R* be the reflection across the line $\overleftrightarrow{OP}$. Let *Q′* be the reflection of point *Q*. Then by *Theorem 6.3*, *Q′* lies on *C*. Since *O* and *P* lie on line $\overleftrightarrow{OP}$, *R(O) = O* and *R(P) = P*. Since reflections preserve degrees of angles, ∠*PQ′O* is a right angle and line $\overleftrightarrow{PQ′}$ is tangent to *C*.

Theorem 6.11: Let *P* be a point outside a given circle *C*, and suppose the points of tangency of the two tangent lines to *C* are *Q* and *R*. Then *PQ = PR*.

In the proof of the *Theorem 6.10*, Δ*PQO* and Δ*PQ′O* are congruent by the HL Theorem (*Theorem 3.20*), *PQ = PQ′*.

Arcs and Inscribed Angles

Central angles, as noted previously, are probably the angles most often associated with a circle, but by no means are they the only ones. Angles may also be inscribed in the circumference of a circle or formed by intersecting chords and other lines.

Given a chord $\overline{AB}$ on a circle *C* with a center *O*, it can be assumed that $\overline{AB}$ is not the diameter unless specifically stated. Then $\overline{AB}$ determines a minor arc and a major arc. Refer to these as *opposite arcs*. The ambiguity can be removed by identifying a point in each arc. In the following figure, $\overset{\frown}{AB}$ denotes the minor arc of $\overline{AB}$ and $\overset{\frown}{AEB}$ denotes the opposite arc.

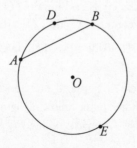

Given a chord $\overline{AB}$ on a circle C with center O, let E be a point on the opposite arc, which is distinct from A and B (see figure above). The angle $\angle AEB$ is called the *inscribed angle intercepting the arc* $\overset{\frown}{AB}$. In summary:

Inscribed angle: In a circle, this is an angle formed by two chords with the vertex on the circle.

Intercepted arc: Corresponding to an angle, this is the portion of the circle that lies in the interior of the angle together with the endpoints of the arc.

An inscribed angle intercepting an arc is also known as the *angle subtended by the arc.*

In the following figure, $\angle AEB$ is an inscribed angle and $\overset{\frown}{AB}$ is its intercepted arc.

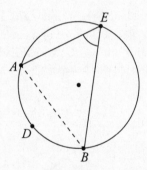

In the case of the major arc $\overset{\frown}{AEB}$, if D is a point on the minor arc, then $\angle ADB$ is an inscribed angle intercepting the major arc $\overset{\frown}{AEB}$, as shown in the following figure.

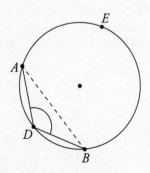

In the following figures, $\angle QRS$ and $\angle TWV$ are *not* inscribed angles.

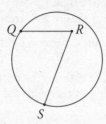 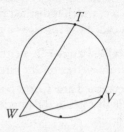

$\angle QRS$ is not an inscribed angle because its vertex is not on the circle.

$\angle TWV$ is not an inscribed angle because its vertex is not on the circle.

Theorem 6.12: Fix an arc on a circle C. Then *any* inscribed angle subtended by the arc is half of the central angle subtended by the arc.

Consider the intercepted arc to be a minor arc. The proof for a major arc is entirely similar. Let $\overline{PQ}$ be a chord of a circle C with center O. Let A be a point on the major arc of $\overline{PQ}$, which is different from P and Q. There are three cases, as shown below.

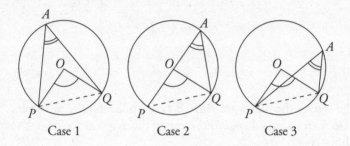

Case 1   Case 2   Case 3

In case 1, the center O lies inside the angle $\angle PAQ$. Draw ray $\overrightarrow{AO}$ and let B be a point on ray $\overrightarrow{AO}$, as shown in the following figure. Using the Exterior Angle Theorem (*Theorem 3.1*) on $\triangle AOQ$, $m\angle QOB = m\angle OAQ + m\angle OQA$.

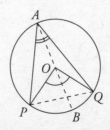

Since $\triangle AOQ$ is an isosceles triangle, $m\angle OAQ = m\angle OQA$. Therefore, $m\angle QOB = 2(m\angle OAQ)$.

Similarly from $\triangle AOP$, $m\angle POB = 2(m\angle OAP)$.

Hence, $m\angle POB + m\angle QOB = 2(\angle OAP + \angle OAQ)$, or $m\angle POQ = 2(m\angle PAQ)$. Since $m\angle POQ = 2(m\angle PAQ)$, then $m\angle PAQ = \frac{1}{2}(m\angle POQ)$.

In case 2, the center of the circle lies on the diameter $\overline{PA}$ and $\triangle OAQ$ is an isosceles triangle. As a result, $m\angle OAQ$ and $m\angle OQA$ are equal. Then, by the Exterior Angle Theorem (*Theorem 3.1*), $m\angle POQ = 2(m\angle OAQ)$.

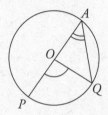

Since $m\angle POQ = 2(m\angle OAQ)$, then $m\angle OAQ = \frac{1}{2}(m\angle POQ)$. Thus, $m\angle PAQ = \frac{1}{2}(m\angle POQ)$.

In case 3, where the center lies outside the inscribed angle, draw ray $\overrightarrow{AO}$ and let B be a point on ray $\overrightarrow{AO}$, where it intersects the circle, as shown in the following figure.

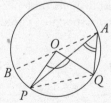

Using the information from case 2, it follows that $m\angle BAQ = \frac{1}{2}(m\angle QOB)$ and that $m\angle BAP = \frac{1}{2}(m\angle POB)$. Then $m\angle BAQ - m\angle BAP = \frac{1}{2}(m\angle QOB) - \frac{1}{2}(m\angle POB)$. But $m\angle BAQ - m\angle BAP = m\angle PAQ$ and $m\angle QOB - m\angle POB = m\angle POQ$. Therefore, $m\angle PAQ = \frac{1}{2}(m\angle POQ)$.

The following theorems follow directly from *Theorem 6.12.*

Theorem 6.13: Two inscribed angles subtended by the same chord of a circle have equal measures.

Theorem 6.14: The measure of an inscribed angle subtended by a diameter of a circle is 90°.

Theorem 6.15: In a circle, if two chords $\overline{AB}$ and $\overline{CD}$ are equal in measure, then the angles subtended by the corresponding minor arcs are equal in measure.

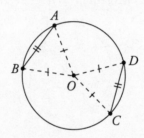

Let O be the center of the circle with equal chords $\overline{AB}$ and $\overline{CD}$ as shown in the above figure. Then $\triangle AOB$ and $\triangle COD$ are congruent triangles by the SSS Theorem for congruence (*Theorem 3.21*), $m\angle AOB = m\angle COD$.

Those are the central angles subtended by $\overline{AB}$ and $\overline{CD}$. By *Theorem 6.12*, the angles subtended by the corresponding minor arcs have equal measure.

Theorem 6.16: In a circle, if angles subtended by two minor arcs are equal in measure, then their corresponding chords are equal in measure.

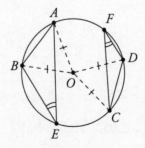

Let O be the center of the circle with angles $m\angle AEB$ and $m\angle CFD$ subtended by the chords $\overline{AB}$ and $\overline{CD}$ respectively, as shown in the above figure. By the hypothesis and by *Theorem 6.12*, $m\angle AOB = m\angle COD$. Then $\triangle AOB$ and $\triangle COD$ are congruent triangles by the SAS Theorem for congruence (*Theorem 3.17*). Hence, $\overline{AB}$ and $\overline{CD}$ are equal in measure.

Example 2: Find the measure of $\angle A$ in the following figure.

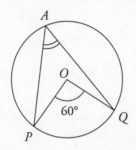

$$m\angle A = \frac{1}{2}\angle POQ, \text{ by } \textit{Theorem 6.12}$$

$$m\angle A = \frac{1}{2}(60°)$$

$$m\angle A = 30°$$

Example 3: In the following figure, suppose the measure of the central angle subtended by arc $\overset{\frown}{DC}$ is 110°. That is, the measure of $\angle DOC$ is 110°. Find the measures of $\angle A$ and $\angle B$.

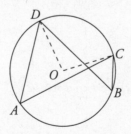

By *Theorem 6.13*, $\angle A$ and $\angle B$ have the same measure because they are angles subtended by the minor arc $\overset{\frown}{DC}$. Then by *Theorem 6.12*,

$$m\angle A = m\angle B = \frac{1}{2}(110°) = 55°$$

Example 4: In the following circle, $\overline{QS}$ is a diameter. Find the measure of $\angle R$.

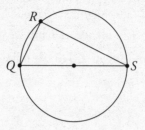

$m\angle R = 90°$, by *Theorem 6.14*.

Example 5: In the circle below, the measure of the central angle subtended by arc $\overset{\frown}{CD}$ is 60° and $m\angle CAB = 25°$. Find the measures of the following angles.

(a) $\angle CAD$

(b) $\angle BOC$

(c) $\angle AOB$

(d) $\angle ACB$

(e) $\angle ABC$

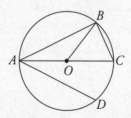

(a) $m\angle CAD = \dfrac{1}{2}(m\angle COD)$ by *Theorem 6.12*

$\qquad = \dfrac{1}{2}(60°)$

$\qquad = 30°$

(b) $m\angle CAB = \dfrac{1}{2}(m\angle BOC)$ by *Theorem 6.12*

$\quad 2(m\angle CAB) = m\angle BOC \qquad$ (Multiply both sides by 2)

$\quad\quad m\angle BOC = 2(25°) = 50°$

(c) $m\angle AOB = 180° - m\angle BOC$

$\quad\quad\quad\quad = 130°$

(d) $m\angle ACB = \dfrac{1}{2}(m\angle AOB)$ by *Theorem 6.12*

$\quad\quad\quad\quad = \dfrac{1}{2}(130°)$

$\quad\quad\quad\quad = 65°$

(e) $m\angle ABC = 90°$ by *Theorem 6.14*

Concyclic Points

It has been previously discussed that there is a unique circle passing through three given noncollinear points. If a collection of points lie on a circle, then those points are said to be **concyclic points.** When can it be said that four given points are concyclic? The following few theorems provide the answer.

Theorem 6.17: Let four points P, Q, R, and S be given. Suppose P and R lie on the same side of the line $\overleftrightarrow{QS}$. If $m\angle QPS = m\angle QRS$, then P, Q, R, and S are concyclic.

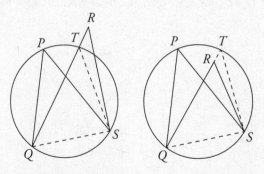

Let C be the circle passing through the points P, Q, and S. If the point R does not lie on C, then R either is inside of C or outside of C, as shown in the figures above. If R is outside of C, then let T be the point where the line $\overleftrightarrow{QR}$ intersects circle C. Then by *Theorem 6.13*, $m\angle QPS = m\angle QTS$. However, $\angle QTS$ is an exterior angle of $\triangle QTS$. By the Exterior Angle Theorem (*Theorem 3.1*), $m\angle QTS > m\angle QRS$. Then $m\angle QPS > m\angle QRS$. This contradicts the hypothesis of the theorem. Hence, P, Q, R, and S are concyclic. You can apply the same line of thinking to show that point R cannot lie inside of circle C either.

Theorem 6.18: Let four points A, B, C, and D be given. Suppose points A and C lie on the same side of line $\overleftrightarrow{BD}$. If A, B, C, and D are concyclic, then $m\angle BAD = m\angle BCD$.

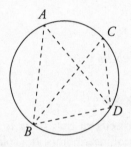

Since points A, B, C, and D are concyclic, $m\angle BAD$ and $m\angle BCD$ are inscribed angles subtended by the same arc $\overparen{BD}$. By *Theorem 6.13*, $m\angle BAD = m\angle BCD$.

Theorem 6.19: Let four points A, B, C, and D be given. Suppose A and C lie on opposite sides of the line $\overleftrightarrow{BD}$, as shown in the following figure. If A, B, C, and D are concyclic, then $m\angle BAD + m\angle BCD = 180°$.

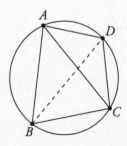

$m\angle BAD + m\angle BCD = (m\angle BAC + m\angle CAD) + m\angle BCD.$

But, $m\angle BAC = m\angle BDC$ and $m\angle CAD = m\angle CBD$, by *Theorem 6.13*, so $m\angle BAD + m\angle BCD = (m\angle BDC + m\angle CBD) + m\angle BCD.$

But, by the Angle Sum Theorem (*Theorem 3.2*) on $\triangle BDC$, $m\angle BDC + m\angle CBD + m\angle BCD = 180°$.

Therefore, $m\angle BAD + m\angle BCD = 180°$.

Theorem 6.20: Let four points P, Q, R, and S be given. Suppose P and R lie on opposite sides of the line $\overleftrightarrow{QS}$, as shown in the figures below. If $m\angle QPS + m\angle QRS = 180°$, then P, Q, R, and S are concyclic.

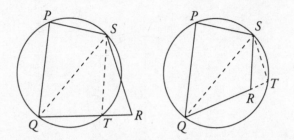

Let C be the circle passing through the points P, Q, and S. If point R does not lie on C then R is either inside of C or outside of C, as shown above. If R is outside of C, then let T be the point where line $\overleftrightarrow{QR}$ intersects C. By *Theorem 6.19*, $m\angle QPS + m\angle QTS = 180°$. But by the Exterior Angle Theorem (*Theorem 3.1*) on $\triangle STR$, $m\angle QTS > m\angle QRS$, and $m\angle QPS + m\angle QRS < 180°$. This contradicts the hypothesis of the theorem. Therefore, R must lie on circle C. The proof of the other case is similar.

Theorem 6.21: The measure of an angle formed by a tangent and a chord meeting at the point of tangency is equal to the measure of an inscribed angle subtended by the chord.

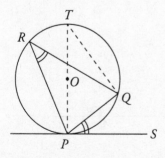

Let C be a circle with center O, as shown above. Let $\overline{PQ}$ be a chord and let line $\overleftrightarrow{PS}$ be the tangent line to C at point P. To show that $m\angle SPQ = m\angle PRQ$, construct the diameter $\overline{PT}$. Since R and T lie on the same side of line $\overleftrightarrow{PQ}$, $m\angle PRQ = m\angle PTQ$ by *Theorem 6.18*. Since $\overline{PT}$ is a diameter, $m\angle PQT = 90°$ by *Theorem 6.14*. Then $m\angle PTQ = 90° - m\angle TPQ$. However, $m\angle TPS = 90°$ by *Theorem 6.5*. That implies $m\angle SPQ = 90° - m\angle TPQ$. As a result, $m\angle SPQ = m\angle PTQ$ and $m\angle SPQ = m\angle PRQ$.

Theorem 6.22: If a diameter is perpendicular to a chord, then it bisects the chord.

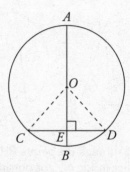

Let the diameter $\overline{AB}$ be perpendicular to the chord $\overline{CD}$ and let E be the point of intersection of $\overline{AB}$ and $\overline{CD}$. Let O be the center of the circle. $OC = OD$ because $\overline{OC}$ and $\overline{OD}$ are radii of the circle. As a result, $\triangle OCE$ and $\triangle ODE$ are congruent by the HL Theorem (*Theorem 3.20*) ($\overline{OE}$ is a common side of the two triangles). Hence, $CE = DE$.

Let ℓ be a line and O be a point not on ℓ. Let line $\overleftrightarrow{OA}$ be the line perpendicular to ℓ at point A. Then OA is called the distance between O and ℓ.

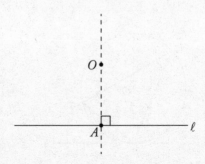

Theorem 6.23: If two chords are equal in measure in a circle, then they are equidistant from the center.

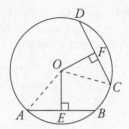

Let $\overline{AB}$ and $\overline{CD}$ be two chords of equal measure of a circle. Let O be the center of the circle. Suppose the line through O and perpendicular to line $\overleftrightarrow{AB}$ intersects line $\overleftrightarrow{AB}$ at point E and the line through O and perpendicular to line $\overleftrightarrow{CD}$ intersects line $\overleftrightarrow{CD}$ at point F. Then OE and OF are distances from O to lines $\overleftrightarrow{AB}$ and $\overleftrightarrow{CD}$. The goal is to show that $OE = OF$. We will show that $\triangle OAE$ and $\triangle OCF$ are congruent to achieve this goal. The lengths OA and OC are radii of the circle and therefore, $OA = OC$. Line $\overleftrightarrow{OE}$ is the perpendicular bisector of $\overline{AB}$, and line $\overleftrightarrow{OF}$ is the perpendicular bisector of $\overline{CD}$. Then by Theorem 3.6. and by the hypothesis, $AE = CF$. Therefore, $\triangle OAE$ and $\triangle OCF$ are congruent by the HL Theorem (*Theorem 3.20*), and, $OE = OF$.

Segments of Intersecting Chords and Tangents

Consider two chords of a circle. They may intersect inside the circle, or not. If the two chords are not intersecting inside the circle, it is possible that the lines containing the chords intersect outside the circle. In this case, we say the chords intersect outside the circle.

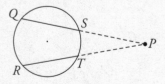

Consider two chords $\overline{QS}$ and $\overline{RT}$ intersecting at P as shown in the figures above. The segments $\overline{PS}$ and $\overline{PQ}$ are also known as **secant segments** of the chord $\overline{QS}$; and the segments $\overline{PR}$ and $\overline{PT}$ are secant segments of the chord $\overline{RT}$.

Theorem 6.24: If two chords of a circle intersect inside the circle, then the product of the lengths of secant segments of one chord is equal to the product of the the lengths of secant segments of the other chord.

Suppose chords $\overline{QS}$ and $\overline{TR}$ intersect at P inside the circle. We want to show that $PQ \cdot PS = PR \cdot PT$. Let $PQ = a$, $PS = b$, $PR = c$, and $PT = d$. Then we want to prove $ab = cd$.

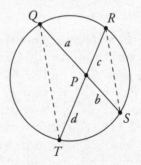

By *Theorem 6.13*, $m\angle Q = m\angle R$ and $m\angle T = m\angle S$. By the AA Theorem for Similarity (*Theorem 5.10*), $\triangle PRS$ and $\triangle PQT$ are similar, and $\dfrac{a}{c} = \dfrac{d}{b}$.

Then, $ab = cd$ by the Cross-Multiplication Algorithm (*Theorem 5.7*).

Theorem 6.25: If two chords of a circle intersect outside the circle, then the product of the lengths of secant segments of one chord is equal to the product of the lengths of secant segments of the other chord.

Suppose chords $\overline{QS}$ and $\overline{TR}$ intersect at P outside the circle as shown in the figure below. We want to show that $PQ \cdot PS = PR \cdot PT$. Let $PQ = a$, $PS = b$, $PR = c$, and $PT = d$. Then we want to prove $ab = cd$.

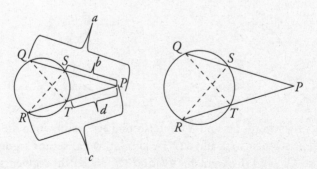

By *Theorem 6.13*, $m\angle Q = m\angle R$ because these are angles subtended by the chord $\overline{TS}$. Since $\angle P$ is common to both $\triangle PRS$ and $\triangle PQT$, by the AA Theorem for Similarity (*Theorem 5.10*), the triangles are similar, and $\dfrac{a}{c} = \dfrac{d}{b}$. Then $ab = cd$, by the Cross-Multiplication Algorithm (*Theorem 5.7*).

Example 6: Find the value of x in figures **(a)** and **(b)** below.

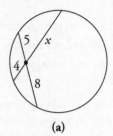

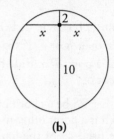

(a)   **(b)**

(a) By *Theorem 6.24*,

$$4(x) = (5)(8)$$
$$4x = 40$$
$$x = 10$$

(b) By *Theorem 6.24*,

$$(x)(x) = (2)(10)$$
$$x^2 = 20$$
$$x = \pm\sqrt{20}$$
$$x = \sqrt{20} \text{ because } x > 0$$
$$x = \sqrt{(4)(5)}$$
$$x = 2\sqrt{5}$$

Example 7: Find the value of x in figures **(a)** and **(b)** below.

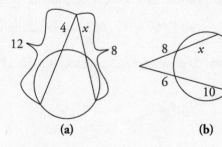

(a)   **(b)**

(a) By *Theorem 6.25,*

$$8(x) = (12)(4)$$
$$8x = 48$$
$$x = 6$$

(b) By *Theorem 6.25,*

$$(x+8)(8) = (10+6)(6)$$
$$8x + 64 = 96$$
$$8x = 32$$
$$x = 4$$

Let $\overline{RS}$ be a chord of a circle C. Let ℓ be a tangent line to C at Q, which is a point other than R or S. If the lines ℓ and $\overleftrightarrow{RS}$ are not parallel, then they intersect at a point P outside the circle. The segment $\overline{PQ}$ is called a **tangent segment** of ℓ.

Theorem 6.26. Let $\overline{RS}$ be a chord of a circle C and let ℓ be a tangent line to C at Q, which is a point other than R or S. Suppose ℓ and $\overleftrightarrow{RS}$ intersect at P. Then the product of the lengths of the secant segments of $\overline{RS}$ is equal to the square of the length of the tangent segment $\overline{PQ}$. That is, $PS \cdot PR = PQ^2$.

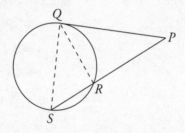

By *Theorem 6.21,* $m\angle PQR = m\angle QSP$, and $\triangle PQR$ and $\triangle PSQ$ share $\angle P$. Thus, $\triangle PQR \sim \triangle PSQ$ by the AA Theorem for Similarity (*Theorem 5.10*).

Therefore, $\dfrac{PQ}{PR} = \dfrac{PS}{PQ}$, and $PQ^2 = PS \cdot PR$ using cross-multiplication.

Theorem 6.27: If two tangent segments intersect outside of a circle, they have equal lengths.

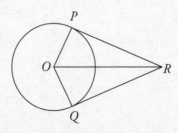

In the figure above, if tangent segments $\overline{PR}$ and $\overline{QR}$ intersect at point R, then $RP = RQ$. Let O be the center of the circle. Construct $\overline{OR}$. Both $\angle P$ and $\angle Q$ are right angles by *Theorem 6.22*, and right triangles $\triangle OPR$ and $\triangle OQR$ share the hypotenuse $\overline{OR}$. Thus, $\triangle OPR$ and $\triangle OQR$ are congruent by the HL Theorem (*Theorem 3.20*) making $RP = RQ$.

Example 8: Find the value of x in figures **(a)**, **(b)**, **(c)**, and **(d)** below.

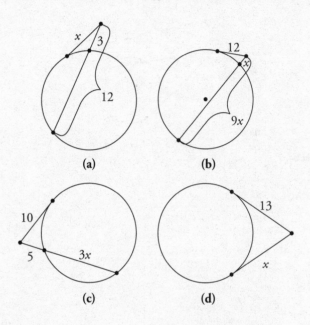

(a)   (b)

(c)   (d)

(a) By *Theorem 6.26*,

$$x^2 = (12)(3)$$
$$x^2 = 36$$
$$x = 6 \text{ since } x > 0$$

(b) By *Theorem 6.26*,

$$12^2 = (9x)(x)$$
$$144 = 9x^2$$
$$16 = x^2$$
$$x = 4 \text{ since } x > 0$$

(c) By *Theorem 6.26*,

$$10^2 = (3x+5)(5)$$
$$100 = 15x + 25$$
$$75 = 15x$$
$$x = 5$$

(d) By *Theorem 6.27*, $x = 13$.

Chapter Check-Out

Questions

1. Determine the measure of an inscribed angle whose intercepted arc on the circle is the same as that of a central angle of degree measure 88°.

2. Compute x in the following figure.

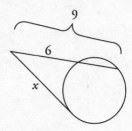

Answers

1. 44°
2. $x = 3\sqrt{6}$

Chapter 7

LENGTH AND AREA

Chapter Check-In

❑ Calculating the lengths of line segments and polygonal curves

❑ Computing the perimeter and the area of squares, rectangles, triangles, parallelograms, trapezoids, and regular polygons

❑ Computing the circumference and the area of a circle

Common Core Standard: Geometric Measurement and Dimension

Solve real-life and mathematical problems involving angle measure, area, and surface area (G.4–6). Give an informal argument for the formulas for the circumference of a circle and area of a circle (G.GMD.1).

In this chapter, we will investigate the measurements of length and area of geometric objects. Let's start with a few simple definitions. **Perimeter** is the distance around any closed figure; that is, the sum of its lengths. **Circumference** is the perimeter of a circle. **Area** is the measure of the interior of a two-dimensional closed figure. It is expressed in square units, such as square inches (in^2) or square centimeters (cm^2) or in special units such as acres.

The critical step in performing any measurement is the choice of a unit. The goal is to assign a numerical value to any length or area measurement relative to the chosen unit. This assignment is assumed to satisfy the following fundamental assumptions.

Measurement assumption 1 (M1): The length or area is the same for congruent objects.

Measurement assumption 2 (M2): The length or area is additive: (a) If two curves meet only at endpoints, then the length of the union of the two curves is the sum of the lengths of the individual curves. (b) If two planar regions meet only at their respective boundary curves, then the area of the union of the two planar regions is the sum of the areas of the individual regions.

Geometry Theorems

The geometry theorems in this book are numbered for organizational purposes. For example, *Theorem 2.2* is the second theorem given in Chapter 2. Study these theorems by their content, not by their number, as the theorem numbering has no significance outside of this book.

Length of a Line Segment

Suppose we want to find the length of a given segment $\overline{AB}$. We need a ruler for this. Consider a number line (a ruler) with tick marks at whole numbers, and the first tick mark is at 0 (zero). The length unit of this ruler is the length of the segment [0, 1], that is, 1. For example, if we place a segment on this number line so that one end point is at 0 and if the other end falls on the tick mark 5, then we say the length of the segment is 5 units.

Place the segment $\overline{AB}$ on the number line so that A is at 0. Then point B falls on some point on the number line. The point B may fall on a tick mark, or not. If it does fall on a tick mark, let's say 4, then we say the length of $\overline{AB}$ is 4.

If B does not fall on a tick mark, then it lies between two tick marks. For example, suppose B lies between 4 and 5. Then the length of $\overline{AB}$ is $4 + t_1$, for some number t_1, where $0 < t_1 < 1$. Our goal now is to find t_1. We adopt the following method.

Partition the segment [4, 5] into 10 equal parts. Then each part has a length of $\frac{1}{10}$ units, or 0.1 units. Then there are nine new tick marks between 4 and 5, and we identify them as 4.1, 4.2, 4.3, 4.4, …,4.9. If B falls on one of these new tick marks, say 4.4, then we say the length of $\overline{AB}$ is 4.4. However, it is possible that B falls between two of the new tick marks and we still do not know the length of $\overline{AB}$. Suppose B lies between 4.4 and 4.5. Then the length of $\overline{AB}$ is $4.4 + t_2$, for some number t_2, where $0 < t_2 < 0.1$. Our goal now is to find t_2. We adopt the same method as before.

Partition the segment [4.4, 4.5] into 10 equal parts. Then each part has a length of $\frac{1}{100}$ units, or 0.01 units. Then there are nine new tick marks between 4.4 and 4.5, and we identify them as 4.41, 4.42, 4.43, …, 4.49.

If B falls on one of these new tick marks, then great. Suppose B is on the tick mark 4.48. Then we say that the length of $\overline{AB}$ is 4.48. However, it is possible that B lies between two of the new tick marks. Then we still do not know the length of $\overline{AB}$.

Suppose B lies between 4.48 and 4.49. Then the length of $\overline{AB}$ is $4.48 + t_3$, for some number t_3, where $0 < t_3 < 0.01$.

Partition the segment [4.48, 4.49] into 10 equal parts, obtaining nine new tick marks between 4.48 and 4.49 identified as, 4.481, 4.482, 4,483, …, 4.489, and each part has a length of $\dfrac{1}{1,000}$ or 0.001 units.

If B falls on one of these new tick marks, then we know the length of $\overline{AB}$, but if not, then we don't. However, we can continue partitioning each new segment into 10 equal parts until we get the length of $\overline{AB}$, or it may continue forever. In that case, we say the length of $\overline{AB}$ is a number with infinite decimal places. In practice, we give up after a certain decimal and declare the length of $\overline{AB}$ as an approximation up to that decimal.

Length of a Polygonal Curve

A **polygonal curve** is a concatenation (the placing of segments end to end) of finite line segments. For example, in the following figure, the curve $\overline{ABCDE}$ is a polygonal curve that is a concatenation of segments $\overline{AB}$, $\overline{BC}$, $\overline{CD}$, and $\overline{DE}$.

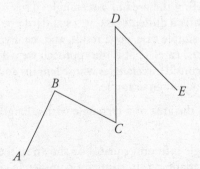

According to M2, the length of a polygonal curve is the sum of the lengths of the segments of the polygonal curve. For example, the length of the polygonal curve $\overline{ABCDE}$ above is $AB + BC + CD + DE$.

Theorem 7.1: The length of a polygonal curve is the sum of the lengths of the segments of the polygonal curve.

Squares and Rectangles

A square with sides of 1 length unit is called a **unit square,** or the area of a unit square is 1 square unit. This is the standard unit for measuring areas of geometric objects on a plane.

Note: When calculating perimeter and area, length and width are measured in positive values.

Two sides of a rectangle are usually called the length, l, and the width, w, of the rectangle. If the length and width have the same measure, then the rectangle is a square. If l and w are the length and width of a rectangle in length units, then the perimeter of the rectangle is a polygonal curve whose length is $l + w + l + w$ by *Theorem 7.1*. The perimeter of a rectangle is $2l + 2w$ or $2(l + w)$. If the length of a side of a square is l, then the perimeter of a square is $4l$.

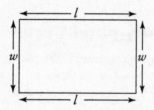

Our goal is to define the area of a rectangle. This is not an easy task. When you encounter a difficult task, it is standard practice in mathematics to start with a simple case, get a result, and see if you can extend that result for the general case. That is the approach we will take here. Therefore, we will first consider rectangles whose lengths and widths are whole numbers. Let us look at an example.

Example 1: Find the area of a rectangle with a length of 4 units and a width of 3 units.

Divide the rectangle into unit squares, as shown in the following figure, so that 12 nonoverlapping unit squares completely cover the rectangle with no gaps. Hence, the area of the rectangle is 12 square units or 3×4 square units.

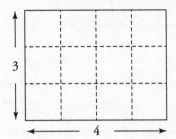

You can prove the following theorem along those lines.

Theorem 7.2: The area of a rectangle with sides m and n units is mn units², where m and n are positive whole numbers.

Now we will see if we can extend *Theorem 7.2* for a rectangle with fractional lengths and widths. Once again, let us look at an example to guide us to the extension of *Theorem 7.2*.

Consider a unit square. Divide each side of the square into six equal parts. Now connect corresponding tick marks by lines parallel to the sides of the square. The resulting figure is as follows.

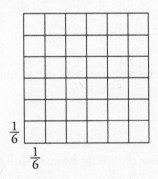

The little squares are congruent to each other. Suppose the area of one such square is A. Then by M2,

$$36A = 1$$

Hence,

$$A = \frac{1}{36} = \frac{1}{6} \times \frac{1}{6}$$

Example 2: Find the area of the rectangle with length $\frac{2}{3}$ and width $\frac{5}{2}$.

In this case, we can repeat the procedure used to measure the length of a segment to measure the area of the given rectangle. Using equivalent fractions, both $\frac{2}{3}$ and $\frac{5}{2}$ can be put on an equal footing. This is known as the *Fundamental Fact of Fraction Pairs* in arithmetic. In this case, $\frac{2}{3} = \frac{4}{6}$ and $\frac{5}{2} = \frac{15}{6}$.

Divide the segment with length $\frac{2}{3}$ into 4 equal parts. Then each part has length $\frac{2}{3 \times 4}$, or $\frac{1}{6}$ length units. Now, divide the segment $\frac{5}{2}$ into 15 equal parts so that each part has a length of $\frac{5}{2 \times 15}$, or $\frac{1}{6}$ length units.

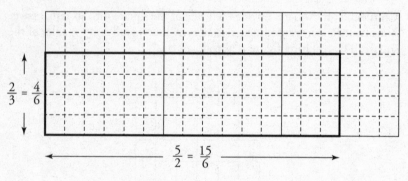

There are exactly 4×15 nonoverlapping squares with sides $\frac{1}{6}$ that cover the given rectangle. Since the area of a square with sides $\frac{1}{6}$ length units is $\frac{1}{6 \times 6}$, the area of the given rectangle is $\frac{4 \times 15}{6 \times 6}$. This is the same as $\frac{4}{6} \times \frac{15}{6}$, or $\frac{2}{3} \times \frac{5}{2}$.

The following theorem can be proven using a similar strategy that was used in Example 2.

Theorem 7.3: The area of a rectangle with sides m and n units is mn units^2, where m and n are positive fractions.

If the lengths of the sides of a rectangle are not fractions, then use the following intuitive argument. For example, find a fraction as close as possible to m, $\frac{p}{q} < m$, and a fraction as close as possible to n, $\frac{r}{s} < n$. Therefore, the area of the rectangle is approximately $\frac{p}{q} \times \frac{r}{s}$. As you may have seen in the argument of finding the length of a line segment, we can find a fraction as close as we please to a given number. Therefore, we say the length of the rectangle is $m \times n$, where m and n may be given as numbers with infinite decimals.

Theorem 7.4: The area of a rectangle with sides m and n units is mn units^2, where m and n are positive real numbers.

Theorem 7.5: The area of a square with side n units is n^2 units^2.

Example 3: Find the perimeter and area of the following square.

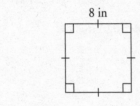

8 in

$$P_{\text{square}} = 4a \qquad\qquad A_{\text{square}} = a^2$$
$$= 4(8 \text{ in}) \qquad\qquad = (8 \text{ in})^2$$
$$= 32 \text{ in} \qquad\qquad = 64 \text{ in}^2$$

Example 4: Find the perimeter and area of the following rectangle.

12 cm

6 cm

$$P_{\text{rectangle}} = 2(l + w) \qquad\qquad A_{\text{rectangle}} = lw$$
$$= 2(12 \text{ cm} + 6 \text{ cm}) \qquad\qquad = (12 \text{ cm})(6 \text{ cm})$$
$$= 36 \text{ cm} \qquad\qquad = 72 \text{ cm}^2$$

Example 5: Find the area of a square with a 36 foot perimeter.

$$P_{square} = 4a \qquad A_{square} = a^2$$
$$36 \text{ ft} = 4a \qquad\qquad = (9 \text{ ft})^2$$
$$9 \text{ ft} = a \qquad\qquad = 81 \text{ ft}^2$$

The area of the square is 81 square feet.

Example 6: For a rectangle with length 9 inches and an area of 36 in², find its perimeter.

$$A_{rectangle} = lw \qquad\qquad P_{square} = 2(l+w)$$
$$36 \text{ in}^2 = (9 \text{ in})(w) \qquad\qquad = 2(9 \text{ in} + 4 \text{ in})$$
$$4 \text{ in} = w \qquad\qquad\qquad = 26 \text{ in}$$

The perimeter of the rectangle is 26 inches.

Triangles

Right triangles

Consider a right triangle $\triangle ABC$ with $m\angle B = 90°$. Let ρ be this 180° rotation around the midpoint M of the side $\overline{AC}$. Then $\rho(A) = C$ and $\rho(C) = A$.

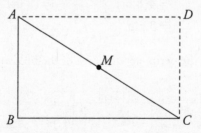

$\rho(\overleftrightarrow{CB}) \parallel \overleftrightarrow{CB}$ and passes through A.

$\rho(\overleftrightarrow{AB}) \parallel \overleftrightarrow{AB}$ and passes through C.

Since B is on $\overleftrightarrow{CB}$, $\rho(B)$ is on $\rho(\overleftrightarrow{CB})$. Also, since B is on $\overleftrightarrow{AB}$, $\rho(B)$ is on $\rho(\overleftrightarrow{AB})$.

Therefore, $\rho(B)$ is at the intersection of $\rho(\overleftrightarrow{CB})$ and $\rho(\overleftrightarrow{AB})$.

Let $\rho(B) = D$. Then $\rho(\triangle ABC) = \triangle CDA$. Therefore, $\triangle ABC$ is congruent to $\triangle CDA$.

$m\angle BAD = 90°$ by *Theorem 2.9*.

$m\angle BCD = 90°$ by *Theorem 2.9*.

$m\angle D = m\angle B = 90°$ since rotations preserve degrees of angles.

Therefore, $ABCD$ is a rectangle, by definition, and the area of $\triangle ABC$ is one-half of the rectangle $ABCD$. This proves the following theorem.

Theorem 7.6: The area of a right triangle is *half* the base times the height: $\frac{1}{2}\left(\text{base} \times \text{height}\right)$ or $\frac{1}{2}(bh)$.

In $\triangle ABC$ above, AB = height and BC = base. Therefore, by *Theorem 7.6*, the area of $\triangle ABC$ with $m\angle B = 90°$ is $\frac{1}{2}(AB)(BC)$.

Arbitrary triangles

If $\triangle ABC$ is an arbitrary triangle, let $\overline{AD}$ be the altitude from A to line $\overline{BC}$. There are two cases to consider. Case 1: D is between B and C. Case 2: D is not between B and C. The two cases are illustrated in the following figure.

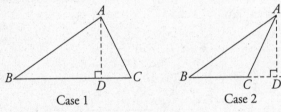

Case 1   Case 2

Case 1:

The area of $\triangle ABC$ = the area of $\triangle ABD$ + the area of $\triangle ACD$. By *Theorem 7.6*, the area of $\triangle ABD = \frac{1}{2}(BD)(AD)$ and the area of $\triangle ACD = \frac{1}{2}(CD)(AD)$. Therefore:

$$\text{The area of } \triangle ABC = \frac{1}{2}(BD)(AD) + \frac{1}{2}(CD)(AD)$$

$$= \frac{1}{2}\left[(BD) + (CD)\right](AD)$$

$$= \frac{1}{2}(BC)(AD)$$

Case 2:

The area of $\triangle ABC =$ the area of $\triangle ABD -$ the area of $\triangle ACD$

$$= \frac{1}{2}(BD)(AD) - \frac{1}{2}(CD)(AD)$$

$$= \frac{1}{2}[(BD) - (CD)](AD)$$

$$= \frac{1}{2}(BC)(AD)$$

Theorem 7.7: The area of a $\triangle ABC$ with altitude $\overline{AD}$ and base $\overline{BC}$ is $\frac{1}{2}(BC)(AD)$.

Example 7: Find the perimeter and area for the triangles in figures **(a)**, **(b)**, and **(c)** below.

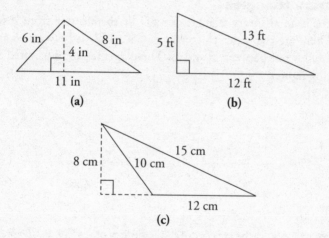

(a) $P_{\text{triangle}} = a + b + c$ $\qquad A_{\text{triangle}} = \frac{1}{2}bh$

$\qquad\qquad = 8 + 11 + 6 \qquad\qquad\qquad = \frac{1}{2}(11)(4)$

$\qquad\qquad = 25 \text{ in} \qquad\qquad\qquad\qquad = 22 \text{ in}^2$

(b) $P_{\text{triangle}} = a + b + c$ $\qquad A_{\text{triangle}} = \dfrac{1}{2} bh$

$\qquad\qquad = 13 + 12 + 5$ $\qquad\qquad = \dfrac{1}{2}(12)(5)$

$\qquad\qquad = 30 \text{ ft}$ $\qquad\qquad = 30 \text{ ft}^2$

(c) $P_{\text{triangle}} = a + b + c$ $\qquad A_{\text{triangle}} = \dfrac{1}{2} bh$

$\qquad\qquad = 15 + 12 + 10$ $\qquad\qquad = \dfrac{1}{2}(12)(8)$

$\qquad\qquad = 37 \text{ cm}$ $\qquad\qquad = 48 \text{ cm}^2$

Example 8: If the area of a triangle is 64 cm² and it has a height of 16 cm, find the length of its base.

$$A_{\text{triangle}} = \frac{1}{2} bh$$

$$64 \text{ cm}^2 = \frac{1}{2}(b)(16 \text{ cm})$$

$128 \text{ cm}^2 = (b)(16 \text{ cm})$ $\qquad$ Multiply both sides by 2.

$8 \text{ cm} = b$ $\qquad\qquad\quad$ Divide both sides by 16.

The triangle will have a base of 8 centimeters.

Parallelograms

Let *ABCD* be a parallelogram (not a rectangle). Drop a perpendicular from *D* to line $\overleftrightarrow{BC}$, and let *E* be the foot of the perpendicular. Here, there are two cases. Case 1: *E* lies between *B* and *C*. Case 2: *E* does not lie between *B* and *C*. The two cases are illustrated in the following figure.

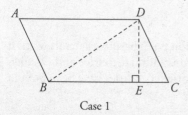

Case 1

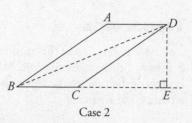

Case 2

In either case, connect B and D by a line segment; then $\triangle ABD$ and $\triangle CDB$ are congruent by the SSS Theorem (*Theorem 3.21*). Therefore, by the assumption M1, their areas are equal. By the assumption M2:

$$\text{The area of the parallelogram } ABCD = 2\left[\frac{1}{2}(BC)(DE)\right]$$
$$= (BC)(DE)$$

Theorem 7.8: The area of a parallelogram is (base)(height) or *bh*.

Therefore, by *Theorem 7.8*, if BC is the *base* and DE is the height, then the area of parallelogram $ABCD$ is $(BC)(DE)$.

Since it has been established that opposite sides of a parallelogram are equal in length, then finding the perimeter of a parallelogram will be similar to finding the perimeter of a rectangle. Thus, if a and b represent the lengths of any two consecutive sides of a parallelogram, the perimeter is $2a + 2b$ or $2(a + b)$.

Example 9: Find the perimeter and area of the following parallelogram.

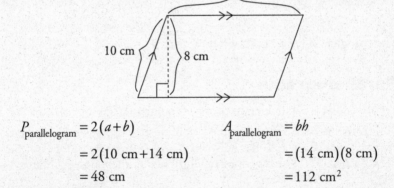

$$P_{\text{parallelogram}} = 2(a+b) \qquad\qquad A_{\text{parallelogram}} = bh$$
$$= 2(10 \text{ cm} + 14 \text{ cm}) \qquad\qquad = (14 \text{ cm})(8 \text{ cm})$$
$$= 48 \text{ cm} \qquad\qquad\qquad = 112 \text{ cm}^2$$

Trapezoids

The trapezoid is one of the most common types of quadrilaterals when it comes to bridge construction. Numerous railroad trestles and wooden bridges of the nineteenth and early twentieth centuries have been built in a trapezoidal shape.

Trapezoid *PQRS* below is labeled so that b_1 and b_2 are the bases (h is the height to these bases) and a and c are the legs. The perimeter is the sum of the bases and leg lengths.

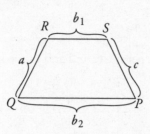

$$P_{\text{trapezoid}} = a + b_1 + c + b_2$$

Let *ABCD* be a trapezoid with $\overleftrightarrow{AD} \parallel \overleftrightarrow{BC}$, as shown in the following figure. Draw perpendiculars from *B* to line $\overleftrightarrow{AD}$ and *D* to line $\overleftrightarrow{BC}$, respectively. Now, *E* and *F* are the feet of those perpendiculars respectively.

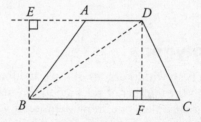

Since $\overleftrightarrow{AD} \parallel \overleftrightarrow{BC}$ and a line perpendicular to one of these two parallel lines is perpendicular to the other, *BEDF* is a rectangle, so $BE = DF$. For this reason, *BE* is the distance between the parallel lines $\overleftrightarrow{AD}$ and $\overleftrightarrow{BC}$. From the assumption M2:

The area of the trapezoid $ABCD$ = the area of $\triangle ABD$ + the area of $\triangle BDC$

$$= \frac{1}{2}(AD)(BE) + \frac{1}{2}(BC)(DF)$$

Since $BE = DF$,

$$= \frac{1}{2}(AD)(BE) + \frac{1}{2}(BC)(BE)$$

$$= \frac{1}{2}(AD + BC)(BE)$$

Theorem 7.9: The area of a trapezoid is $\frac{1}{2}(\text{base}_1 + \text{base}_2)(\text{height})$.

Therefore, by *Theorem 7.9*, the area of trapezoid $ABCD$ with $\overrightarrow{AD} \parallel \overrightarrow{BC}$ is $\frac{1}{2}(AD + BC)(BE)$.

Example 10: Find the perimeter and area of the following trapezoid.

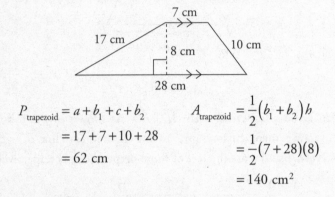

$$P_{\text{trapezoid}} = a + b_1 + c + b_2$$
$$= 17 + 7 + 10 + 28$$
$$= 62 \text{ cm}$$

$$A_{\text{trapezoid}} = \frac{1}{2}(b_1 + b_2)h$$
$$= \frac{1}{2}(7 + 28)(8)$$
$$= 140 \text{ cm}^2$$

Regular Polygons

Thus far, we have dealt with polygons of three and four sides. But there is really no limit to the number of sides a polygon may have. The only practical limit is that unless you draw them on a very large sheet of paper, after about 20 sides or so, the polygon begins to look very much like a circle.

Parts of a regular polygon

As discussed in Chapter 4, a regular polygon is both equilateral and equiangular. In a regular polygon, there is one point in its interior that is equidistant from its vertices. This point is called the **center of the regular polygon.** In the regular polygon that follows, O is the center.

The **radius of a regular polygon** is a segment that goes from the center to any vertex of the regular polygon. In the regular polygon below, $\overline{OC}$ is a radius.

The **apothem of a regular polygon** is any segment that goes from the center to the midpoint of one of the sides and is perpendicular to one of the polygon's sides. In the regular polygon below, $\overline{OX}$ is an apothem.

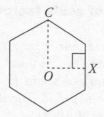

Finding the perimeter

Because a regular polygon is equilateral, to find its perimeter you need to know only the length of one of its sides and multiply that by the number of sides. Using n-gon to represent a polygon with n sides, and s as the length of each side, produces the following formula.

$$P_{\text{regular } n\text{-gon}} = ns$$

Finding the area

Since we can triangulate a regular polygon, the following result follows from the area of a triangle.

Theorem 7.10: The area of a regular n-gon is $\frac{1}{2}(a)(p)$, where p is the perimeter of the n-gon ($p = ns$) and a is the length of the apothem.

Example 11: Find the perimeter and area of the regular pentagon below, with apothem 5.5 in.

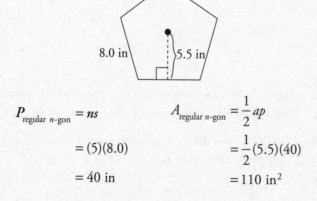

$$P_{\text{regular } n\text{-gon}} = ns \qquad\qquad A_{\text{regular } n\text{-gon}} = \frac{1}{2}ap$$

$$= (5)(8.0) \qquad\qquad = \frac{1}{2}(5.5)(40)$$

$$= 40 \text{ in} \qquad\qquad = 110 \text{ in}^2$$

Effect of a dilation of scale factor *r* on the area of a polygon

Let T be a dilation with the scale factor $r > 0$. If $ABCD$ is a rectangle whose consecutive sides have lengths a and b, let $T(ABCD) = ABCD'$. Then $ABCD'$ is also a rectangle (dilations preserve degrees of angles) with consecutive sides of lengths ra and rb. Therefore, the area of the dilated rectangle is r^2 times the area of $ABCD$.

Theorem 7.11: Let T be a dilation with the scale factor $r > 0$. Let $ABCD$ be a rectangle so that $T(ABCD) = ABCD'$. Then the area of $ABCD'$ is $r^2 \cdot$ area of $ABCD$.

Suppose $\triangle ABC$ is a triangle with the height h and the base b. Let $T(\triangle ABC) = \triangle ABC'$. Then by the Fundamental Theorem of Similarity (*Theorem 5.1*), $\triangle ABC'$ has the height rh and the base rb as shown in the following figure. Hence, the area of $\triangle ABC'$ is $\frac{1}{2}(rh)(rb) = r^2\left(\frac{1}{2}bh\right)$.

Theorem 7.12: Let T be a dilation with the scale factor $r > 0$. Let $\triangle ABC$ be a triangle so that $T(ABC) = \triangle ABC'$. Then the area of $\triangle ABC'$ is $r^2 \cdot$ area of $\triangle ABC$.

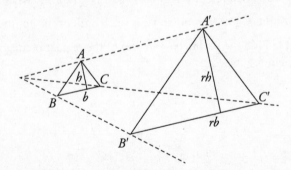

Given a polygon P, we can triangulate it to a collection of concatenated triangles. Then the following theorem follows from *Theorem 7.2* and M2.

Theorem 7.13: Let T be a dilation with the scale factor $r > 0$. Let P be a polygon so that $T(P) = P'$. Then the area of $P' = r^2 \cdot$ area of P.

Area and Circumference of a Circle

Recall that the unit circle is the circle with radius 1. We define the *circumference of the unit circle* as pi (the symbol is π), a number that is approximately equal to 3.14 when rounded to two decimal places.

Our first goal is to find the **area of the unit circle.** We will achieve this by inscribing a sequence of regular polygons in the unit circle so that the area of each iteration gives a better approximation for the area of the unit circle.

First, inscribe a square $ABCD$ (a regular 4-gon) in the circle. We will denote this polygon as P_4.

Draw perpendicular bisectors of each side of P_4. Those perpendicular bisectors intersect the unit circle at four new points: let's say at P, Q, R, and S. Then, since each triangle formed, $\triangle APB$, $\triangle BQC$, $\triangle CRD$, and $\triangle DSA$, is a congruent isosceles triangle, $APBQCRDS$ is a regular 8-gon. Denote this regular polygon as P_8. The regular polygons P_4 and P_8 are shown in the following figure.

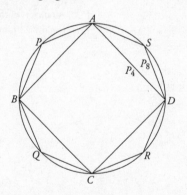

Use the same method of obtaining P_8 from P_4 again to get a regular 16-gon P_{16} from P_8. Continue to use this method to produce regular polygons that are inscribed in the unit circle, each of which has twice as many sides as the previous one. The area of each new polygon is closer to the area of the unit circle than to the area of the previous polygon after each iteration. We can expect that we can create an n-gon, P_n, for an arbitrarily large n, so that its boundary can be made as close as we please to the boundary of the unit circle.

Consider a regular n-gon, P_n, of this sequence for some arbitrarily large n. We can triangulate P_n by connecting each vertex of P_n to the center O of the unit circle. By the SSS Theorem (*Theorem 3.21*), all of the newly created triangles are congruent. Clearly, there are n such triangles and they are isosceles triangles. The following figure shows three of those congruent triangles and a portion of the n-gon.

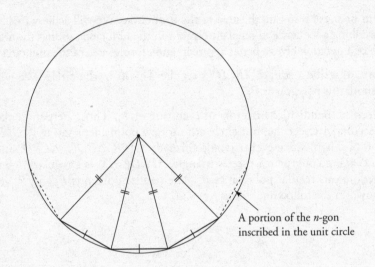

A portion of the n-gon inscribed in the unit circle

Consider one of those n triangles.

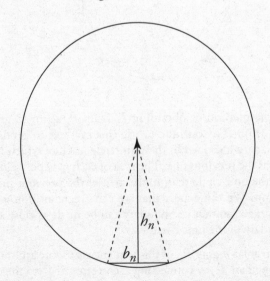

Let the length of a side of P_n be b_n, which is also the length of the base of the triangle. Let the length of a perpendicular from O to the base of the triangle be h_n. Then the area of the triangle is $\frac{1}{2} b_n h_n$. Since the n triangles are congruent, they all have the same area: $n\left(\frac{1}{2} b_n h_n\right)$.

By M2, the area of P_n is the sum of the areas of the n congruent triangles:

$$\text{area}(P_n) = n\left(\frac{1}{2} h_n b_n\right) = \frac{1}{2} h_n (n b_n)$$

Clearly, $n b_n$ is the perimeter of P_n, and the above result indicates that the area of P_n is one half of h_n times the perimeter of P_n.

As n gets arbitrarily large, $n b_n$ gets arbitrarily close to the circumference of the unit circle and h_n gets arbitrarily close to the radius of the unit circle.

Let A be the area of the unit circle. Since the circumference of the unit circle is 2π and the radius of unit circle is 1, we can say that

$$A = \frac{1}{2} \cdot 1 \cdot 2\pi$$

This leads to:

$$A = \pi$$

Thus, we have the following theorem:

Theorem 7.14: The area of the unit circle is π.

Let U be the unit circle with center O.

A circle of radius $r > 0$ can be obtained from U by using a dilation, $P_n{}'$, with center O and the scale factor r. Since the area of P_n gets arbitrarily close to the area of the unit circle, the area of $P_n{}'$ gets arbitrarily close to U'. Then by *Theorem 7.13*,

$$\text{area } P_n{}' = r^2 \cdot \text{area } P_n$$

Therefore, the area of $P_n{}'$ gets arbitrarily close to $r^2 \cdot C(1)' = \pi r^2$. Thus, we have the following theorem.

Theorem 7.15: The area of a circle with radius r is πr^2.

Let the circumference of the circle with center O and radius r be C_r. As n gets arbitrarily large, the perimeter of $P_n{}'$ gets arbitrarily close to C_r. By *Theorem 7.13*, the perimeter of $P_n{}'$ is $r(nb_n)$ and

$$C_r = r(nb_n) = r(C) = r(2\pi) = 2\pi r$$

This leads to the following theorem:

Theorem 7.16: The circumference of a circle with radius r is $2\pi r$.

Consequently, if d is the diameter of a circle with radius r, then the circumference is πd.

To get a good approximation for the value of π, you can conduct the following experiment. In a pair of perpendicular diameters partition the unit circle into 4 congruent *quarter circles*. Then the area of a quarter circle is $\dfrac{\pi}{4}$, by definition.

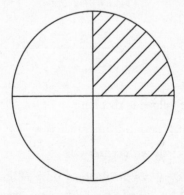

Suppose the shaded quarter circle within a quarter square was placed on a grid so that the radius of the circle was 20 units. Count the total number of grid squares that lie entirely in the quarter circle. For those partial grid squares inside the circle, make the best possible estimate in terms of decimals. For example, if half of a grid square lies inside the quarter circle, then count it as a 0.5 of a grid square. Make the radius as large as possible.

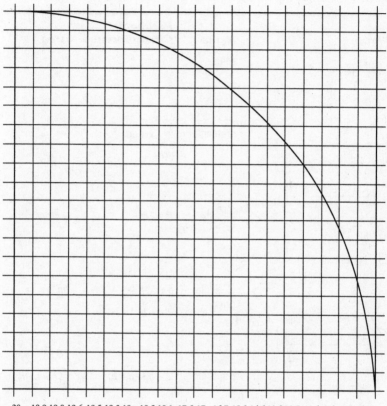

20   19.9 19.8 19.6 19.5 19.3 19   18.5 18.1 17.6 17   16.7 15.5 14.6 13.5 12.5 11.4 9.6   7.6   4.3

The area of the quarter circle is then approximately 314 square units (20 + 19.9 + 19.8 + 19.6 + 19.5 + 19.3 + 19 + 18.5 + 18.1 + 17.6 + 17 + 16.7 + 15.5 + 14.6 + 13.5 + 12.5 + 11.4 + 9.6 + 7.6 + 4.3 = 314). The area of the quarter square is 400 square units ($20^2 = 400$).

Therefore, $\dfrac{\pi}{4} \approx \dfrac{314}{400} \approx 0.785$ or $\pi \approx 3.14$.

Summary of Perimeter, Circumference, and Area Formulas

With a simple formula, you can find the perimeter or area for any shape. Review the following summary of formulas for each shape.

Figure	Name	Perimeter/ Circumference	Area
a (square figure)	square	$4a$	a^2
l, w (rectangle figure)	rectangle	$2l + 2w$ or $2(l + w)$	lw
a, h, b, c (triangle figure)	triangle	$a + b + c$	$\frac{1}{2}bh$
a, h, b (parallelogram figure)	parallelo-gram	$2a + 2b$ or $2(a + b)$	bh
b_1, a, h, c, b_2 (trapezoid figure)	trapezoid	$a + b_1 + c + b_2$	$\frac{1}{2}(b_1 + b_2)h$
a, s (regular polygon figure)	regular polygon	ns n = number of sides	$\frac{1}{2}ap$ a = apothem p = perimeter
d, r (circle figure)	circle	πd or $2\pi r$	πr^2

Chapter Check-Out

Questions

1. Compute the perimeter and the area of a rectangle with base 7 cm and height 4 cm.

2. Compute the perimeter and the area of an isosceles triangle with height 12 inches and sides 10, 13, and 13 inches.

3. Compute the circumference and the area of a circle of radius 5 inches. Use 3.14 as an approximation for π.

4. Find the **(a)** area and **(b)** perimeter of the following trapezoid.

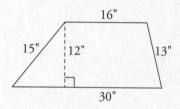

Answers

1. $P = 22$ cm; $A = 28$ cm^2

2. $P = 36$ in; $A = 60$ in^2

3. $C = 10\pi \approx 31.4$ in; $A = 25\pi \approx 78.5$ in^2

4. **(a)** $\text{area} = \dfrac{1}{2}(a + b)h$

$$= \dfrac{1}{2}(16 + 30)12$$

$$= \dfrac{1}{2}(46)12$$

$$= 23(12)$$

$$= 276 \text{ in}^2$$

(b) perimeter $= 16 + 13 + 30 + 15 = 74$ in

Chapter 8

GEOMETRIC SOLIDS

Chapter Check-In

❏ Computing the lateral area and the total surface area for a right prism, a right circular cylinder, a regular pyramid, a right circular cone, and a sphere

❏ Computing the volume of a right prism, a right circular cylinder, a regular pyramid, a right circular cone, and a sphere

> **Common Core Standard: Extending to Three Dimensions**
>
> Give an informal argument for the formulas for the volume of a cylinder, pyramid, and cone. Use volume formulas for cylinders, pyramids, cones, and spheres to solve problems (G.GMD.3).

Different types of geometric solids affect your life in many ways. For example, since containers of various shapes and sizes are frequently used to store liquids, knowing the volume of a right circular cylinder of paint will help you calculate how much paint to purchase for a specific surface area.

> ### Geometry Theorems
> The geometry theorems in this book are numbered for organizational purposes. For example, *Theorem 2.2* is the second theorem given in Chapter 2. Study these theorems by their content, not by their number, as the theorem numbering has no significance outside of this book.

Prisms

Prisms are solids (three-dimensional figures) that, unlike planar figures, occupy space. They come in many shapes and sizes. Every prism has the following characteristics:

■ **Bases:** A prism has two bases, which are congruent polygons lying in **parallel planes**.

- **Lateral edges:** The line segments obtained by connecting the corresponding vertices of the two bases so that any two of these edges lie on two parallel lines.

- **Lateral faces:** Each parallelogram formed by the lateral edges.

- **Altitude:** A segment perpendicular to the planes of the bases with an endpoint in each plane.

A prism is named by the polygon that forms its base, as follows:

- **Oblique prism:** A prism whose lateral edges are not perpendicular to the planes of its bases.

- **Right prism:** A prism whose lateral edges are perpendicular to the planes of its bases. In a right prism, a lateral edge is also an altitude.

  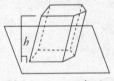

Right triangular prism   Right rectangular prism   Oblique pentagonal prism

In the oblique pentagonal prism above, the altitude is labeled h.

Right Prisms

As stated above, in certain prisms, the lateral faces are each perpendicular to the plane of the bases. As a group, these are known as right prisms.

Lateral area of a right prism

The **lateral area of a right prism** is the sum of the areas of all the lateral faces.

Theorem 8.1: The lateral area, *LA*, of a right prism with altitude h and base perimeter p is given by the following equation:

$$LA_{\text{right prism}} = (p)(h) \text{ units}^2$$

Example 1: Find the lateral area of the following right hexagonal prism.

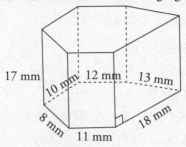

$$LA_{\text{right prism}} = (p)(h) \text{ units}^2$$
$$= (11+18+13+12+10+8)(17) \text{ mm}^2$$
$$= (72)(17) \text{ mm}^2$$
$$= 1,224 \text{ mm}^2$$

Total surface area of a right prism

The **total surface area of a right prism** is the sum of the lateral area and the areas of the two bases. Because the bases are congruent, their areas are equal.

Theorem 8.2: The total surface area, *TA*, of a right prism with lateral area *LA* and a base area *B* is given by the following equation:

$$TA_{\text{right prism}} = LA + 2B \text{ or } TA_{\text{right prism}} = (p)(h) + 2B$$

Example 2: Find the total surface area of the following triangular prism.

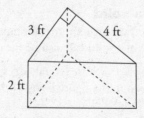

The base of this prism is a right triangle with legs of 3 feet and 4 feet (see figure below).

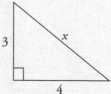

$$\text{hypotenuse}^2 = 3^3 + 4^2 \text{ (Pythagorean Theorem)}$$

$$\text{hypotenuse}^2 = 9 + 16$$

$$\text{hypotenuse}^2 = 25$$

$$\text{hypotenuse} = \sqrt{25}$$

$$\text{hypotenuse} = 5 \text{ ft}$$

The perimeter of the base is $(3 + 4 + 5)$ feet, or 12 feet.

Because the triangle is a right triangle, its legs can be used as base and height of the triangle.

$$B = \text{Area}_{\text{triangle}} = \frac{1}{2}(b)(h)$$

$$= \frac{1}{2}(3)(4) \text{ ft}^2$$

$$= 6 \text{ ft}^2$$

The altitude of the prism is given as 2 feet. Therefore,

$$TA_{\text{right prism}} = LA + 2B \text{ units}^2$$

$$= (p)(h) + 2B \text{ units}^2$$

$$= (12 \text{ ft})(2 \text{ ft}) + (2)(6) \text{ ft}^2$$

$$= 24 \text{ ft}^2 + 12 \text{ ft}^2$$

$$= 36 \text{ ft}^2$$

Interior space of a solid

Lateral area and total surface area are measurements of the surface of a solid. The interior space of a solid can also be measured.

A **cube** is a square right prism whose lateral edges are the same length as a side of the base, as shown in the figure below. A *unit cube* is a cube with each edge 1 unit length long.

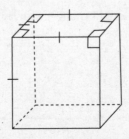

The **volume** of a cube is the number of unit cubes necessary to entirely fill the interior of the solid. The following right rectangular prism measures 3 inches by 4 inches by 5 inches.

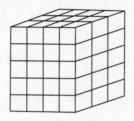

The top layer has 12 unit cubes. Because the above prism has 5 such layers, it takes 60 of these cubes to fill this solid. Thus, the volume of this prism is 60 cubic inches, which is the same as 3 × 4 × 5 cubic inches.

The following theorem is true for a right prism even if the base of the prism is not a rectangle.

Theorem 8.3: The volume, V, of a right prism with a base area B and an altitude h is given by the following equation:

$$V_{\text{right prism}} = (B)(h) \text{ units}^3$$

Example 3: The following figure is an isosceles trapezoidal right prism. Find **(a)** LA, **(b)** TA, and **(c)** V.

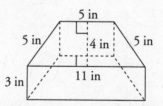

(a) *Note:* The h refers to the altitude of the prism, not the height of the trapezoid.

$$LA_{\text{right prism}} = (p)(h) \text{ units}^2 = (5+5+5+11)(3) \text{ in}^2$$
$$= (26)(3) \text{ in}^2$$
$$= 78 \text{ in}^2$$

(b) $B = \text{Area}_{\text{trapezoid}}$ $\qquad\qquad$ $TA_{\text{right prism}} = LA + 2B$ units^2

$\quad B = \dfrac{1}{2}(5+11)(4)$ in^2 $\qquad\qquad = 78 + 2(32)$

$\quad B = \dfrac{1}{2}(16)(4)$ in^2 $\qquad\qquad\quad = 78 + 64$

$\quad B = 32$ in^2 $\qquad\qquad\qquad\quad\; = 142$ in^2

(c) *Note:* The h refers to the altitude of the prism, not the height of the trapezoid.

$$V_{\text{right prism}} = (B)(h) \text{ units}^3$$
$$= (32)(3) \text{ in}^3$$
$$= 96 \text{ in}^3$$

Right Circular Cylinders

A prism-shaped solid whose bases are circles is a *circular cylinder.* If the segment joining the centers of the circles of a cylinder is perpendicular to the planes of the bases, the cylinder is a **right circular cylinder.**

Right circular cylinder   Oblique circular cylinder

Lateral area, total surface area, and volume for right circular cylinders are found in the same way as they are for right prisms.

If a cylinder is pictured as a soup can, its lateral area is the area of the label. If the label is carefully peeled off, the label becomes a rectangle, as detailed in the following figure.

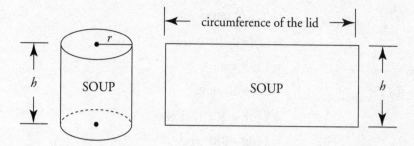

circumference of the lid

SOUP

SOUP

The area of the label is the area of a rectangle with a height the same as the altitude of the can and a base the same as the circumference of the lid of the can.

Theorem 8.4: The lateral area, LA, of a right circular cylinder with a base circumference C and an altitude h is given by the following equation:

$$LA_{\text{right circular cylinder}} = (C)(h) \text{ units}^2$$

$$= (2\pi r)(h) \text{ units}^2$$

Theorem 8.5: The total surface area, TA, of a right circular cylinder with lateral area LA and a base area B is given by the following equation:

$$TA_{\text{right circular cylinder}} = LA + 2B \text{ units}^2$$

$$= (2\pi r)(h) + 2\pi r^2 \text{ units}^2$$

$$= 2\pi r(h + r) \text{ units}^2$$

Theorem 8.6: The volume of a right circular cylinder, V, with a base area B and altitude h is given by the following equation:

$$V_{\text{right circular cylinder}} = (B)(h) \text{ units}^3$$

$$= (\pi r^2)(h) \text{ units}^3$$

Example 4: In the following right circular cylinder; find **(a)** LA, **(b)** TA, and **(c)** V.

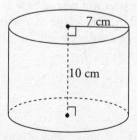

7 cm

10 cm

(a) $LA_{\text{right circular cylinder}} = (C)(h) \text{ units}^2$

$$= (2)(\pi)(7)(10) \text{ cm}^2$$

$$= 140\pi \text{ cm}^2$$

(b) $TA_{\text{right circular cylinder}} = LA + 2B \text{ units}^2$

$$= 140\pi + 2(\pi)(7)^2 \text{ cm}^2$$

$$= 140\pi + 98\pi \text{ cm}^2$$

$$= 238\pi \text{ cm}^2$$

(c) $V_{\text{right circular cylinder}} = (B)(h) \text{ units}^3$

$$= (\pi)(7)^2(10) \text{ cm}^3$$

$$= (49\pi)(10) \text{ cm}^3$$

$$= 490\pi \text{ cm}^3$$

Pyramids

A **pyramid** is a solid that has the following characteristics:

- It has one base, which is a polygon.

- The vertices of the base are each joined to a point, not in the plane of the base. This point is called the **vertex of the pyramid.**

- The triangular sides, all of which meet at the vertex, are its **lateral faces.**

- The edges where pairs of lateral faces intersect are **lateral edges.**

- The perpendicular segment from the vertex to the plane of the base is the **altitude of the pyramid.**

Regular pyramids

A **regular pyramid** is a pyramid whose base is a regular polygon and whose lateral edges are all equal in length. A pyramid is named by its base. Here are some examples of regular pyramids.

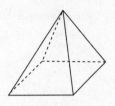
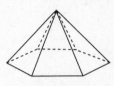

Regular
triangular pyramid

Regular
square pyramid

Regular
hexagonal pyramid

The lateral faces of a regular pyramid are congruent isosceles triangles. The altitude of any of these triangles is the **slant height of the regular pyramid.** Pyramid *ABCD*, below, is a square pyramid.

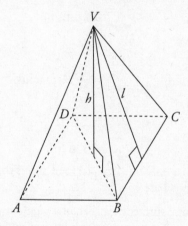

Square *ABCD* is its base.
V is the vertex.
Triangle *VAB* is a lateral face.
VA is a lateral edge.
h is the altitude.
l is the slant height.

Pyramids also have a lateral area, total area, and volume.

Theorem 8.7: The lateral area, *LA*, of a regular pyramid with slant height *l* and base perimeter *p* is given by the following equation:

$$LA_{\text{regular pyramid}} = \frac{1}{2}(p)(l) \text{ units}^2$$

Example 5: In the following square pyramid, find the lateral area, *LA*.

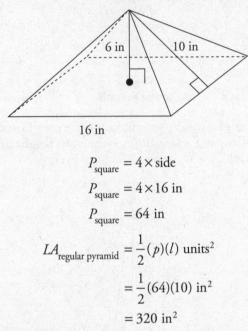

$$P_{\text{square}} = 4 \times \text{side}$$

$$P_{\text{square}} = 4 \times 16 \text{ in}$$

$$P_{\text{square}} = 64 \text{ in}$$

$$LA_{\text{regular pyramid}} = \frac{1}{2}(p)(l) \text{ units}^2$$

$$= \frac{1}{2}(64)(10) \text{ in}^2$$

$$= 320 \text{ in}^2$$

Because a pyramid has only one base, its total area is the sum of the lateral area and the area of its base.

Theorem 8.8: The total surface area, *TA*, of a regular pyramid with lateral area *LA* and base area *B* is given by the following equation:

$$TA_{\text{regular pyramid}} = LA + B \text{ units}^2$$

$$= \frac{1}{2}(p)(l) + B \text{ units}^2$$

Example 6: In the following square pyramid, find the total surface area, *TA*.

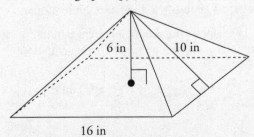

The base of the regular pyramid is a square. Hence, $B = 16^2$ in^2, or $B = 256$ in^2.

$$TA_{\text{regular pyramid}} = LA + B \text{ units}^2$$

From Example 5,

$$LA = 320 \text{ in}^2$$
$$TA = 320 + 256 \text{ in}^2$$
$$= 576 \text{ in}^2$$

Theorem 8.9: The volume, V, of a regular pyramid with base area B and altitude h is given by the following equation:

$$V_{\text{regular pyramid}} = \frac{1}{3}(B)(h) \text{ units}^3$$

Example 7: In the following square pyramid, find the volume.

From Example 6, $B = 256$ in^2. The figure indicates that $h = 6$ in.

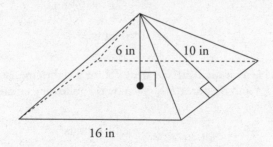

$$V_{\text{regular pyramid}} = \frac{1}{3}(B)(h) \text{ units}^3$$
$$= \frac{1}{3}(256)(6) \text{ in}^3$$
$$= 512 \text{ in}^3$$

Right Circular Cones

A **right circular cone** is similar to a regular pyramid except that its base is a circle. The vocabulary and equations pertaining to the right circular cone are similar to those for the regular pyramid. The following figure shows the vocabulary regarding right circular cones.

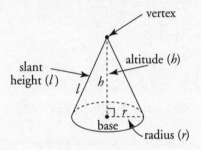

Theorem 8.10: The lateral area, *LA*, of a right circular cone with base circumference *C* and slant height *l* is given by the following equation:

$$LA_{\text{right circular cone}} = \frac{1}{2}(C)(l) \text{ units}^2$$

$$= \frac{1}{2}(2\pi)(r)(l) \text{ units}^2$$

$$= \pi rl \text{ units}^2$$

Theorem 8.11: The total surface area, *TA*, of a right circular cone with lateral area *LA* and base area *B* is given by the following equation:

$$TA_{\text{right circular cone}} = LA + B \text{ units}^2$$

$$= \pi rl + \pi r^2 \text{ units}^2$$

$$= \pi r(l+r) \text{ units}^2$$

Theorem 8.12: The volume, *V*, of a right circular cone with base area *B* and altitude *h* is given by the following equation:

$$V_{\text{right circular cone}} = \frac{1}{3}(B)(h) \text{ units}^3$$

$$= \frac{1}{3}(\pi r^2)(h) \text{ units}^3$$

Example 8: In the following right circular cone, find **(a)** *LA*, **(b)** *TA*, and **(c)** *V*.

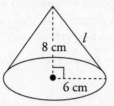

(a) The slant height, radius, and altitude of a right circular cone form a right triangle, as shown in the following figure.

$$l^2 = 8^2 + 6^2 \quad \text{(Pythagorean Theorem)}$$
$$l^2 = 64 + 36$$
$$l^2 = 100$$
$$l = \sqrt{100}$$
$$l = 10 \text{ cm}$$

$$LA_{\text{right circular cone}} = \pi r l \text{ units}^2$$
$$= \pi(6)(10) \text{ cm}^2$$
$$= 60\pi \text{ cm}^2$$

(b) $$TA_{\text{right circular cone}} = LA + B \text{ units}^2$$
$$= 60\pi + \pi(6)^2 \text{ cm}^2$$
$$= 60\pi + 36\pi \text{ cm}^2$$
$$= 96\pi \text{ cm}^2$$

(c) $$V_{\text{right circular cone}} = \frac{1}{3}(B)(h) \text{ units}^3$$
$$= \frac{1}{3}(36\pi)(8) \text{ cm}^3$$
$$= 96\pi \text{ cm}^3$$

Spheres

A **sphere** is the set of all points in space that are equidistant from a fixed point (the *center*); this distance is the radius of the sphere. Because a sphere has no bases, its area is referred to as its surface area.

Theorem 8.13: The surface area, *SA*, of a sphere with radius *r* is given by the following equation:

$$SA_{\text{sphere}} = 4\pi r^2 \text{ units}^2$$

Theorem 8.14: The volume of a sphere, *V*, with radius *r* is given by the following equation:

$$V_{\text{sphere}} = \frac{4}{3}\pi r^3 \text{ units}^3$$

Example 9: In the following sphere with radius *r*, if *r* = 9 cm, find **(a)** *SA* and **(b)** *V*.

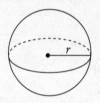

(a) $SA_{\text{sphere}} = 4\pi r^2 \text{ units}^2$

$$= 4\pi(9)^2 \text{ cm}^2$$

$$= 4\pi(81) \text{ cm}^2$$

$$= 324\pi \text{ cm}^2$$

(b) $V_{\text{sphere}} = \frac{4}{3}\pi r^3 \text{ units}^3$

$$= \frac{4}{3}\pi(9)^3 \text{ cm}^3$$

$$= \frac{4}{3}\pi(729) \text{ cm}^3$$

$$= 972\pi \text{ cm}^3$$

Summary of Lateral Area, Total Area, and Volume Formulas

Review the following summary of area and volume formulas for each shape.

Key:

C = circumference of a base B = area of a base
r = radius of a circle h = altitude
p = perimeter of a base l = slant height

Figure	Name	Lateral Area	Total Area	Volume
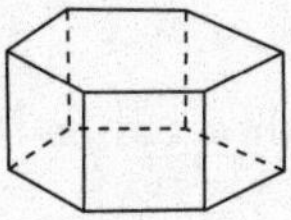	right prism	ph	$LA + 2B = ph + 2B$	Bh
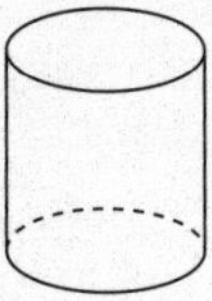	right circular cylinder	$Ch = 2\pi rh$	$LA + 2B = 2\pi rh + 2\pi r^2$ $= 2\pi r(h + r)$	Bh
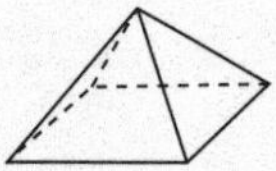	regular pyramid	$\frac{1}{2}pl$	$LA + B = \frac{1}{2}pl + B$	$\frac{1}{3}Bh$
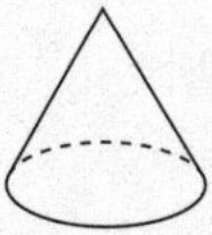	right circular cone	$\frac{1}{2}Cl = \frac{1}{2}(2\pi r)l$ $= \pi rl$	$LA + B = \pi rl + \pi r^2$ $= \pi r(l + r)$	$\frac{1}{3}Bh = \frac{1}{3}\pi r^2 h$
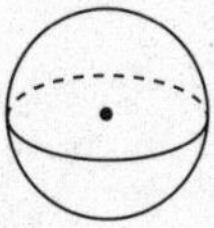	sphere	none	$SA = 4\pi r^2$	$\frac{4}{3}\pi r^3$

Chapter Check-Out

Questions

1. Find the following measurements for a right circular cylinder with a radius of 4 inches and a height of 10 inches.

   (a) lateral area
   (b) total surface area
   (c) volume

2. Find the following measurements for a regular pyramid with an altitude of 12 inches and a square base with side measuring 6 inches. (*Hint:* Use the Pythagorean Theorem to compute the slant height.)

   (a) lateral area
   (b) total surface area
   (c) volume

3. Find the following measurements for a sphere with a radius of 2 inches.

   (a) surface area
   (b) volume

Answers

1. (a) $LA = 80\pi$ in^2
   (b) $TA = 112\pi$ in^2
   (c) $V = 160\pi$ in^3

2. (a) $LA = 36\sqrt{17}$ in^2
   (b) $TA = \left(36\sqrt{17} + 36\right)$ in^2
   (c) $V = 144$ in^3

3. (a) $SA = 16\pi$ in^2
   (b) $V = \dfrac{32}{3}\pi$ in^3

Chapter 9

COORDINATE GEOMETRY

Chapter Check-In

❏ Computing the distance between two points on a number line and two points in a plane

❏ Finding the midpoint of a line segment connecting two points

❏ Finding the equation of a circle

❏ Determining the slope of a line

❏ Determining whether lines are parallel or perpendicular or neither

❏ Determining an equation for a straight line

Common Core Standard: Connecting Algebra and Geometry Through Coordinates

Derive the equation of a circle of given center and radius using the Pythagorean Theorem; complete the square to find the center and radius of a circle given by an equation (G.GPE.1). Use coordinates to prove simple geometric theorems algebraically. For example, prove or disprove that a figure defined by four given points in the coordinate plane is a rectangle; prove or disprove that the point $\left(1, \sqrt{3}\right)$ lies on the circle centered at the origin and containing the point (0, 2) (G.GPE.4). Prove the slope criteria for parallel and perpendicular lines and use them to solve geometric problems (e.g., find the equation of a line parallel or perpendicular to a given line that passes through a given point) (G.GPE.5).

Geometry Theorems

The geometry theorems in this book are numbered for organizational purposes. For example, *Theorem 2.2* is the second theorem given in Chapter 2. Study these theorems by their content, not by their number, as the theorem numbering has no significance outside of this book.

Consider a line ℓ. Pick a point on ℓ and assign the number 0 to this point. Choose a fixed segment and consider the length of this segment to be 1. Use this segment to mark points on ℓ that represent integers. Imagine assigning each point on ℓ a number using this method. For example, the number $\frac{1}{2}$ is assigned to the midpoint between the points 0 and 1. The line ℓ with numbers assigned to each point in this manner is called a *number line*. A number line is also called the *one-dimensional space* (or *1-space*) and the number associated with each point is called the **coordinate** of that point. Use the notation $P(x_1)$ to identify the point P with the associated number x_1. The following figure is an example of a number line.

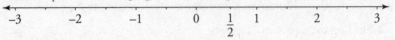

Draw two number lines that are perpendicular to each other on the plane so that they intersect at the point where 0 is the assigned number to the point of intersection on both lines. To distinguish between the two number lines, identify the horizontal line as the **x-axis** and the vertical line as the **y-axis**. The point of intersection is called the **origin,** or just O. Identify O by the two zeros on the two number lines. Write this as an **ordered pair** $(0, 0)$ so that the first zero in the ordered pair is the 0 on the x-axis and the second zero is the 0 on the y-axis.

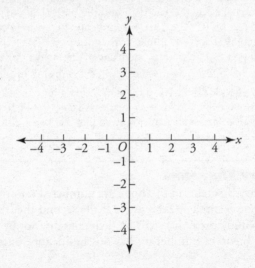

Now we can identify *any* point P on the plane by an ordered pair (x_1, y_1) obtained as follows: Drop a perpendicular from P to the x-axis. The foot of the perpendicular to the x-axis is the point with the associated number x_1. Drop a perpendicular from P to the y-axis. The foot of the perpendicular to the y-axis is the point with the associated number y_1. Now, it is possible to rename the points on the x-axis and the y-axis using the same convention. For example, the point 1 on the x-axis now has the associated ordered pair $(1, 0)$ and the point -1 on the y-axis has the associated ordered pair $(0, -1)$. The first number of the ordered pair associated with a point P is the **x-coordinate** of P, and the second number is the **y-coordinate** of P. Since you can drop only one perpendicular from a given point to a line, the coordinates of a point are *unique* to that point.

The two axes are called the *coordinate axes,* and the plane with coordinate axes is called the *Cartesian coordinate system* in honor of seventeenth-century French mathematician Rene Descartes. A plane with coordinate axes is also identified as a rectangular coordinate system. The plane with a rectangular coordinate system is simply identified as a **coordinate plane.** The coordinate plane is also known as the *two-dimensional space* (or *2-space*). We will use the notation $P(x_1, y_1)$ to identify a point P with coordinates (x_1, y_1).

The x-axis and y-axis separate the coordinate plane into four regions called **quadrants.** (See the figure below.) The upper right quadrant is quadrant I (or the first quadrant), the upper left quadrant is quadrant II (or the second quadrant), the lower left quadrant is quadrant III (or the third quadrant), and the lower right quadrant is quadrant IV (or the fourth quadrant).

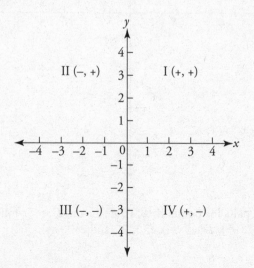

Note the following:

- For a point in quadrant I, both coordinates of the point are positive.

- For a point in quadrant II, the x-coordinate of the point is negative and the y-coordinate is positive.

- For a point in quadrant III, both coordinates of the point are negative.

- For a point in quadrant IV, the x-coordinate of the point is positive and the y-coordinate is negative.

Example 1: Identify the ordered pairs for points A, B, C, D, E, and F on the following coordinate plane.

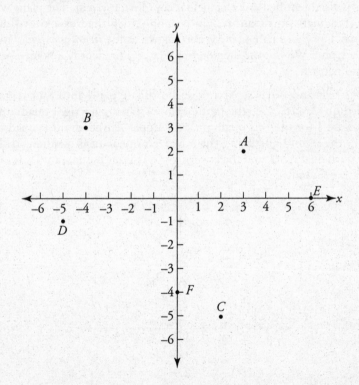

The ordered pairs for points A, B, C, D, E, and F are as follows: $A(3, 2)$, $B(-4, 3)$, $C(2, -5)$, $D(-5, -1)$, $E(6, 0)$, and $F(0, -4)$.

Example 2: The vertices of the rectangle $ABCD$ have coordinates as follows: $A(-5, 2)$, $B(8, 2)$, and $C(8, -4)$. Find the coordinates of point D.

See the following figure. The coordinates of point D must be $(-5, -4)$ for the following reasons: Line $\overleftrightarrow{AB}$ is perpendicular to the y-axis by the way coordinates are defined. The y-axis is perpendicular to the line $\overleftrightarrow{DC}$ since a line perpendicular to one of two parallel lines is perpendicular to the other. By similar reasoning, the x-axis is perpendicular to the line $\overleftrightarrow{AD}$.

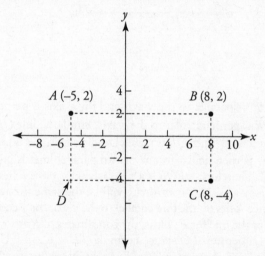

One-Dimensional Distance Formula

Consider a horizontal number line ℓ. Let $P(x_1)$ and $Q(x_2)$ be two points on ℓ. Find the distance between points P and Q denoted by PQ. If P is to the left of Q, then $x_1 < x_2$ and $PQ = x_2 - x_1$. If $P = Q$, then $x_1 = x_2$ and $PQ = x_2 - x_1 = 0$. If P is to the right of Q, then $x_1 > x_2$ and PQ is $x_1 - x_2 = -(x_2 - x_1)$. The following theorem summarizes the above observations.

Theorem 9.1 (One-Dimensional Distance Formula): The distance between two points $P(x_1)$ and $Q(x_2)$ in 1-space is $|x_2 - x_1|$.

Two-Dimensional Distance Formula

Consider two points $P(x_1, y_1)$ and $Q(x_2, y_2)$ in 2-space. Suppose $x_1 \neq x_2$ and $y_1 \neq y_2$. Draw a line through P parallel to the x-axis and draw a line through Q parallel to the y-axis. Let R be the point of intersection of these two lines, as shown in the following figure.

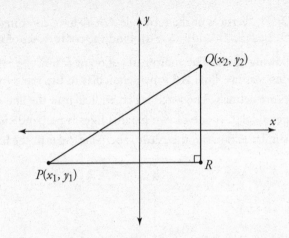

Since line $\overleftrightarrow{PR}$ is parallel to the x-axis and the x-axis is perpendicular to the y-axis, $\overleftrightarrow{PR}$ is perpendicular to the y-axis. Similarly, line $\overleftrightarrow{QR}$ is perpendicular to the x-axis. Since $\overleftrightarrow{QR}$ is parallel to the y-axis, $\overleftrightarrow{PR}$ is perpendicular to $\overleftrightarrow{QR}$ (a line perpendicular to one of two parallel lines is perpendicular to the other). Therefore, ΔPQR is a right triangle. Since R lies on the line parallel to the y-axis, its x-coordinate will be the same as the one for Q. Similarly, since R lies on the line parallel to the x-axis, its y-coordinate will be the same as the one for P. Thus, the coordinates of R are (x_2, y_1). Then by the One-Dimensional Distance Formula, $PR = |x_2 - x_1|$. Using similar reasoning, you can show that $QR = |y_2 - y_1|$. Now, by the Pythagorean Theorem:

$$PQ^2 = PR^2 + QR^2$$

$$PQ^2 = |x_2 - x_1|^2 + |y_2 - y_1|^2$$

Since the square of a number is nonnegative,

$$PQ^2 = (x_2 - x_1)^2 + (y_2 - y_1)^2$$

Since PQ is nonnegative,

$$PQ = \sqrt{\left(x_2 - x_1\right)^2 + \left(y_2 - y_1\right)^2}$$

If $x_1 = x_2$ and $y_1 \neq y_2$, then by the One-Dimensional Distance Formula, $PQ = |y_2 - y_1|$. But since $\sqrt{\left(y_2 - y_1\right)^2} = |y_2 - y_1|$, this result is contained in the formula obtained for PQ in the previous case. Similarly, the results of the two cases ($x_1 \neq x_2$ and $y_1 = y_2$; $x_1 = x_2$ and $y_1 = y_2$) are contained in the above formula. Therefore, the following theorem is proved.

Theorem 9.2 (Two-Dimensional Distance Formula): If the coordinates of two points in 2-space are (x_1, y_1) and (x_2, y_2), then the distance, d, between the two points is given by the following formula:

$$d = \sqrt{\left(x_2 - x_1\right)^2 + \left(y_2 - y_1\right)^2}$$

Example 3: Use the Two-Dimensional Distance Formula to find the distance between the points with coordinates $(-3, 4)$ and $(5, 2)$.

Let $(-3, 4) = (x_1, y_1)$ and $(5, 2) = (x_2, y_2)$. Then,

$$d = \sqrt{\left(5 - (-3)\right)^2 + \left(2 - 4\right)^2}$$
$$d = \sqrt{\left(8\right)^2 + \left(-2\right)^2}$$
$$d = \sqrt{64 + 4}$$
$$d = \sqrt{68}$$
$$d = \sqrt{(4)(17)}$$
$$d = 2\sqrt{17}$$

Example 4: A triangle has vertices $A(12, 5)$, $B(5, 3)$, and $C(12, 1)$. Show that the triangle is isosceles.

By the distance formula,

$$AB = \sqrt{\left(5 - 12\right)^2 + \left(3 - 5\right)^2} \qquad BC = \sqrt{\left(12 - 5\right)^2 + \left(1 - 3\right)^2}$$
$$AB = \sqrt{\left(-7\right)^2 + \left(-2\right)^2} \qquad BC = \sqrt{\left(7\right)^2 + \left(-2\right)^2}$$
$$AB = \sqrt{49 + 4} \qquad BC = \sqrt{49 + 4}$$
$$AB = \sqrt{53} \qquad BC = \sqrt{53}$$

Because $AB = BC$, $\triangle ABC$ is isosceles. (*Note:* If the first two sides chosen to test are not equal, then try the third side and see if it's equal to one of the first two sides.)

Midpoint Formula for One-Dimensional Space

Consider two points $P(x_1)$ and $P(x_2)$ in 1-space. Without loss of generality, assume $x_1 < x_2$. Then the distance between P and Q is $x_2 - x_1$; therefore, the distance to the midpoint R of $\overline{PQ}$ from P is $\dfrac{x_2 - x_1}{2}$.

Therefore, the coordinate of R is $x_1 + \dfrac{x_2 - x_1}{2}$, and the coordinate of the midpoint is $\dfrac{2x_1 + \left(x_2 - x_1\right)}{2} = \dfrac{x_1 + x_2}{2}$.

If $x_1 = x_2$, then the midpoint is x_1 as expected and the formula holds.

Theorem 9.3 (Midpoint Formula for One-Dimensional Space): The midpoint between $P(x_1)$ and $Q\left(x_2\right)$ is $\dfrac{x_1 + x_2}{2}$.

Midpoint Formula for Two-Dimensional Space

Consider two points $P(x_1, y_1)$ and $Q(x_2, y_2)$ in 2-space. Suppose $x_1 \neq x_2$ and $y_1 \neq y_2$. Draw a line through P parallel to the x-axis and draw a line through Q parallel to the y-axis. Let R be the point of intersection of these two lines, as shown in the following figure.

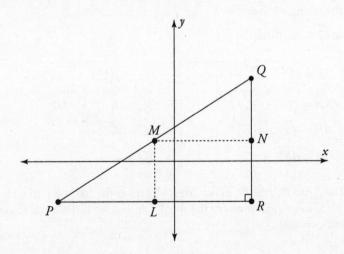

Let M be the midpoint of $\overline{PQ}$, L be the midpoint of $\overline{PR}$, and N be the midpoint of $\overline{QR}$. Then by the Midpoint Theorem (*Theorem 4.21*), line $\overleftrightarrow{ML}$ is parallel to line $\overleftrightarrow{QR}$, and by *Theorem 1.8*, the line $\overleftrightarrow{ML}$ is parallel to the y-axis. Therefore, line $\overleftrightarrow{ML}$ is perpendicular to the x-axis. Therefore, the x-coordinate of M is same as the x-coordinate of L. By the Midpoint Formula for One-Dimensional Space (*Theorem 9.3*), the x-coordinate of L is $\dfrac{x_1 + x_2}{2}$. Therefore, the x-coordinate of M is also $\dfrac{x_1 + x_2}{2}$. By a similar argument, you can show that the y-coordinate of M is $\dfrac{y_1 + y_2}{2}$. It is also easy to see that the special cases, where $x_1 = x_2$ or $y_1 = y_2$, are contained in the following theorem.

Theorem 9.4 (Midpoint Formula for Two-Dimensional Space): Suppose $P(x_1, y_1)$ and $Q(x_2, y_2)$ are two points in 2-space. Then the coordinates of the midpoint M of $\overline{PQ}$ are $\left(\dfrac{x_1 + x_2}{2}, \dfrac{y_1 + y_2}{2} \right)$.

Example 5: In the following figure, R is the midpoint between $Q(-9, -1)$ and $T(-3, 7)$. Find its coordinates and use the Two-Dimensional Distance Formula to verify that it is in fact the midpoint of $\overline{QT}$.

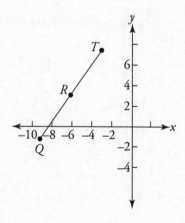

By the Midpoint Formula for Two-Dimensional Space,

$$R = \left(\frac{-9 + -3}{2}, \ \frac{-1 + 7}{2} \right)$$

$$R = \left(\frac{-12}{2}, \ \frac{6}{2} \right)$$

$$R = (-6, \ 3)$$

By the Two-Dimensional Distance Formula,

$$QR = \sqrt{(-6 - (-9))^2 + (3 - (-1))^2} \qquad TR = \sqrt{(-6 - (-3))^2 + (3 - 7)^2}$$

$$QR = \sqrt{3^3 + 4^2} \qquad\qquad\qquad TR = \sqrt{(-3)^2 + (-4)^2}$$

$$QR = \sqrt{25} \qquad\qquad\qquad\qquad TR = \sqrt{9 + 16}$$

$$QR = 5 \qquad\qquad\qquad\qquad\quad TR = \sqrt{25}$$

$$\qquad\qquad\qquad\qquad\qquad\qquad\quad TR = 5$$

Because $QR = TR$ and Q, T, and R are collinear, R is the midpoint of $\overline{QT}$.

Example 6: If the midpoint of $\overline{AB}$ is $(-3, 8)$ and A is $(12, -1)$, find the coordinates of B.

Let the coordinates of B be (x, y). Then by the Midpoint Formula for Two-Dimensional Space,

$$(-3, \ 8) = \left(\frac{12 + x}{2}, \ \frac{-1 + y}{2} \right)$$

$$-3 = \frac{12 + x}{2} \quad \text{and} \quad 8 = \frac{-1 + y}{2}$$

Multiply each side of each equation by 2.

$$-6 = 12 + x \quad \text{and} \quad 16 = -1 + y$$

$$-18 = x \qquad\quad \text{and} \quad 17 = y$$

The coordinates of B are $(-18, 17)$.

Equation of a Circle

Consider a circle with a center at point $C(h, k)$ and radius r. Let $P(x, y)$ be an arbitrary point on the circle, as shown in the following figure.

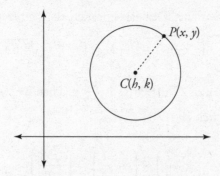

Since P is on the circle, the distance between C and P is r. By the Two-Dimensional Distance Formula, the distance between P and C is

$$\sqrt{(x-h)^2+(y-k)^2} \text{ or } \sqrt{(x-h)^2+(y-k)^2} = r.$$

By squaring both sides, the result is:

$$(x-h)^2 + (y-k)^2 = r^2$$

Since P is an arbitrary point on the circle, this equation is true for *any* point on the circle.

Theorem 9.5: Consider a circle with a center at point $C(h, k)$ and radius r. Then the equation of the circle is $(x-h)^2 + (y-k)^2 = r^2$.

Example 7: Find the equation of the circle with center $(-3, 8)$ and radius 2.

The equation of the circle is:

$$\left(x-(-3)\right)^2 + \left(y-8\right)^2 = 2^2$$
$$\left(x+3\right)^2 + \left(y-8\right)^2 = 4$$

Example 8: Suppose $P(2, -3)$ and $Q(5, 4)$ are endpoints of a diameter of a circle. Find the equation of the circle.

By the Midpoint Formula for Two-Dimensional Space, the center of the circle has the following coordinates:

$$\left(\frac{2+5}{2}, \frac{-3+4}{2}\right) = \left(\frac{7}{2}, \frac{1}{2}\right)$$

By the Two-Dimensional Distance Formula, the diameter of the circle is:

$$\sqrt{(2-5)^2 + (-3-4)^2} = \sqrt{(-3)^2 + (-7)^2} = \sqrt{9+49} = \sqrt{58}$$

Therefore, the radius of the circle is $\dfrac{\sqrt{58}}{2}$. Then by *Theorem 9.5*, the equation of the circle is:

$$\left(x - \frac{7}{2}\right)^2 + \left(y - \frac{1}{2}\right)^2 = \left(\frac{\sqrt{58}}{2}\right)^2$$

$$\left(x - \frac{7}{2}\right)^2 + \left(y - \frac{1}{2}\right)^2 = \frac{58}{4}$$

$$\left(x - \frac{7}{2}\right)^2 + \left(y - \frac{1}{2}\right)^2 = \frac{29}{2}$$

Lines on a Coordinate Plane

If a line ℓ is perpendicular to the *x*-axis, then line ℓ is a vertical line. All other lines are characterized as nonvertical lines. However, a line perpendicular to the *y*-axis is called a horizontal line.

A measure associated with any nonvertical line ℓ is called a *slope* and is described as follows. Pick any arbitrary point P on line ℓ. Draw a horizontal line through P. Pick point Q on this horizontal line one unit from P. Draw a vertical line through Q. Make this vertical line a number line so that 0 is at Q, positive numbers are above Q, and the negative numbers are below Q. This can easily be completed if you translate the *y*-axis along the vector $\overrightarrow{OQ}$. Since ℓ is nonvertical, it intersects the vertical number line at point R. The number (say, m) on the number line at R is called the **slope of the line**. See the following figure.

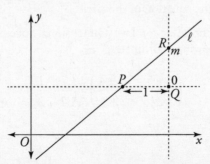

The slope of a line is a measurement of the steepness of the line. As you can see in the following figure, line ℓ_2 is steeper than line ℓ_1 and clearly the slope m_1 of line ℓ_1 is less than the slope m_2 of line ℓ_2.

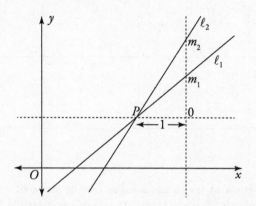

The line in the next figure has a negative slope since it intersects the vertical number line below 0.

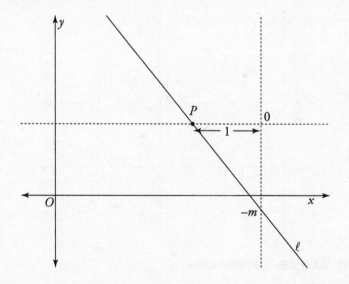

By definition, the slope of a horizontal line is 0, as shown in the following figure.

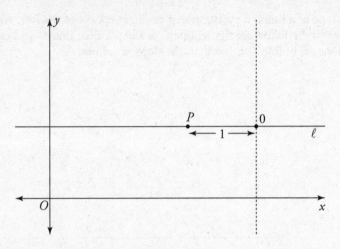

Notice that you can try to get a value for the slope of a vertical line using the same definition. However, since two vertical lines do not intersect, the vertical line has no slope; therefore, the slope is undefined for a vertical line.

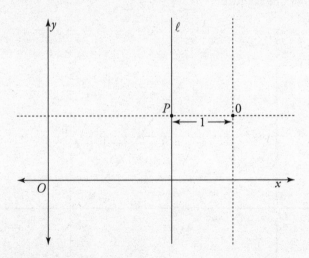

The Slope Theorem

Theorem 9.6 (Slope Theorem): Consider a nonvertical line ℓ. Suppose $A(x_1, y_1)$ and $B(x_2, y_2)$ are two points on ℓ. Then the slope m of ℓ is

$$m = \frac{y_1 - y_2}{x_1 - x_2}.$$

Since A and B are points on a nonvertical line, x_1 and x_2 cannot be equal to one another.

Three cases are described below.

Case 1: The line is horizontal. Then $y_2 = y_1$. By definition, the slope of a horizontal line is 0. The above formula gives $m = 0$ since $y_2 = y_1$.

Case 2: Suppose the slope of the line is positive. Without loss of generality, suppose $x_2 > x_1$ and $y_2 > y_1$.

Let the line passing through point A and parallel to the x-axis and the line passing through point B and parallel to the y-axis meet at point C. Let point D be on line $\overline{AC}$, one unit from point A, as shown in the following figure. Let the line parallel to the y-axis passing through point D intersect line ℓ at point E.

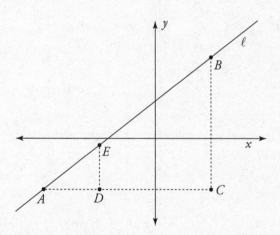

Let m be the length of the segment $\overline{DE}$. By definition, the slope of line ℓ is m. $\angle D$ and $\angle C$ are right angles by construction, and $\angle A$ is common to $\triangle ADE$ and $\triangle ACB$. By the AA Theorem for Similarity (*Theorem 5.10*), $\triangle ADE$ and $\triangle ACB$ are similar.

$$\frac{DE}{AD} = \frac{CB}{AC}$$

By construction, $AD = 1$, and by the One-Dimensional Distance Formula, $BC = y_2 - y_1$ and $AC = x_2 - x_1$.

$$m = \frac{y_2 - y_1}{x_2 - x_1}$$

Case 3: Suppose the slope of the line is negative. Without loss of generality, suppose $x_2 > x_1$ and $y_2 < y_1$.

Let the line passing through point A and parallel to the x-axis and the line passing through point B and parallel to the y-axis meet at point C. Let point D be on line $\overrightarrow{AC}$ one unit from point A, as shown in the following figure. Let the line parallel to the y-axis passing through point D intersect line ℓ at point E.

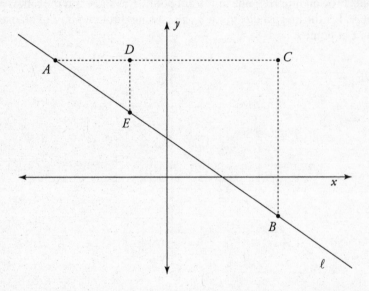

Let $DE = -m$ for some number $m < 0$. By definition, the slope of line ℓ is m. $\angle D$ and $\angle C$ are right angles by construction, and $\angle A$ is common to $\triangle ADE$ and $\triangle ACB$. By the AA Theorem for Similarity (*Theorem 5. 10*), $\triangle ADE$ and $\triangle ACB$ are similar.

$$\frac{DE}{AD} = \frac{CB}{AC}$$

By construction, $AD = 1$, and by the One-Dimensional Distance Formula, $BC = y_1 - y_2$ and $AC = x_2 - x_1$.

$$-m = \frac{y_1 - y_2}{x_2 - x_1}$$

If both sides of the above equation are multiplied by -1,

$$m = \frac{y_2 - y_1}{x_2 - x_1}$$

Example 9: In the following figure, find the slopes of lines a, b, c, and d.

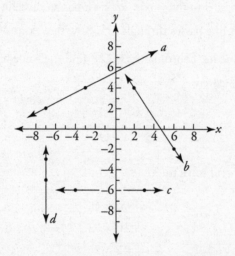

(a) Let m be the slope of line a. Line a passes through the points $(-7, 2)$ and $(-3, 4)$.

$$m = \frac{4-2}{-3-(-7)}$$

$$m = \frac{2}{4}$$

$$m = \frac{1}{2}$$

(b) Let m be the slope of line b. Line b passes through the points $(2, 4)$ and $(6, -2)$.

$$m = \frac{-2 - 4}{6 - 2}$$

$$m = \frac{-6}{4}$$

$$m = \frac{3}{2}$$

(c) Let m be the slope of line c. Line c is parallel to the x-axis, and $m = 0$.

(d) Line d is parallel to the y-axis, so line d has an undefined slope.

Example 10: A line passes through $(-5, 8)$ with a slope of $\frac{2}{3}$. If another point on this line has coordinates $(x, 12)$, find the value of x.

By the Slope Theorem,

$$\frac{2}{3} = \frac{12 - 8}{x - (-5)}$$

Cross multiply and solve for x,

$$2(x + 5) = 4(3)$$
$$2x + 10 = 12$$
$$2x = 2$$
$$x = 1$$

Slopes of parallel lines

If a line ℓ is not parallel to the x-axis or if line ℓ is not the x-axis, then line ℓ intersects the x-axis at only one point. The point of intersection of ℓ and the x-axis is called the **x-intercept** of ℓ. Since the x-intercept of a line is on the x-axis, the y-coordinate of the x-intercept is zero. Clearly, a horizontal line that is not the x-axis has no x-intercept.

If a line ℓ is not parallel to the y-axis or if line ℓ is not the y-axis, then line ℓ intersects the y-axis at only one point. The point of intersection of ℓ and the y-axis is called the **y-intercept** of ℓ. Since the y-intercept of a line is on the y-axis, the x-coordinate of the y-intercept is zero. Clearly, a vertical line that is not the y-axis has no y-intercept.

If two lines are horizontal and parallel, then their slopes are 0, by definition.

Let ℓ_1 and ℓ_2 be two nonvertical, nonhorizontal lines so that $\ell_1 \parallel \ell_2$. Let $P(x_1, 0)$ be the x-intercept of ℓ_1 and let $Q(x_2, 0)$ be the x-intercept of ℓ_2. Without loss of generality, assume Q is located to the right of P on the x-axis, or $x_2 > x_1$. Let the line through Q and parallel to the y-axis intersect line ℓ_1 at $R(x_2, y_3)$, and let the line through R parallel to the x-axis intersect line ℓ_2 at $S(x_4, y_3)$. Two such lines are shown in the following figure.

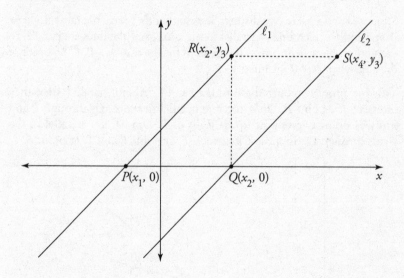

Suppose the slope of ℓ_1 is m_1 and the slope of ℓ_2 is m_2. Since $R(x_2, y_3)$ and $P(x_1, 0)$ are two points on ℓ_1, then by the Slope Theorem,

$$m_1 = \frac{y_3 - 0}{x_2 - x_1} = \frac{y_3}{x_2 - x_1}$$

Since $S(x_4, y_3)$ and $Q(x_2, 0)$ are two points on ℓ_2, then by the Slope Theorem,

$$m_2 = \frac{y_3 - 0}{x_4 - x_2} = \frac{y_3}{x_4 - x_2}$$

By construction, $PQSR$ is a parallelogram and $RS = PQ$. By the One-Dimensional Distance Formula, $PQ = x_2 - x_1$ and $RS = x_4 - x_2$. That is, $x_4 - x_2 = x_2 - x_1$, so $m_1 = m_2$. As a result, we have the following theorem.

Theorem 9.7: If two nonvertical lines are parallel, then they have the same slope.

The converse of *Theorem 9.7* is also true. This is stated in *Theorem 9.8*.

Theorem 9.8: If two lines have the same slope, then the lines are nonvertical parallel lines.

Suppose ℓ_1 and ℓ_2 are two distinct lines so that they have the same slope m. If $m = 0$, then each line is parallel to the x-axis and the lines are parallel to each other. Now, let's prove the theorem for the case $m > 0$. (The proof of the case when $m < 0$ is similar.)

This is a proof by contradiction. If ℓ_1 and ℓ_2 are not parallel, then they intersect at a point P. Draw the line parallel to the x-axis through P and find the point Q one unit to the right of P. Draw line ℓ parallel to the y-axis through Q. Suppose ℓ intersects ℓ_1 at point R and ℓ_2 at point S.

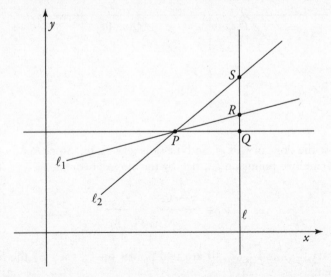

Then by the definition of the slope of a line, $QR = m$ and $QS = m$, or $R = S$ so that both ℓ_1 and ℓ_2 pass through two distinct points. This contradicts the fact that ℓ_1 and ℓ_2 are distinct lines. Therefore, our assumption that ℓ_1 and ℓ_2 are not parallel is false, and if two lines have the same slope, then the two lines must be parallel.

Slopes of perpendicular lines

Now suppose two lines ℓ_1 and ℓ_2 are perpendicular to each other at P. If one of the lines is vertical, then the other line is horizontal. Then the slope of one line is 0, and the slope of the other line is undefined.

Without loss of generality, suppose ℓ_1 is nonvertical and nonhorizontal. Then clearly, ℓ_2 is also nonvertical and nonhorizontal. The following theorems are for those types of perpendicular lines.

Theorem 9.9: Suppose ℓ_1 and ℓ_2 are two perpendicular lines with slopes m_1 and m_2, respectively. Then $m_1 = -\dfrac{1}{m_2}$.

Let the x-intercept of ℓ_1 be $P(x_1, 0)$. Draw a line ℓ_3 parallel to ℓ_2 through P. Then by *Theorem 9.7*, ℓ_3 has the slope m_2 since $\ell_2 \parallel \ell_3$. Without loss of generality, assume $m_1 > 0$. Select the point Q one unit right of P on the x-axis. Let ℓ be the line passing through Q parallel to the y-axis. Suppose ℓ intersects ℓ_1 at R and ℓ_3 at S. Since $m_1 > 0$, by definition of the slope of a line, R lies above the x-axis, as shown in the following figure.

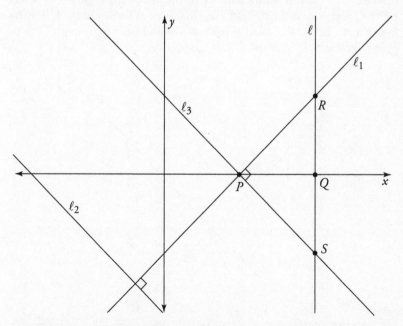

Since ℓ_1 is not vertical, $m\angle RPQ < 90°$. However, $m\angle RPS = 90°$ and S lies below the x-axis. Then by definition of the slope of a line, $m_2 < 0$. $m\angle RPQ = 90 - m\angle QPS$ and $m\angle PSQ = 90 - m\angle QPS$. Therefore,

$m\angle RPQ = m\angle PSQ$ and the right triangle $\triangle RQP$ and the right triangle $\triangle PQS$ are similar by the AA Theorem for Similarity (*Theorem 5.10*).

$$\frac{RQ}{PQ} = \frac{PQ}{QS}$$

$$\frac{m_1}{1} = \frac{1}{-m_2}$$

$$m_1 = -\frac{1}{m_2}$$

Theorem 9.10: Suppose ℓ_1 and ℓ_2 are two lines with slopes m_1 and m_2, respectively. If $m_1 = -\dfrac{1}{m_2}$, then $\ell_1 \perp \ell_2$.

Without loss of generality, assume $m_1 > 0$. Then by hypothesis, $m_2 < 0$. Therefore, ℓ_1 and ℓ_2 are not parallel by *Theorem 9.7*. Suppose ℓ_1 and ℓ_2 intersect at P. Draw a line parallel to the x-axis through P and select point Q one unit to the right of P on that line, as shown in the following figure. Let ℓ be the line parallel to the y-axis and passing through Q. Suppose ℓ intersects ℓ_1 at R and ℓ_2 at S, respectively.

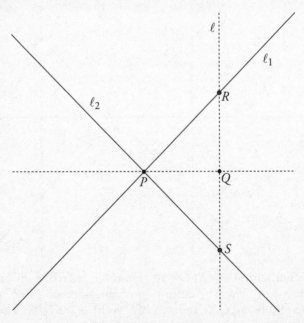

Since $m_1 > 0$, point R lies above line $\overrightarrow{PQ}$ and since $m_2 < 0$, point S lies below $\overrightarrow{PQ}$, as shown in the figure above. By definition of the slope of a line, $QR = m_1$ and $QS = -m_2$.

$$\frac{QR}{PQ} = \frac{m_1}{1}$$

$$\frac{PQ}{QS} = \frac{1}{-m_2}$$

Then, by the hypothesis of the theorem, that $m_1 = -\dfrac{1}{m_2}$, $\dfrac{QR}{PQ} = \dfrac{PQ}{QS}$.

Both $\angle PQR$ and $\angle SQP$ are right angles. Therefore, by the SAS Theorem for Similarity (*Theorem 5.9*), $\triangle PQR$ and $\triangle SQP$ are similar. As a result, $m\angle RPQ = m\angle PSQ$.

From right $\triangle SQP$, $m\angle PSQ + m\angle QPS = 90°$. Hence, $m\angle RPQ + m\angle QPS = 90°$, or $m\angle RPS = 90°$ and $\ell_1 \perp \ell_2$.

Example 11: If line ℓ has slope $\dfrac{3}{4}$, then find **(a)** the slope of any line parallel to ℓ and **(b)** the slope of any line perpendicular to ℓ.

(a) By *Theorem 9.7*, any line parallel to ℓ has the slope $\dfrac{3}{4}$.

(b) By *Theorem 9.9*, any line perpendicular to ℓ has the slope $-\dfrac{4}{3}$.

Example 12: Given points Q, R, S, and T in the following figure, determine which sides, if any, of quadrilateral $QRST$ are parallel or perpendicular.

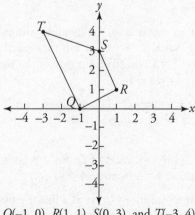

$Q(-1, 0)$, $R(1, 1)$, $S(0, 3)$, and $T(-3, 4)$

Let the slopes of lines $\overrightarrow{QR}$, $\overrightarrow{RS}$, $\overrightarrow{ST}$, and $\overrightarrow{TQ}$ be m_1, m_2, m_3, and m_4, respectively. Then by the Slope Theorem,

$$m_1 = \frac{1-0}{1-(-1)} = \frac{1}{2}$$

$$m_2 = \frac{3-1}{0-1} = -2$$

$$m_3 = \frac{4-3}{-3-0} = -\frac{1}{3}$$

$$m_4 = \frac{0-4}{-1-(-3)} = -2$$

So, $\overrightarrow{QR}$ is perpendicular to both $\overrightarrow{RS}$ and $\overrightarrow{TQ}$ by *Theorem 9.10*, and in a plane, if two lines are perpendicular to the same line, the two lines are parallel. Therefore, $\overrightarrow{RS} \parallel \overrightarrow{TQ}$ by *Theorem 2.4*.

Linear Equations in x and y

An equation of the form $ax + by = c$ is called a **linear equation in two variables x and y,** where a, b, and c are constants and at least one of a and b is not zero.

For example, $2x + y = 3$, $x = 4$, $y = -3$, $-2x + 4y = 7$, and $\frac{1}{2}x - \frac{3}{4}y = \frac{61}{7}$ are all linear equations in two variables. If $x = 4$ is a linear equation in two variables, it is understood that y is arbitrary. That is, think of the equation $x = 4$ as $x + 0 \cdot y = 4$.

Not every pair of numbers (x, y) makes an equation a true statement. For example, $(1, -1)$ makes $2x + y = 3$ a false statement. The left side of the equation is $2(1) - 1 = 1$ and the right side of the equation is 3. So, when $x = 1$ and $y = -1$, $2x + y \neq 3$.

An ordered pair of numbers (x_1, y_1) that would make $ax_1 + by_1 = c$ a true statement is called a *solution* of the linear equation in two variables, $ax + by = c$.

For example, $(1, 1)$ is a solution of $2x + y = 3$ because $2(1) + 1 = 3$, and $(4, 5)$ is a solution of $x = 4$ because $4 = 4$.

The collection of all solutions (x, y) of a linear equation in two variables is called the *solution set* of the linear equation in two variables. A graph is a representation of the solution set. Since any ordered pair of numbers (x, y) can be plotted as a point with coordinates (x, y) on the Cartesian coordinate plane, the graph of a linear equation in two variables can be thought of as a curve on the Cartesian coordinate plane.

Theorem 9.11: The graph of a linear equation $x = c$, where c is a constant, is the vertical line passing through the point $(c, 0)$.

Any point of the form (c, y), for any arbitrary y, is a solution of the equation $x = c$ because $c + 0 \cdot y = c$ is a true statement. Therefore, the solutions of the equation $x = c$ are exactly all ordered pairs of the form (c, y), where y is any arbitrary number. The points with coordinates (c, y) always lie on the vertical line passing through $(c, 0)$. Since y can be any number, the collection of all points (c, y) is the complete vertical line passing through $(c, 0)$.

Theorem 9.12: Every vertical line is a graph of a linear equation of the form $x = c$, where $(c, 0)$ is the point of intersection of the vertical line and the x-axis.

By definition, any vertical line is parallel to the y-axis, and the x-axis is perpendicular to the y-axis. Therefore, the x-axis is perpendicular to the vertical line, by *Theorem 2.7*. That is, any vertical line intersects the x-axis at a point $(c, 0)$ for some constant c. By the Parallel Postulate (*Postulate 10*), there is exactly one vertical line passing through $(c, 0)$ and parallel to the y-axis. By *Theorem 9.11*, the graph of the linear equation $x = c$ is *this* vertical line passing through $(c, 0)$ so that every vertical line is a graph of a linear equation of the form $x = c$, where $(c, 0)$ is the point of intersection of the vertical line and the x-axis.

Proofs of the following theorems are similar to the proofs of *Theorems 9.11* and *9.12*.

Theorem 9.13: The graph of a linear equation $y = c$, where c is a constant, is the horizontal line passing through the point $(0, c)$.

Theorem 9.14: Every horizontal line is a graph of a linear equation of the form $y = c$, where $(0, c)$ is the point of intersection of the horizontal line and the y-axis.

Is it also true that the graph of a linear equation $ax + by = c$, where both a and b are nonzero, is a line? Conversely, is it also true that any nonvertical, nonhorizontal line is a graph of a linear equation of the form $ax + by = c$, where both a and b are nonzero? The answers to these questions will now be discussed.

First, observe that $ax + by = c$ can be written as $y = mx + k$, for some non-zero constant m and a constant k, as follows.

Assume $ax + by = c$ is a true statement. Then, $by = -ax + c$. Since $b \neq 0$, by dividing both sides by b, $y = -\dfrac{a}{b} + \dfrac{c}{b}$. Now, let $m = -\dfrac{a}{b}$ and let $k = \dfrac{c}{b}$.

Theorem 9.15: The line joining any two distinct points of a graph of $y = mx + k$, $m \neq 0$ has the slope m.

Suppose $P(x_1, y_1)$ and $Q(x_2, y_2)$ are any two points on the graph of $y = mx + k$. Then,

$$y_1 = mx_1 + k$$

And

$$y_2 = mx_2 + k$$

By the Slope Theorem, the slope of a line passing through P and Q is:

$$\frac{y_2 - y_1}{x_2 - x_1} = \frac{(mx_2 + k) - (mx_1 + k)}{x_2 - x_1}$$

$$= \frac{mx_2 + k - mx_2 - k}{x_2 - x_1}$$

$$= \frac{mx_2 - mx_1}{x_2 - x_1}$$

$$= \frac{m(x_2 - x_1)}{(x_2 - x_1)}$$

$$= m$$

By the definition of the slope of a line, *Theorem 9.16* (below) follows.

Theorem 9.16: There is only one line passing through a given point with a given slope.

Now let's prove the following theorem.

Theorem 9.17: The graph of a linear equation $y = mx + k$, where $m \neq 0$, is a nonvertical line with slope m and passing through $(0, k)$.

Let G be the graph of $y = mx + k$. Let P and Q be two points on G, and let ℓ be the line passing through P and Q. If we can show that

(1) any point on G is on ℓ and

(2) any point on ℓ is on G,

then $G = \ell$.

(1) Consider that R is any point on G. If R is one of either P or Q, then there is nothing to prove. Now, suppose R is distinct from both P and Q. Since P and Q are on G, the slope of ℓ is m, by *Theorem 9.15*. Now, suppose that ℓ_1 is the line passing through P and R. By *Theorem 9.15*, the slope of ℓ_1 is also m. But both ℓ and ℓ_1 pass through P and have the slope m. By *Theorem 9.16*, ℓ_1 is ℓ. Hence, R is on ℓ.

(2) Consider that $S(x_0, y_0)$ is any point on ℓ. If S is either P or Q, then there is nothing to prove. Consider that S is distinct from $P(x_1, y_1)$ and Q. Since P is on G:

$$y_1 = mx_1 + k$$

The coordinates of P are $(x_1, mx_1 + k)$. Since both P and S lie on ℓ, use the Slope Theorem to find the slope of ℓ.

The slope of $\ell = \dfrac{y_0 - (mx_1 + k)}{x_0 - x_1}$.

That is:

$$m = \frac{y_0 - (mx_1 + k)}{x_0 - x_1}$$

Cross multiply and then add mx_1 to both sides to solve for y_0:

$$m\left(x_0 - x_1\right) = y_0 - \left(mx_1 + k\right)$$
$$mx_0 - mx_1 = y_0 - mx_1 - k$$
$$mx_0 = y_0 - k$$
$$y_0 = mx_0 + k$$

The point S is on G.

By combining the results of *Theorems 9.11, 9.13,* and *9.17,* the following theorem results.

Theorem 9.18: The graph of a linear equation is a line.

Now let's answer the second question: Is any line a graph of a linear equation? The answer is "yes," when the line is either a horizontal line or a vertical line by *Theorems 9.12* and *9.14*.

Theorem 9.19: Any nonvertical and nonhorizontal line is the graph of a linear equation.

Let ℓ be a nonvertical and nonhorizontal line with slope $m \neq 0$. Suppose the y-intercept of the line is the point $Q(0, k)$. In order to prove the claim that ℓ is the graph of the linear equation $y = mx + k$, we need to prove the following two statements:

(1) Any point on ℓ is a point on the graph of $y = mx + k$.

(2) Any point on the graph of $y = mx + k$ is on ℓ.

(1) Suppose $P(x_0, y_0)$ is any arbitrary point on ℓ other that Q. Then by using P and Q, it is possible to find the slope m of the line.

$$m = \frac{y_0 - k}{x_0 - 0}$$

Cross multiply and solve for y_0:

$$mx_0 = y_0 - k$$
$$y_0 = mx_0 + k$$

$P(x_0, y_0)$ is a point on the graph of the linear equation $y = mx + k$.

(2) Suppose R is any arbitrary point on the graph of $y = mx + k$. If R is Q, then there is nothing to prove. Suppose $R \neq Q$. Then the slope of line ℓ_1 passing through R and Q is m by *Theorem 9.15*. But ℓ is a line passing through Q with slope m. By *Theorem 9.16*, $\ell_1 = \ell$. Therefore, R is on ℓ.

By combining *Theorems 9.12*, *9.14*, and *9.19*, we get the following theorem.

Theorem 9.20: Any line is a graph of a linear equation.

Linear equation $y = mx + k$ is the equation of the line with slope m and y-intercept k. This is also known as the **slope-intercept form** of an equation of a line.

The equation $ax + by = c$ is known as the **standard form** of an equation of a line.

Theorem 9.21: The equation of a line passing through $P(x_1, y_1)$ and $Q(x_2, y_2)$ is $y - y_1 = m(x - x_1)$, where $m = \dfrac{y_2 - y_1}{x_2 - x_1}$ and $x_2 \neq x_1$.

Let ℓ_1 be the line passing through P and Q and let ℓ_2 be the graph of the equation $y - y_1 = m(x - x_1)$. By *Theorem 9.18*, ℓ_2 is a line. The slope of ℓ_1 by the Slope Theorem is $\dfrac{y_2 - y_1}{x_2 - x_1}$. Therefore, the slope of ℓ_1 is m. Clearly, P is on ℓ_2, and the slope of ℓ_2 is m by hypothesis. Then by *Theorem 9.16*, $\ell_1 = \ell_2$.

The equation $y - y_1 = m(x - x_1)$ is called the **point-slope form** of the equation of the line with slope m and passing through $P(x_1, y_1)$.

Example 13: Draw the graph of $2x + 3y = 12$ by finding the x-intercept and the y-intercept.

The x-intercept has a y-coordinate of zero. Substituting zero for y, the resulting equation is $2x + 3(0) = 12$. Now, solving for x,

$$2x = 12$$

$$x = 6$$

The x-intercept is $(6, 0)$. However, it is an accepted convention to just say the x-intercept is 6.

The y-intercept has an x-coordinate of zero. Substituting zero for x, the resulting equation is $2(0) + 3y = 12$. Now, solving for y,

$$3y = 12$$

$$y = 4$$

The y-intercept is $(0, 4)$. However, it is an accepted convention to just say the y-intercept is 4.

The line can now be graphed by graphing these two points and then drawing the line they determine, as shown in the following figure.

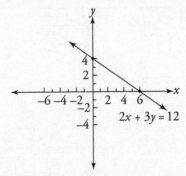

Example 14: Draw the graph of $x = 2$.

$x = 2$ is a vertical line whose x-coordinate is always 2, as shown in the following figure.

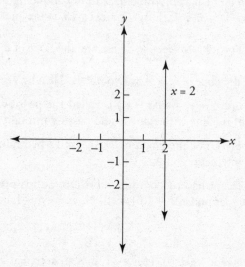

Example 15: Draw the graph of $y = -1$.

$y = -1$ is a horizontal line whose y-coordinate is always -1, as shown in the following figure.

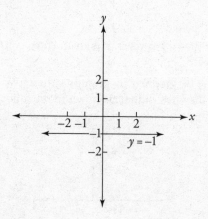

Example 16: Find the equation of a line containing the points $(-3, 4)$ and $(7, 2)$ and write the equation in **(a)** point-slope form and **(b)** standard form.

(a) For the point-slope form, first find the slope, m.

$$m = \frac{2-4}{7-(-3)}$$

$$m = \frac{-2}{10}$$

$$m = \frac{-1}{5}$$

Now choose either original point—say, $(-3, 4)$.

So, $y - 4 = -\frac{1}{5}\left(x - (-3)\right)$ or $y - 4 = -\frac{1}{5}(x + 3)$.

(b) Begin with the point-slope form and clear it of fractions by multiplying both sides by the least common denominator.

$$y - 4 = -\frac{1}{5}(x + 3)$$

Multiply both sides by 5.

$$5(y - 4) = 5\left[-\frac{1}{5}(x + 3)\right]$$

$$5y - 20 = -(x + 3)$$

$$5y - 20 = -x - 3$$

Get x and y on one side and the constants on the other side by adding x to both sides and adding 20 to both sides.

$$x + 5y = 17$$

Example 17: Find the slope and y-intercept of the line with equation $3x - 4y = 20$.

Solve $3x - 4y = 20$ for y.

$$-4y = -3x + 20$$

$$y = \frac{3}{4}x - 5$$

The slope of the line is $\frac{3}{4}$ and the y-intercept is -5.

Example 18: Line ℓ_1 has equation $2x + 5y = 10$, line ℓ_2 has equation $4x + 10y = 30$, and line ℓ_3 has equation $15x - 6y = 12$. Which lines, if any, are parallel? Which lines are perpendicular?

Suppose the slopes of ℓ_1, ℓ_2, and ℓ_3 are m_1, m_2, and m_3, respectively. Put each equation into slope-intercept form and determine the slope of each line.

The equation of ℓ_1 can be written in slope-intercept form as follows:

$$2x + 5y = 10$$

$$5y = -2x + 10$$

$$y = -\frac{2}{5}x + 2$$

Hence, $m_1 = -\frac{2}{5}$.

The equation of ℓ_2 can be written in slope-intercept form as follows:

$$4x + 10y = 30$$

$$10y = -4x + 30$$

$$y = -\frac{2}{5}x + 3$$

Therefore, $m_2 = -\frac{2}{5}$.

The equation of ℓ_3 can be written in slope-intercept form as follows:

$$15x - 6y = 12$$

$$-6y = -15x + 12$$

$$y = \frac{5}{2}x - 2$$

Hence, $m_3 = \dfrac{5}{2}$.

Since $m_1 = m_2$, ℓ_1 and ℓ_2 are parallel by *Theorem 9.7*.

Since $m_3 = \dfrac{-1}{m_1}$, ℓ_3 is perpendicular to both ℓ_1 and ℓ_2.

Summary of Coordinate Geometry Formulas

Review the following summary of coordinate geometry formulas.

If $A(x_1, y_1)$ and $B(x_2, y_2)$, then distance d, from A to B, is

$$d = \sqrt{\left(x_2 - x_1\right)^2 + \left(y_2 - y_1\right)^2}$$

The midpoint, M, of $\overline{AB}$ is

$$M = \left(\frac{x_1 + x_2}{2}, \; \frac{y_1 + y_2}{2} \right)$$

The slope, m, of the line passing through A and B is

$$m = \frac{y_2 - y_1}{x_2 - x_1}$$

Following is a list of the different forms for equations of lines:

Standard form: $ax + by = c$
a, b, and c are real numbers.
a and b are not both zero.

Point-slope form: $y - y_1 = m(x - x_1)$
(x_1, y_1) is a point on the line and m is the slope of the line.

Slope-intercept form:
$y = mx + b$
m is the slope of the line and b is the y-intercept value.

Chapter Check-Out

Questions

1. What is the distance from $(3, 3)$ to $(10, -1)$?

2. What is the midpoint of the line segment with endpoints $(3, 3)$ and $(10, -1)$?

3. What is the slope of a line passing through $(3, 3)$ and $(10, -1)$?

4. Find the following forms for the equation of the line passing through $(3, 3)$ and $(10, -1)$:

   (a) point-slope form
   (b) slope-intercept form
   (c) standard form

5. **(a)** Find the slope and the y-intercept of the line with equation $4x + 5y = 6$.

   (b) Find an equation of the line passing through $(3, 3)$ and perpendicular to the line from item **(a)**.

Answers

1. $\sqrt{65}$

2. $\left(\dfrac{13}{2}, 1\right)$

3. $-\dfrac{4}{7}$

4. **(a)** $y - 3 = -\dfrac{4}{7}(x - 3)$ or $y + 1 = -\dfrac{4}{7}(x - 10)$

   (b) $y = -\dfrac{4}{7}x + \dfrac{33}{7}$

   (c) $4x + 7y = 33$

5. **(a)** $m = -\dfrac{4}{5}$, $b = \dfrac{6}{5}$

   (b) $y - 3 = \dfrac{5}{4}(x - 3)$

REVIEW QUESTIONS

Use this review to practice what you've learned in this book and to build your confidence in working with geometry. After you work through the review questions, you'll be well on your way to achieving your goal of being proficient in the use of geometry.

Questions

Chapter 1

1. In the following diagram, determine the degree measure of **(a)** ∠a and **(b)** ∠b.

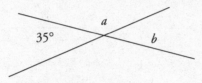

2. If two lines are parallel, then how many points are in their intersection?

3. True or False: Only one plane passes through any three given points.

4. What information is necessary to completely describe a circle?

5. True or False: A square, by definition, is a rectangle.

6. True or False: Given a line ℓ and a point P not on the line ℓ, there is exactly one plane passing through ℓ and P.

7. True or False: Given a line ℓ and a point P not on the line ℓ, there is exactly one line passing through P and parallel to ℓ.

Chapter 2

8. True or False: In a plane, two lines perpendicular to the same line are perpendicular to each other.

9. True or False: Any rotation maps lines to lines, rays to rays, segments to segments, and angles to angles.

10. True or False: Any rotation maps a line segment to a segment with the same length.

11. True or False: Any rotation maps an angle to an angle of the same degree.

12. True or False: Any 180° rotation maps a line to a line parallel to it.

13. True or False: Any 180° rotation maps a line not passing through the center of rotation to a line parallel to it.

14. True or False: If ρ is a 180° rotation with center O, and if P is a point other than O, then $\rho(P)$, P, and O are collinear.

15. In the following diagram, two parallel lines are intersected by a transversal. What is the degree measure of **(a)** $\angle a$, **(b)** $\angle b$, and **(c)** $\angle c$?

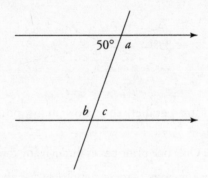

Chapter 3

16. True or False: An exterior angle of a triangle is equal to the sum of two remote interior angles.

17. In the following diagram, determine the degree measure of $\angle a$.

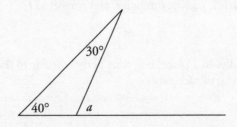

18. In a triangle with two angles of measure 30° and 40°, what must be the measure of the third angle?

19. In the following figure, $m\angle a = 45°$ and $m\angle d = 145°$. What is the degree measure of $\angle f$?

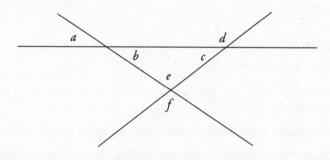

20. True or False: An equilateral triangle, by definition, is an isosceles triangle.

21. True or False: In an isosceles triangle, the angle bisector of the vertex angle is the perpendicular bisector of the base.

22. True or False: The base angles of an isosceles triangle are equal.

23. True or False: The angle measure of any angle of an equilateral triangle is 60°.

24. Which set of numbers may be the lengths of the sides of a triangle?

   A. {1, 3, 5}

   B. {4, 5, 6}

   C. {4, 5, 9}

   D. {4, 5, 10}

25. True or False: A rotation followed by a reflection is a congruence.

26. True or False: We say that two figures S and T are congruent to each other if there is a congruence C so that C maps S to T.

27. True or False: Given two triangles $\triangle ABC$ and $\triangle DEF$ so that $m\angle B = m\angle E$, $AB = DE$, and $BC = EF$, then the two triangles are congruent.

28. True or False: Given two triangles $\triangle ABC$ and $\triangle DEF$ so that $m\angle B = m\angle E$, $AB = DE$, and $m\angle A = m\angle D$, then the two triangles are congruent.

29. True or False: Given two triangles $\triangle ABC$ and $\triangle DEF$ so that $AB = DE$, $BC = EF$, and $CA = FD$, then the two triangles are congruent.

30. True or False: Given two right triangles $\triangle ABC$ and $\triangle DEF$ so that $m\angle B = m\angle E = 90°$ and $AB = DE$, then the two triangles are congruent.

Chapter 4

31. Draw a quadrilateral that is not convex.

32. What is the degree measure of each interior angle in a regular pentagon?

33. What is the degree measure of an exterior angle of a regular nonagon?

34. True or False: A parallelogram, by definition, is a quadrilateral with both pairs of opposite sides parallel.

35. True or False: If a pair of opposite sides of a quadrilateral are parallel and equal, then the quadrilateral is a parallelogram.

36. True or False: If the diagonals of a quadrilateral bisect each other, then the quadrilateral is a parallelogram.

37. True or False: If all interior angles of a quadrilateral are equal, then the quadrilateral is a rectangle.

38. True or False: The diagonals of a rectangle are equal.

39. True or False: A square is a rhombus.

40. True or False: A rhombus is a square.

41. True or False: The diagonals of a rhombus are perpendicular to each other.

42. True or False: The base angles of any trapezoid are equal.

43. True or False: The base angles of an isosceles trapezoid are equal.

44. True or False: The perpendicular bisectors of the three sides of a triangle meet at a point.

45. True or False: The circumcenter of a triangle is the point where perpendicular bisectors of the three sides of the triangle meet.

46. True or False: The orthocenter of a triangle is the point where three altitudes of the triangle meet.

47. True or False: The incenter of a triangle is the point where three angle bisectors of the triangle meet.

48. True or False? The centroid of a triangle is the point where three medians of the triangle meet.

49. Each side of an equilateral triangle has a length of 6. A second triangle is formed by the segments that join the midpoints of the sides of the equilateral triangle. What is the perimeter of the second triangle?

Chapter 5

50. True or False: Any congruence is a similarity.

51. True or False: Any similarity is a congruence.

52. Let D be a dilation with scale factor 2 and center of dilation O.
    True or False: $D(O) = O$.

53. Let D be a dilation with scale factor 2 and center of dilation O. Suppose P is a point other than O and $D(P) = P'$.
    True or False: $OP = \dfrac{1}{2} OP'$.

54. True or False: Any similarity maps angles to angles of the same degree.

55. True or False: Any similarity maps segments to segments of the same length.

56. True or False: Any two circles are similar.

57. True or False: If $\triangle ABC$ and $\triangle PQR$ are similar triangles, then $\dfrac{AB}{PQ} = \dfrac{BC}{QR} = \dfrac{CA}{RP}$.

58. True or False: If $\triangle ABC$ and $\triangle PQR$ are triangles so that $\dfrac{AB}{PQ} = \dfrac{BC}{QR} = \dfrac{CA}{RP}$, then the triangles are similar.

59. True or False: If $\triangle ABC$ and $\triangle PQR$ are triangles so that $m\angle A = m\angle P$ and $m\angle B = m\angle Q$, then the triangles are similar.

60. Suppose $\triangle ABC \sim \triangle PQR$, $\dfrac{AB}{PQ} = \dfrac{1}{2}$, and $QR = 6$ length units. What is the measure of BC?

61. The three angles of a triangle are in the ratio $1 : 2 : 6$. What is the measure of the smallest angle?

62. What is the degree measure of the angle formed by the hands of a clock at 4:00?

63. True or False: The area of a square will be doubled if the length of each side is multiplied by $\sqrt{2}$.

64. True or False: All isosceles right triangles must be similar.

Chapter 6

65. True or False: Let P be a point on a circle C. Then the line passing through the center O and point P is perpendicular to the line tangent to the circle at the point P.

66. Let P, Q, and R be three points on a circle C so that $\overline{PQ}$ is a diameter of the circle. What is the degree measure of $\angle PRQ$?

67. Let P and Q be two points on a circle C so that $\overline{PQ}$ is a chord of C. Suppose R and S are two points that lie on the major arc of $\overline{PQ}$. If $m\angle PRQ = 60°$, then what is the degree measure of $\angle PSQ$?

68. Let P, Q, and R be three points on a circle C so that $\overline{PQ}$ is a chord of C and R lies on the major arc of $\overline{PQ}$. Let S be a point on the tangent line to circle C at point P so that R and S lie on opposite half-planes of the line $\overline{PQ}$. If $m\angle PRQ = 30°$, then what is the degree measure of $\angle QPS$?

69. True or False: Let A, B, C, and D be four points so that A and C lie on the same half-plane of line $\overleftrightarrow{BD}$. If $m\angle BAD = m\angle BCD$, then the four points lie on a circle.

70. Let A, B, C, and D be four points that lie on a circle so that A and C lie on the same half-plane of line $\overleftrightarrow{BD}$. If $m\angle BAD = 30°$, then what is the degree measure of $\angle BCD$?

71. True or False: A diameter of a circle is perpendicular to a chord of the circle.

72. True or False: If a diameter and a chord of a circle intersect, then the diameter is perpendicular to the chord.

73. Two chords $\overline{AB}$ and $\overline{CD}$ of a circle intersect at point E. If $AE = 4$, $EB = 6$, $CE = 2$, then what is the measure of ED?

Chapter 7

74. If the legs of an isosceles triangle are each 17 inches long and the altitude to the base is 15 inches long, how long is the base of the triangle?

75. In a square, the perimeter is how many times as long as a diagonal?

76. What is the area of an equilateral triangle whose side has a length of 8?

77. In the following diagram, lines $\overleftrightarrow{AE}$ and $\overleftrightarrow{BD}$ are both perpendicular to line $\overleftrightarrow{EC}$. If $BC = 5$ and $BD = 3$, what is the ratio of AE to EC?

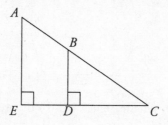

78. Which of the following sets of numbers may be the lengths of the sides of a right triangle?

   A. {4, 6, 8}

   B. {12, 16, 20}

   C. {7, 17, 23}

   D. {9, 20, 27}

79. Jeremy lives on the corner of a rectangular field that measures 120 yards by 160 yards. If he wants to walk to the diagonally opposite corner, he can either go along the boundary of the field or cut across in a straight line. How many yards does he save by taking the direct route?

80. In the following diagram, $ABDE$ is a parallelogram and $BCEF$ is a square. If $AB = 10$ and $CD = 6$, what is the perimeter of the parallelogram $ABDE$?

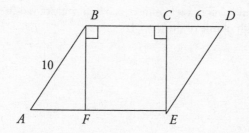

81. The following figure shows a rectangle inscribed in a circle. If the measurements of the rectangle are 8 inches by 14 inches, what is the area of the circle in terms of π?

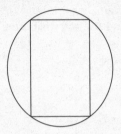

82. Compute (a) the circumference and (b) the area of a circle of radius $r = 5$ in terms of π.

83. Determine (a) the perimeter and (b) the area of $\triangle ABC$ in the following diagram.

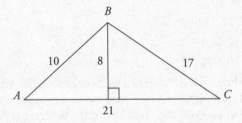

84. The measure of the central angle of a sector is 120°. If the radius of the circle is 6 centimeters, determine the area of the sector.

85. If a central angle of 45° intercepts an arc 5 inches long on a circle, what is the radius of the circle in terms of π?

86. If an equilateral triangle is inscribed in a circle of radius 1 inch, what is the length of one of the triangle's sides?

Chapter 8

87. Determine **(a)** the total surface area and **(b)** the volume of the rectangular solid in the following figure.

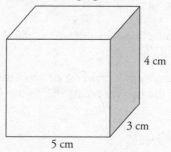

4 cm

3 cm

5 cm

88. Find **(a)** the lateral area, **(b)** the total area, and **(c)** the volume of a right circular cone with radius 4 inches and height 10 inches.

89. Find **(a)** the surface area and **(b)** the volume of a sphere of radius $r = 7$ inches.

Chapter 9

90. The vertices of rectangle $ABCD$ are $A(2, 0)$, $B(5, 0)$, $C(5, 4)$, and $D(2, 4)$. How long is the diagonal $\overline{AC}$?

91. The coordinates of the endpoints of the diameter of a circle are $(-1, 5)$ and $(3, -1)$. Specify the coordinates of the center of the circle.

92. True or False: If two points have the same y-coordinate, then they lie on the same horizontal line.

93. What is the distance between the points $(2, 5)$ and $(10, 20)$?

94. Find the slope-intercept form of the equation of the line passing through points $(2, 5)$ and $(5, 9)$.

95. Suppose $O(2, 3)$ is the center of a circle of radius 2. What is the equation of the circle?

96. True or False: The points $P(2, 3)$ and $Q(3, 3)$ lie on a vertical line.

97. True or False: The points $P(2, 3)$ and $Q(3, 3)$ lie on a horizontal line.

98. True or False: The slope of any horizontal line is 0.

99. True or False: The slope of the line passing through the points $P(2, 3)$ and $Q(3, 7)$ is 4.

100. Find the slope-intercept form of the equation of the line passing through the points $P(2, 3)$ and $Q(3, 7)$.

101. Find the slope of a line parallel to the line passing through the points $P(2, 3)$ and $Q(3, 7)$.

102. Find the slope of a line perpendicular to the line passing through the points $P(2, 3)$ and $Q(3, 7)$.

103. Find the slope-intercept form of the equation of a line perpendicular to the line passing through the points $P(2, 3)$ and $Q(3, 7)$ at P.

Answers

Chapter 1

1. (a) $m\angle a = 145°$;
   (b) $m\angle b = 35°$

2. 0

3. False

4. The center of the circle and the radius of the circle

5. True

6. True

7. True

Chapter 2

8. False

9. True

10. True

11. True

12. False

13. True

14. True

15. (a) $m\angle a = 130°$;
    (b) $m\angle b = 130°$;
    (c) $m\angle c = 50°$

Chapter 3

16. True

17. $m\angle a = 70°$

18. 110°

19. $m\angle f = 100°$

20. True

21. True

22. True

23. True

24. B

25. True

26. True

27. True

28. True

29. True

30. False

Chapter 4

31.

32. 108°

33. 40°

34. True

35. True

36. True

37. True

38. True

39. True

40. False

41. True

42. False

43. True

44. True

45. True

46. True

47. True

48. True

49. 9

Chapter 5

50. True

51. False

52. True

53. True

54. True

55. False

56. True

57. True

58. True

59. True

60. 3 length units

61. 20°

62. 120°

63. True

64. True

Chapter 6

65. True

66. $m\angle PRQ = 90°$

67. $m\angle PSQ = 60°$

68. $m\angle QPS = 30°$

69. True

70. $m\angle BCD = 30°$

71. False

72. False

73. $ED = 12$

Chapter 7

74. 16 inches

75. $2\sqrt{2}$

76. $16\sqrt{3}$ square units

77. 3 : 4

78. B

79. 80 yards

80. 48

81. 65π square units

82. (a) 10π; (b) 25π square units

83. (a) 48; (b) 84 square units

84. 12π cm^2

85. $\dfrac{20}{\pi}$ inches

86. $\sqrt{3}$

Chapter 8

87. (a) 94 cm²; (b) 60 cm³

88. (a) $8\sqrt{29}\,\pi$ in.²;
(b) $(8\sqrt{29}+16)\pi$ in.²;
(c) $\dfrac{160}{3}\pi$ in³

89. (a) 196π in²; (b) $\dfrac{1{,}372}{3}\pi$ in³

Chapter 9

90. 5

91. $(1, 2)$

92. True

93. 17

94. $y = \dfrac{4}{3}x + \dfrac{7}{3}$

95. $(x-2)^2 + (y-3)^2 = 4$

96. False

97. True

98. True

99. True

100. $y = 4x - 5$

101. $m = 4$

102. $m = -\dfrac{1}{4}$

103. $y = -\dfrac{1}{4}x + \dfrac{7}{2}$

GLOSSARY

acute angle: A positive angle whose measure is less than 90°.

acute triangle: A triangle having all acute angles in its interior.

adjacent angles: Any two angles that share a common vertex and a common side that separates them.

alternate exterior angles: The nonadjacent angles outside two lines being intersected by a transversal, on opposite sides of the transversal.

alternate interior angles: The nonadjacent angles inside two lines being intersected by a transversal, on opposite sides of the transversal.

altitude of a prism: A segment perpendicular to the planes of the bases with an endpoint in each plane.

altitude of a pyramid: The perpendicular line segment from the vertex to the plane of the base.

altitude of a triangle: The perpendicular line segment from a vertex to the side opposite (or its extension).

angle: Formed by two rays with the same endpoint (vertex).

angle bisector: A ray that divides an angle into two angles of equal measure.

apothem of a regular polygon: A line segment that goes from the center of the polygon to the midpoint of one of the sides; it is perpendicular to the side.

arc of a circle: The intersection of a central angle of a circle and the circle; the arc is made of the points on the circle.

area: A measure of the interior of a planar (flat) figure. It is expressed in square units such as square inches (in^2) or square centimeters (cm^2), or in special units such as acres.

area of a unit circle: The area of a unit circle is π area units.

base angles of an isosceles triangle: The two angles other than the vertex angle.

base angles of a trapezoid: A pair of angles sharing the same base.

base of an isosceles triangle: The third side, as distinguished from the other two equal sides.

base of a triangle: Any side of the triangle.

bases of a prism: The two congruent polygons lying in parallel planes.

bases of a trapezoid: The pair of parallel sides.

basic rigid motions of a plane: Plane transformations; a *reflection,* a *rotation,* and a *translation* of a plane are known as basic rigid motions of a plane.

center of a circle (sphere): The (fixed) interior point that is equidistant from all points on the circle (sphere).

center of a regular polygon: The interior point that is equidistant from each of the vertices.

central angle of a circle: An angle with its vertex at the center of the circle.

centroid of a triangle: The point where three medians of the triangle meet.

chord of a circle: A line segment whose endpoints lie on a circle.

circle: The collection of all points equidistant from a fixed point O on the plane. The fixed point O is called the center of the circle.

circumcenter of a triangle: The point at which perpendicular bisectors of the sides of the triangle meet.

circumcircle of a triangle: A circle that passes through all vertices of a triangle is called the circumcircle of that triangle.

circumference: The distance around a circle.

collinear points: Points that lie on the same line.

complementary angles: Two positive angles whose sum is 90°.

concave polygon: A polygon that is not convex. A line segment connecting two vertices may pass outside the figure. See *convex polygon.*

concurrent lines: Three or more lines that pass through the same point.

concyclic points: A collection of points that lie on a circle.

congruence: A composition of basic rigid motions. A congruence: maps lines to lines, rays to rays, and segments to segments; maps line segments to line segments of equal length; and maps an angle to an angle of the same degree.

congruent triangles: Two triangles are congruent if there is a congruence that maps one triangle onto the other triangle, meaning when the three sides and the three angles of one triangle have the same measurements as the three sides and the three angles of another triangle.

consecutive exterior angles: Exterior angles on the same side of the transversal.

consecutive interior angles: Interior angles on the same side of the transversal.

consecutive sides of a polygon: Two sides that have a common endpoint.

Converse of the Pythagorean Theorem: If the lengths of the three sides of a triangle are a, b, and c, and if $a^2 + b^2 = c^2$, then the triangle is a right triangle. The side of the length c is the hypotenuse of the right triangle. See *Pythagorean Theorem.*

convex polygon: A polygon for which any two interior points can be connected by a line segment that stays entirely inside the polygon.

coordinate: One real number paired with each point on a number line.

coordinate plane: The x-axis, the y-axis, and all the points in the plane they determine.

coordinates of a point: The ordered pair of numbers assigned to a point in a plane.

corresponding angles: Angles that occur in the same relative position in each group of four angles created when a transversal intersects two lines.

corresponding parts of triangles: The parts of two (usually) congruent or similar triangles that are in the same relative positions.

cube: A square right prism whose lateral edges are the same length as a side of the base.

cubic inch: A measure of the interior of a cube whose lateral edge has a length of 1 inch.

cylinder: A prismlike solid whose bases are circles.

decagon: A ten-sided polygon.

degree: A measure of an angle. It is one three-hundred-and-sixtieth $\left(\dfrac{1}{360}\right)$ of a revolution.

degree measure of a major arc: 360° minus the degree measure of the minor arc that has the same endpoints as the major arc.

degree measure of a minor arc: The degree measure of the central angle associated with the arc.

degree measure of a semicircle: 180°.

diagonal of a polygon: Any line segment that joins two nonconsecutive vertices of the polygon.

diameter of a circle: A chord that passes through the center of the circle.

dilation: A dilation with center O and a scale factor $r > 0$ moves each point P other than O to a point on the ray $\overrightarrow{OP}$ so that the distance between O and the image of P is $r(OP)$. The dilation does not move point O.

equiangular triangle: A triangle with all angles equal in measure.

equilateral triangle: A triangle with all sides equal in measure.

exterior angle of a triangle: The nonstraight angle formed outside the triangle when one of its sides is extended; it is adjacent to an interior angle of the triangle.

exterior angle sum: The sum of the measures of all the exterior angles of a polygon, one angle at each vertex.

heptagon: A seven-sided polygon (also: septagon).

hexagon: A six-sided polygon.

hypotenuse: The side opposite the right angle in a right triangle.

incenter of a triangle: The point where three angle bisectors of the triangle meet.

inscribed angle: An angle formed by two chords with the vertex on the circle.

intercepted arc: The connected portion of a circle that lies in the interior of the intercepting angle, together with the endpoints of the arc.

interior angle sum: The sum of the measures of all the interior angles of a polygon.

intersecting lines: Two or more lines that meet at a single point.

isosceles triangle: A triangle with at least two sides with equal measures.

isosceles right triangle: A triangle with two equal sides, two equal angles, and a right angle.

isosceles trapezoid: A trapezoid whose two legs are equal.

lateral area of a right prism: The sum of the areas of all the lateral faces.

lateral edges of a prism: The parallel line segments formed by connecting the corresponding vertices of the two base polygons.

lateral edges of a pyramid: The edges where pairs of lateral faces intersect.

lateral faces of a prism: The parallelograms formed by the lateral edges.

lateral faces of a pyramid: The triangular sides; they all meet at the vertex.

legs of an isosceles triangle: The two equal sides.

legs of a right triangle: The two sides other than the hypotenuse.

legs of a trapezoid: The nonparallel sides.

line: An undefined term. A line can be visualized as a connected set of infinitely many points extending (without curves) infinitely far in opposite directions.

linear equation in two variables x and y: An equation of the form $ax + by = c$, where a, b, and c are constants and at least one of a and b is nonzero.

line segment: A connected piece of a line with two endpoints.

line separation: Any point O on a line ℓ separates the line into two half-lines so that any point other than O on ℓ belongs to exactly one of those half-lines.

major arc: An arc that is larger than a semicircle.

median of a trapezoid: A segment that joins the midpoints of the legs.

median of a triangle: A line segment drawn from a vertex to the midpoint of the opposite side.

midpoint of a line segment: The point on the segment equidistant from the endpoints; the halfway point.

minor arc: An arc that is smaller than a semicircle.

***n*-gon:** A polygon with n sides.

nonagon: A nine-sided polygon.

noncollinear points: Points that do not all lie on a single line.

oblique prism: A prism whose lateral edges are not perpendicular to the planes of its bases.

obtuse angle: An angle whose measure is more than 90° but less than 180°.

obtuse triangle: A triangle having an obtuse angle in its interior.

octagon: An eight-sided polygon.

ordered pair: A pair of numbers whose order is important; these are used to locate points in the plane.

origin: In two dimensions, the point $(0, 0)$; it is the intersection of the x-axis and the y-axis.

orthocenter of a triangle: The point where three altitudes of the triangle meet.

parallel lines: Two lines that lie in the same plane and never intersect.

parallel planes: Two planes that do not intersect.

parallelogram: Any quadrilateral with both pairs of opposite sides parallel.

pentagon: A five-sided polygon.

perimeter: The distance around a figure (polygon).

perpendicular bisector of a line segment: A line that is perpendicular to a line segment and intersects the line segment at the segment's midpoint.

perpendicular lines: Lines that intersect to form right angles.

plane: An undefined term. A plane can be visualized as a flat surface that extends infinitely far in all directions.

plane separation: Any line ℓ on a plane P separates the plane into two half-planes so that any point not on ℓ belongs to exactly one of those half-planes.

point: An undefined term. A point is represented by a dot; it represents position only.

point of tangency: The point where a tangent line intersects a circle.

point-slope form of the equation of a line: The form $y - y_1 = m(x - x_1)$, where m is the slope of the line and (x_1, y_1) is a specific point on the line.

polygon: A closed planar figure with three or more sides, but not infinitely many.

polygonal curve: A concatenation of a finite number of line segments.

postulate: A statement that is assumed to be true (without proof).

prism: A type of solid with two congruent polygons lying in parallel planes for bases and with three or more lateral faces.

pyramid: A solid with one base (a polygon) whose vertices are each joined by line segments to a special point not in the plane of the base; these segments form edges for the lateral faces.

Pythagorean Theorem: In a right triangle, the square of the length of the hypotenuse is equal to the sum of the squares of the lengths of other two sides of the triangle.

quadrants: The four regions of the coordinate plane separated by the x-axis and the y-axis.

quadrilateral: A four-sided polygon.

radius of a circle (sphere): A line segment with the center of the circle (sphere) and a point on the circle (sphere) as its endpoints (plural: *radii*).

radius of a regular polygon: A segment that goes from the center to any vertex.

ray: A connected piece of a line with one endpoint and extending infinitely far in one direction; a "half-line."

rectangle: A quadrilateral in which all the angles are right angles.

reflection: A reflection across a fixed line is a plane transformation so that it moves any point not on the line to its mirror image across the line. Reflection does not move points on the line.

regular polygon: A polygon that is both equilateral and equiangular.

regular pyramid: A pyramid whose base is a regular polygon and whose lateral edges are all equal.

rhombus: A quadrilateral with all four sides equal.

right angle: A 90° angle.

right circular cone: Similar to a regular pyramid, except that its base is a circle.

right circular cylinder: A cylinder with the property that the segment joining the centers of the circular bases is perpendicular to the planes of the bases.

right prism: A prism whose lateral edges are perpendicular to the planes of its bases.

right triangle: A triangle that has a right angle in its interior.

rotation: A rotation around a point O by a fixed angle θ moves a point P other than O to a point P' on the circle with center O and radius $\overline{OP}$ so that $\angle POP' = \theta$. If the angle θ is positive, then the rotation is counterclockwise,

and if the angle θ is negative, then the rotation is clockwise.

scalene triangle: A triangle in which all three sides have different lengths.

secant line to a circle: A line that intersects a circle at two points.

sector of a circle: A region bounded by two radii and an arc of the circle intercepted by (an angle formed by) those two radii.

semicircle: An arc whose endpoints are the endpoints of a diameter of the circle.

septagon: A seven-sided polygon (also: heptagon).

set: A collection of points.

sides of an angle: The rays that form the angle.

similar polygons: Two polygons are similar if there is a similarity that maps one onto the other.

similarity: A plane transformation that is a composition of a dilation and a congruence.

slant height of a regular pyramid: The altitude of any of the congruent isosceles triangles that form the lateral faces.

slope-intercept form of the equation of a line: The form $y = mx + k$ where m is the slope of the line and k is the y-intercept.

slope of a line: A measurement of the steepness of a nonvertical line. If two points (x_1, y_1) and (x_2, y_2) on the line are known, then the slope m of the line can be calculated by using the Slope Theorem: $m = \dfrac{y_2 - y_1}{x_2 - x_1}$.

sphere: The set of all points in space that are equidistant from a fixed point (the center).

square: A quadrilateral in which all the angles are right angles and all the sides are equal.

standard form for the equation of a line: The form $Ax + By = C$, where A, B, and C are real numbers and A and B are not both zero.

straight angle: A 180° angle.

supplementary angles: Two positive angles whose sum is 180°.

tangent: A line that lies on the same plane as a circle and intersects the circle in exactly one point.

theorem: A statement that can be proven using definitions, postulates, and previously proven theorems.

total surface area of a right prism: The sum of the lateral area and the areas of the two bases.

translation: A plane transformation that moves any point on the plane to a point along a fixed vector so that the distance between the point and its image is equal to the magnitude of the vector.

transversal: A line that intersects two or more lines in the same plane at different points.

trapezoid: A quadrilateral with at least one pair of opposite sides parallel.

triangle: A three-sided figure (polygon).

triangulation of a polygon: Partition of the polygon into triangles so that any two of these triangles either do not intersect, intersect at a vertex, or intersect along an edge.

unit circle: A circle with radius 1.

unit square: A square whose sides have lengths of 1 unit.

vector: A line segment with one endpoint identified as a starting point and the other endpoint identified as the ending point. A vector has two properties: the magnitude and the direction. The magnitude is the length of the segment and the direction is given by the starting point and the ending point.

vertex: (1) The endpoint of a ray; (2) the common endpoint for the two rays that determine an angle; (3) an endpoint of a side of a polygon.

vertex angle of an isosceles triangle: The angle formed by the two equal sides.

vertex of a pyramid: The special point, not in the plane of the base, joined to each vertex of the base by a line segment that forms an edge of a lateral face.

vertical angles: Any pair of nonadjacent angles formed when two lines intersect.

volume: A measure of the interior of a solid; the number of unit cubes necessary to fill the interior of such a solid.

***x*-axis:** The horizontal number line of the two lines that define the *xy*-coordinate system of the plane.

***x*-coordinate (of a point):** The first term of the ordered pair that describes the point in the *xy*-coordinate system.

x-intercept: The point where a graph intersects the *x*-axis.

y-axis: A vertical number line of the two lines that defines the *xy*-coordinate system of the plane.

y-coordinate (of a point): The second term of an ordered pair that describes the point in the *xy*-coordinate system.

y-intercept: The point where a graph intersects the *y*-axis.

Appendix

POSTULATES AND THEOREMS

There are numerous geometry postulates and theorems given in this book. They are numbered for organizational purposes. As a handy study reference, the postulates and theorems are compiled in this appendix.

Postulates

Postulate 1: A line contains at least two points.

Postulate 2: A plane contains at least three noncollinear points.

Postulate 3: Through any two points, there is exactly one line.

Postulate 4: Through any three noncollinear points, there is exactly one plane.

Postulate 5: If two points lie in a plane, then the line joining them lies in that plane.

Postulate 6: If two different planes intersect, then their intersection is a line.

Postulate 7 (Ruler Postulate): Each point on a line can be paired with exactly one real number called its coordinate. The distance between two points is the positive difference of their coordinates.

Postulate 8 (Segment Addition Postulate): If B lies between A and C on a line, then $AB + BC = AC$.

Postulate 9 (Protractor Postulate): If the distance around a unit circle is made into 360 adjacent arcs of equal length, then the central angle whose rays pass through the ends of any one of these arcs will have a measure of one degree.

Postulate 10 (Parallel Postulate): Given a line ℓ and a point P not on ℓ, there is exactly one line in the plane passing through P parallel to ℓ, in the plane containing ℓ and P.

Postulate 11 (Line Separation): A point O on a line ℓ separates the line into two nonempty subsets called half-lines, so that every point other than O

in the line belongs on only one of those half-lines, and if two points A and B belong to different half-lines, then O belongs to the segment $\overline{AB}$.

Postulate 12 (Plane Separation): A line ℓ separates the plane into two nonempty convex subsets called *half-planes,* so that every point in the plane belongs on only one of those half-planes or the line ℓ, and if two points A and B belong to different half-planes, then the line segment $\overline{AB}$ intersects ℓ.

Postulate 13 (Properties of Rotations):
(i) Rotations map lines to lines, rays to rays, and segments to segments.
(ii) Rotations map segments to segments of the same length.
(iii) Rotations map angles to angles of the same degree.

Postulate 14 (Properties of Reflections):
(i) Reflections map lines to lines, rays to rays, and segments to segments.
(ii) Reflections map segments to segments of the same length.
(iii) Reflections map angles to angles of the same degree.

Postulate 15 (Properties of Translations):
(i) Translations map lines to lines, rays to rays, and segments to segments.
(ii) Translations map segments to segments of the same length.
(iii) Translations map angles to angles of the same degree.

Postulate 16: (Properties of Rigid Motions)
(i) Rigid motions map lines to lines, rays to rays, and segments to segments.
(ii) Rigid motions map segments to segments of the same length.
(iii) Rigid motions map angles to angles of the same degree.

Postulate 17 (Crossbar Postulate): Given a triangle ABC and a point D in the triangle, a ray emanating from any vertex of the triangle and passing through D intersects the opposite side.

Theorems

Chapter 1: Fundamental Ideas

Theorem 1.1: If two different lines intersect, then they intersect in exactly one point.

Theorem 1.2: If a point lies outside a line, then exactly one plane contains both the line and the point.

Theorem 1.3: If two different lines intersect, then exactly one plane contains both lines.

Theorem 1.4: A line segment has exactly one midpoint.

Theorem 1.5: If two angles are complementary to the same angle, or to equal angles, then they are equal to each other.

Theorem 1.6: If two angles are supplementary to the same angle, or to equal angles, then they are equal to each other.

Theorem 1.7: Given two distinct lines in a plane, either they are parallel or they intersect at exactly one point.

Theorem 1.8: Let ℓ, m, and n be three distinct lines in a plane. If $\ell \parallel m$ and $m \parallel n$, then $\ell \parallel n$.

Theorem 1.9: Vertical angles are equal in measure.

Theorem 1.10: In a plane, if ℓ is a line and P is a point on ℓ, then there is exactly one line passing through P and perpendicular to ℓ.

Theorem 1.11: A nonzero angle has exactly one bisector.

Theorem 1.12: A line segment has exactly one perpendicular bisector.

Chapter 2: Basic Rigid Motions

Theorem 2.1: Given a point O and an angle $0 \le \theta \le 180°$, there is a clockwise or counterclockwise rotation of θ degrees around O.

Theorem 2.2: Let ρ be the 180° rotation around a given point O and let P be a point other than O. Then P, O, and $\rho(P)$ are collinear and P and $\rho(P)$ lie in different half-lines separated by O.

Theorem 2.3: Let ℓ be a line and O be a point not on ℓ. Let ρ be the 180° rotation around O. Then ρ maps ℓ to a line parallel to ℓ.

Theorem 2.4: In a plane, two distinct lines perpendicular to the same line are parallel.

Theorem 2.5: Given a line ℓ and a point P not on line ℓ, there is exactly one line passing through P and perpendicular to ℓ.

Theorem 2.6: Suppose ℓ_1 and ℓ_2 are two parallel lines and ℓ is a transversal intersecting ℓ_1 and ℓ_2. Then alternate interior angles are equal.

Theorem 2.7: Suppose ℓ_1 and ℓ_2 are two parallel lines and ℓ is a transversal intersecting ℓ_1 and ℓ_2. Then corresponding angles are equal.

Theorem 2.8: Suppose ℓ_1 and ℓ_2 are two parallel lines and ℓ is a transversal intersecting ℓ_1 and ℓ_2. Then alternate exterior angles are equal.

Theorem 2.9: Suppose ℓ_1 and ℓ_2 are two parallel lines and ℓ is a transversal intersecting ℓ_1 and ℓ_2. Then consecutive interior angles are supplementary.

Theorem 2.10: Suppose ℓ_1 and ℓ_2 are two parallel lines and ℓ is a transversal intersecting ℓ_1 and ℓ_2. Then consecutive exterior angles are supplementary.

Theorem 2.11: Suppose ℓ_1 and ℓ_2 are two lines and ℓ is a transversal intersecting ℓ_1 and ℓ_2. If alternate interior angles are equal, then $\ell_1 \parallel \ell_2$.

Theorem 2.12: Suppose ℓ_1 and ℓ_2 are two lines and ℓ is a transversal intersecting ℓ_1 and ℓ_2. If corresponding angles are equal, then $\ell_1 \parallel \ell_2$.

Theorem 2.13: Suppose ℓ_1 and ℓ_2 are two lines and ℓ is a transversal intersecting ℓ_1 and ℓ_2. If alternate exterior angles are equal, then $\ell_1 \parallel \ell_2$.

Theorem 2.14: Suppose ℓ_1 and ℓ_2 are two lines and ℓ is a transversal intersecting ℓ_1 and ℓ_2. If consecutive interior angles are supplementary, then $\ell_1 \parallel \ell_2$.

Theorem 2.15: Suppose ℓ_1 and ℓ_2 are two lines and ℓ is a transversal intersecting ℓ_1 and ℓ_2. If consecutive exterior angles are supplementary, then $\ell_1 \parallel \ell_2$.

Theorem 2.16: Opposite sides of a parallelogram are equal.

Theorem 2.17: The angles of a parallelogram at opposite vertices are equal.

Theorem 2.18: Given a line in the plane, there is a reflection across that line.

Theorem 2.19: Given any vector, there is a translation along that vector.

Chapter 3: Triangles and Congruence

Theorem 3.1 (Exterior Angle Theorem): An exterior angle of a triangle is equal to the sum of the two remote (nonadjacent) interior angles.

Theorem 3.2 (Angle Sum Theorem): The sum of the interior angles of any triangle is 180°.

Theorem 3.3: Each angle of an equiangular triangle has a measure of 60°.

Theorem 3.4: The base angles of an isosceles triangle are equal.

Theorem 3.5: In an isosceles triangle, the perpendicular bisector of the base, the angle bisector of the vertex angle, the median from the top vertex to the base, and the altitude from the top vertex to the base all coincide.

Theorem 3.6: A point is on the perpendicular bisector of a line segment if and only if it is equidistant from the endpoints of the segment.

Theorem 3.7: A triangle is equilateral if and only if the triangle is equiangular.

Theorem 3.8: If two sides of a triangle are unequal, then the measures of the angles opposite these sides are unequal, and the greater angle is opposite the greater side.

Theorem 3.9: If two angles of a triangle are unequal, then the measures of the sides opposite these angles are also unequal, and the longer side is opposite the greater angle.

Theorem 3.10 (Triangle Inequality Theorem): The sum of the lengths of any two sides of a triangle is greater than the length of the third side.

Theorem 3.11: If R is a reflection across a line ℓ, then $R \circ R = I$.

Theorem 3.12: If ρ_1 is the counterclockwise rotation around a point O by an angle θ and if ρ_2 is a clockwise rotation around the same point O by the same angle θ, then $\rho_1 \circ \rho_2 = I$.

Theorem 3.13: If T_1 is the translation along the vector $\overline{AB}$ and T_2 is the translation along the vector $\overline{BA}$, then $T_1 \circ T_2 = I$.

Theorem 3.14: A congruence:
(i) maps lines to lines, rays to rays, and segments to segments.
(ii) maps line segments to line segments of equal length.
(iii) maps an angle to an angle of the same degree.

Theorem 3.15: A line segment is congruent to a line segment of equal length.

Theorem 3.16: An angle is congruent to an angle of the same degree.

Theorem 3.17 (SAS Theorem): Given two triangles $\triangle ABC$ and $\triangle DEF$ so that $m\angle A = m\angle D$, $AB = DE$, and $AC = DF$, then the triangles are congruent.

Theorem 3.18 (ASA Theorem): Given two triangles $\triangle ABC$ and $\triangle DEF$ so that $m\angle A = m\angle D$, $m\angle B = m\angle E$, and $AB = DE$, then the triangles are congruent.

Theorem 3.19 (AAS Theorem): If two angles and a side not between them in one triangle are congruent to the corresponding parts in another triangle, then the triangles are congruent.

Theorem 3.20 (HL Theorem): If two right triangles have equal hypotenuses and one pair of equal legs, then the two triangles are congruent.

Theorem 3.21 (SSS Theorem): Two triangles with three equal sides are congruent.

Theorem 3.22: Two circles of the same radius are congruent. Let C_1 and C_2 be the two circles so that their centers are O_1 and O_2. Let r be the common radius. Let T be the translation along the vector $\overrightarrow{O_2O_1}$. Then $T(C_2) = C_1$, because translation preserves lengths of line segments.

Chapter 4: Polygons

Theorem 4.1: The sum of the interior angles of a quadrilateral is 360°.

Theorem 4.2: The sum of the angles of a pentagon is 540°.

Theorem 4.3: The sum of the interior angles of a hexagon is four times 180°.

Theorem 4.4: Any n-gon can be triangulated.

Theorem 4.5: The sum of the interior angles of an n-gon is $(n-2)$ times 180°.

Theorem 4.6: The sum of the exterior angles of a convex n-gon, one at each vertex, is 360°.

Theorem 4.7: In a quadrilateral, if a pair of opposite sides are both parallel and equal in length, then the quadrilateral is a parallelogram.

Theorem 4.8: Consecutive angles of a parallelogram are supplementary.

Theorem 4.9: The opposite angles of a parallelogram are equal.

Theorem 4.10: If an angle of a quadrilateral is supplementary to both of its consecutive angles, then the quadrilateral is a parallelogram.

Theorem 4.11: If both pairs of opposite angles of a quadrilateral are equal, then it is a parallelogram.

Theorem 4.12: The diagonals of a parallelogram bisect each other.

Theorem 4.13: If the diagonals of a quadrilateral bisect each other, then it is a parallelogram.

Theorem 4.14: A rectangle is a parallelogram.

Theorem 4.15: The diagonals of a rectangle are equal.

Theorem 4.16: A rhombus is a parallelogram.

Theorem 4.17: The diagonals of a rhombus bisect opposite angles.

Theorem 4.18: The diagonals of a rhombus are perpendicular to one another.

Theorem 4.19: Base angles of an isosceles trapezoid are equal.

Theorem 4.20: Diagonals of an isosceles trapezoid are equal.

Theorem 4.21 (Midpoint Theorem): The segment joining the midpoints of two sides of a triangle is parallel to the third side and is half as long as the third side.

Theorem 4.22: The perpendicular bisectors of the three sides of a triangle are concurrent.

Theorem 4.23: There is a unique circle passing through the vertices of a triangle whose center is the circumcenter.

Theorem 4.24: The three altitudes of a triangle are concurrent.

Theorem 4.25: The angle bisector of an angle is the collection of all points equidistant from the two sides of the angle.

Theorem 4.26: The three angle bisectors of a triangle are concurrent.

Theorem 4.27: The incenter of a triangle is equidistant from all three sides of the triangle.

Theorem 4.28: The three medians of a triangle are concurrent.

Theorem 4.29: If F is the centroid of a triangle, then on each median, the distance from F to the vertex is twice the distance from F to the opposite side.

Chapter 5: Similarity

Theorem 5.1 (Fundamental Theorem of Similarity, or *FTS):* Let D be the dilation with center O and scale factor $r > 0$ and $r \neq 1$. Let P and Q be two points so that O, P, and Q are noncollinear. If $D(P) = P'$ and $D(Q) = Q'$, then $\overline{P'Q'} \parallel \overline{PQ}$ and $P'Q' = r(PQ)$.

Theorem 5.2: Let D be the dilation with center O and scale factor $r > 0$. If P and Q are two points in the plane, then $D(PQ) = r(PQ)$. That is, the dilation changes distance by a factor of r.

Theorem 5.3: A dilation
(i) maps lines to lines, rays to rays, and segments to segments.
(ii) maps a line passing through the center O to itself.
(iii) maps a line not passing through O to a line parallel to it.

Theorem 5.4: A dilation preserves degrees of angles.

Theorem 5.5 (Fundamental Theorem of Similarity 2): Let $\triangle ABC$ be a triangle and let P be a point on ray $\overrightarrow{AB}$. Suppose a line passing through P and parallel to line $\overleftrightarrow{BC}$ intersects ray $\overrightarrow{AC}$ at Q. Then $\dfrac{AP}{AB} = \dfrac{AQ}{AC} = \dfrac{PQ}{BC}$.

Theorem 5.6: Any two circles are similar.

Theorem 5.7 (Cross-Multiplication Algorithm): If a, b, c, and d are nonzero real numbers, then $\dfrac{a}{b} = \dfrac{c}{d}$ if and only if $ad = bc$.

Theorem 5.8: Suppose ABC and PQR are two triangles so that $\triangle ABC \sim \triangle PQR$. Then $m\angle A = m\angle P$, $m\angle B = m\angle Q$, $m\angle C = m\angle R$, and $\dfrac{AB}{PQ} = \dfrac{BC}{QR} = \dfrac{CA}{RP}$.

Theorem 5.9 (SAS Theorem for Similarity): Given two triangles $\triangle ABC$ and $\triangle PQR$, if $m\angle A = m\angle P$ and $\dfrac{AB}{PQ} = \dfrac{AC}{PR}$, then $\triangle ABC \sim \triangle PQR$.

Theorem 5.10 (AA Theorem for Similarity): Two triangles with two pairs of equal angles are similar.

Theorem 5.11 (SSS Theorem for Similarity): If $\triangle ABC$ and $\triangle PQR$ are triangles so that $\dfrac{AB}{PQ} = \dfrac{BC}{QR} = \dfrac{AC}{PR}$, then $\triangle ABC \sim \triangle PQR$.

Theorem 5.12: Suppose $\triangle ABC$ and $\triangle PQR$ are triangles so that $\triangle ABC \sim \triangle PQR$. Then $\dfrac{AB}{AC} = \dfrac{PQ}{PR}, \dfrac{AB}{BC} = \dfrac{PQ}{QR}$, and $\dfrac{AC}{BC} = \dfrac{PR}{QR}$.

Theorem 5.13: If two triangles are similar, then the ratio of any two corresponding segments (such as altitudes, medians, or angle bisectors) equals the ratio of any two corresponding sides.

Theorem 5.14 (Pythagorean Theorem): Let $\triangle ABC$ be a right triangle with $m\angle B = 90°$. Then $AC^2 = AB^2 + BC^2$.

Theorem 5.15 (Converse of the Pythagorean Theorem): Suppose $\triangle ABC$ is a right triangle so that $AB^2 + BC^2 = AC^2$. Then $\triangle ABC$ is a right triangle with $m\angle B = 90°$.

Theorem 5.16: Let $\triangle ABC$ be a triangle so that D and E are the midpoints of the segments $\overline{AC}$ and $\overline{AB}$. Suppose segments $\overline{CD}$ and $\overline{BE}$ meet at F; then $FE = \dfrac{1}{2} BF$.

Chapter 6: Circles

Theorem 6.1: In a circle, if two central angles have equal measures, then their corresponding arcs have equal measures.

Theorem 6.2: In a circle, if two arcs have equal measures, then their corresponding central angles have equal measures.

Theorem 6.3: Let C be a circle with center O and let ℓ be a line passing through O. If R is the reflection across ℓ, then $R(C) = C$. $R(C) = C$ means R maps C to C. We say C is symmetric with respect to ℓ.

Theorem 6.4: A circle and a line meet at no more than two points.

Theorem 6.5: Let C be a circle with center O. If a line ℓ is tangent to C at a point P, then ℓ is perpendicular to the line $\overrightarrow{OP}$.

Theorem 6.6: Let C be a circle with center O and let P be a point on C. If a line ℓ passing through P is perpendicular to the line $\overrightarrow{OP}$, then ℓ is tangent to C.

Theorem 6.7: There is exactly one circle tangent to all three sides of a triangle.

Theorem 6.8: Let $\overline{PQ}$ be a diameter of a circle C with center O and let R be a point on C distinct from points P and Q. Then $m\angle PQR = 90°$.

Theorem 6.9: Let $\overline{PQ}$ be a chord of C and let R be a point on C distinct from points P and Q. If the $m\angle PRQ = 90°$, then $\overline{PQ}$ is a diameter.

Theorem 6.10: From a point P outside a given circle C, there are exactly two lines tangent to C.

Theorem 6.11: Let P be a point outside a given circle C, and suppose the points of tangency of the two tangent lines to C are Q and R. Then $PQ = PR$.

Theorem 6.12: Fix an arc on a circle C. Then *any* inscribed angle subtended by the arc is half of the central angle subtended by the arc.

Theorem 6.13: Two inscribed angles subtended by the same chord of a circle have equal measures.

Theorem 6.14: The measure of an inscribed angle subtended by a diameter of a circle is $90°$.

Theorem 6.15: In a circle, if two chords $\overline{AB}$ and $\overline{CD}$ are equal in measure, then the angles subtended by the corresponding minor arcs are equal in measure.

Theorem 6.16: In a circle, if angles subtended by two minor arcs are equal in measure, then their corresponding chords are equal in measure.

Theorem 6.17: Let four points P, Q, R, and S be given. Suppose P and R lie on the same side of the line $\overleftrightarrow{PS}$. If $m\angle QPS = m\angle QRS$, then P, Q, R, and S are concyclic.

Theorem 6.18: Let four points A, B, C, and D be given. Suppose points A and C lie on the same side of line $\overleftrightarrow{BD}$. If A, B, C, and D are concyclic, then $m\angle BAD = m\angle BCD$.

Theorem 6.19: Let four points A, B, C, and D be given. Suppose A and C lie on opposite sides of the line $\overleftrightarrow{BD}$. If A, B, C, and D are concyclic, then $m\angle BAD + m\angle BCD = 180°$.

Theorem 6.20: Let four points P, Q, R, and S be given. Suppose P and R lie on opposite sides of the line $\overleftrightarrow{QS}$. If $m\angle QPS + m\angle QRS = 180°$, then P, Q, R, and S are concyclic.

Theorem 6.21: The measure of an angle formed by a tangent and a chord meeting at the point of tangency is equal to the measure of an inscribed angle subtended by the chord.

Theorem 6.22: If a diameter is perpendicular to a chord, then it bisects the chord.

Theorem 6.23: If two chords are equal in measure in a circle, then they are equidistant from the center.

Theorem 6.24: If two chords of a circle intersect inside the circle, then the product of the lengths of secant segments of one chord is equal to the product of the lengths of secant segments of the other chord.

Theorem 6.25: If two chords of a circle intersect outside the circle, then the product of the lengths of secant segments of one chord is equal to the product of the lengths of secant segments of the other chord.

Theorem 6.26. Let $\overline{RS}$ be a chord of a circle C and let ℓ be a tangent line to C at Q, which is a point other than R or S. Suppose ℓ and $\overleftrightarrow{RS}$ intersect at P. Then the product of the lengths of the secant segments of $\overline{RS}$ is equal to the square of the length of the tangent segment $\overline{PQ}$. That is, $PS \cdot PR = PQ^2$.

Theorem 6.27. If two tangent segments intersect outside of a circle, they have equal lengths.

Chapter 7: Length and Area

Theorem 7.1: The length of a polygonal curve is the sum of the lengths of the segments of the polygonal curve.

Theorem 7.2: The area of a rectangle with sides m and n units is mn units^2, where m and n are positive whole numbers.

Theorem 7.3: The area of a rectangle with sides m and n units is mn units^2, where m and n are positive fractions.

Theorem 7.4: The area of a rectangle with sides m and n units is mn units^2, where m and n are positive real numbers.

Theorem 7.5: The area of a square with side n units is n^2 units^2.

Theorem 7.6: The area of a right triangle is *half* the base times the height: $\frac{1}{2}\left(\text{base} \times \text{height}\right)$ or $\frac{1}{2}(bh)$.

Theorem 7.7. The area of a $\triangle ABC$ with altitude $\overline{AD}$ and base $\overline{BC}$ is $\frac{1}{2}(BC)(AD)$.

Theorem 7.8: The area of a parallelogram is (base)(height) or bh.

Theorem 7.9: The area of a trapezoid is $\frac{1}{2}\left(\text{base}_1 + \text{base}_2\right)\left(\text{height}\right)$.

Theorem 7.10: The area of a regular n-gon is $\frac{1}{2}(a)(p)$, where p is the perimeter of the n-gon ($p = ns$) and a is the length of the apothem.

Theorem 7.11: Let T be a dilation with the scale factor $r > 0$. Let $ABCD$ be a rectangle so that $T(ABCD) = ABCD'$. Then the area of $ABCD'$ is $r^2 \cdot$ area of $ABCD$.

Theorem 7.12: Let T be a dilation with the scale factor $r > 0$. Let $\triangle ABC$ be a triangle so that $T(ABC) = \triangle ABC'$. Then the area of $\triangle ABC'$ is $r^2 \cdot$ area of $\triangle ABC$.

Theorem 7.13: Let T be a dilation with the scale factor $r > 0$. Let P be a polygon so that $T(P) = P'$. Then the area of $P' = r^2 \cdot$ area of P.

Theorem 7.14: The area of the unit circle is π.

Theorem 7.15: The area of a circle with radius r is πr^2.

Theorem 7.16: The circumference of a circle with radius r is $2\pi r$.

Chapter 8: Geometric Solids

Theorem 8.1: The lateral area, *LA*, of a right prism with altitude *h* and base perimeter *p* is given by the following equation:

$$LA_{\text{right prism}} = (p)(h) \text{ units}^2$$

Theorem 8.2: The total surface area, *TA*, of a right prism with lateral area *LA* and a base area *B* is given by the following equation:

$$TA_{\text{right prism}} = LA + 2B \text{ or } TA_{\text{right prism}} = (p)(h) + 2B$$

Theorem 8.3: The volume, *V*, of a right prism with a base area *B* and an altitude *h* is given by the following equation:

$$V_{\text{right prism}} = (B)(h) \text{ units}^3$$

Theorem 8.4: The lateral area, *LA*, of a right circular cylinder with a base circumference *C* and an altitude *h* is given by the following equation:

$$LA_{\text{right circular cylinder}} = (C)(h) \text{ units}^2$$
$$= (2\pi r)(h) \text{ units}^2$$

Theorem 8.5: The total surface area, *TA*, of a right circular cylinder with lateral area *LA* and a base area *B* is given by the following equation:

$$TA_{\text{right circular cylinder}} = LA + 2B \text{ units}^2$$
$$= (2\pi r)(h) + 2\pi r^2 \text{ units}^2$$
$$= 2\pi r(h + r) \text{ units}^2$$

Theorem 8.6: The volume of a right circular cylinder, *V*, with a base area *B* and altitude *h* is given by the following equation:

$$V_{\text{right circular cylinder}} = (B)(h) \text{ units}^3$$
$$= (\pi r^2)(h) \text{ units}^3$$

Theorem 8.7: The lateral area, *LA*, of a regular pyramid with slant height *l* and base perimeter *p* is given by the following equation:

$$LA_{\text{regular pyramid}} = \frac{1}{2}(p)(l) \text{ units}^2$$

Theorem 8.8: The total surface area, *TA*, of a regular pyramid with lateral area *LA* and base area *B* is given by the following equation:

$$TA_{\text{regular pyramid}} = LA + B \text{ units}^2$$

$$= \frac{1}{2}(p)(l) + B \text{ units}^2$$

Theorem 8.9: The volume, *V*, of a regular pyramid with base area *B* and altitude *h* is given by the following equation:

$$V_{\text{regular pyramid}} = \frac{1}{3}(B)(h) \text{ units}^3$$

Theorem 8.10: The lateral area, *LA*, of a right circular cone with base circumference *C* and slant height *l* is given by the following equation:

$$LA_{\text{right circular cone}} = \frac{1}{2}(C)(l) \text{ units}^2$$

$$= \frac{1}{2}(2\pi)(r)(l) \text{ units}^2$$

$$= \pi rl \text{ units}^2$$

Theorem 8.11: The total surface area, *TA*, of a right circular cone with lateral area *LA* and base area *B* is given by the following equation:

$$TA_{\text{right circular cone}} = LA + B \text{ units}^2$$

$$= \pi rl + \pi r^2 \text{ units}^2$$

$$= \pi r(l + r) \text{ units}^2$$

Theorem 8.12: The volume, *V*, of a right circular cone with base area *B* and altitude *h* is given by the following equation:

$$V_{\text{right circular cone}} = \frac{1}{3}(B)(h) \text{ units}^3$$

$$= \frac{1}{3}(\pi r^2)(h) \text{ units}^3$$

Theorem 8.13: The surface area, *SA*, of a sphere with radius *r* is given by the following equation:

$$SA_{\text{sphere}} = 4\pi r^2 \text{ units}^2$$

Theorem 8.14: The volume of a sphere, *V*, with radius *r* is given by the following equation:

$$V_{\text{sphere}} = \frac{4}{3}\pi r^3 \text{ units}^3$$

Chapter 9: Coordinate Geometry

Theorem 9.1 (One-Dimensional Distance Formula): The distance between two points $P(x_1)$ and $Q(x_2)$ in 1-space is $|x_2 - x_1|$.

Theorem 9.2 (Two-Dimensional Distance Formula): If the coordinates of two points in 2-space are (x_1, y_1) and (x_2, y_2), then the distance, *d*, between the two points is given by the following formula:

$$d = \sqrt{\left(x_2 - x_1\right)^2 + \left(y_2 - y_1\right)^2}$$

Theorem 9.3 (Midpoint Formula for One-Dimensional Space): The midpoint between $P(x_1)$ and $Q\left(x_2\right)$ is $\dfrac{x_1 + x_2}{2}$.

Theorem 9.4 (Midpoint Formula for Two-Dimensional Space): Suppose $P(x_1, y_1)$ and $Q(x_2, y_2)$ are two points in 2-space. Then the coordinates of the midpoint *M* of $\overline{PQ}$ are $\left(\dfrac{x_1 + x_2}{2}, \dfrac{y_1 + y_2}{2}\right)$.

Theorem 9.5: Consider a circle with a center at point *C*(*h*, *k*) and radius *r*. Then the equation of the circle is $(x - h)^2 + (y - k)^2 = r^2$.

Theorem 9.6 (Slope Theorem): Consider a nonvertical line ℓ. Suppose $A(x_1, y_1)$ and $B(x_2, y_2)$ are two points on ℓ. Then the slope *m* of ℓ is $m = \dfrac{y_1 - y_2}{x_1 - x_2}$.

Theorem 9.7: If two nonvertical lines are parallel, then they have the same slope.

Theorem 9.8: If two lines have the same slope, then the lines are nonvertical parallel lines.

Theorem 9.9: Suppose ℓ_1 and ℓ_2 are two perpendicular lines with slopes m_1 and m_2, respectively. Then $m_1 = -\dfrac{1}{m_2}$.

Theorem 9.10: Suppose ℓ_1 and ℓ_2 are two lines with slopes m_1 and m_2, respectively. If $m_1 = -\dfrac{1}{m_2}$, then $\ell_1 \perp \ell_2$.

Theorem 9.11: The graph of a linear equation $x = c$, where c is a constant, is the vertical line passing through the point $(c, 0)$.

Theorem 9.12: Every vertical line is a graph of a linear equation of the form $x = c$, where $(c, 0)$ is the point of intersection of the vertical line and the x-axis.

Theorem 9.13: The graph of a linear equation $y = c$, where c is a constant, is the horizontal line passing through the point $(0, c)$.

Theorem 9.14: Every horizontal line is a graph of a linear equation of the form $y = c$, where $(0, c)$ is the point of intersection of the horizontal line and the y-axis.

Theorem 9.15: The line joining any two distinct points of a graph of $y = mx + k$, $m \neq 0$ has the slope m.

Theorem 9.16: There is only one line passing through a given point with a given slope.

Theorem 9.17: The graph of a linear equation $y = mx + k$, where $m \neq 0$, is a nonvertical line with slope m and passing through $(0, k)$.

Theorem 9.18: The graph of a linear equation is a line.

Theorem 9.19: Any nonvertical and nonhorizontal line is the graph of a linear equation.

Theorem 9.20: Any line is a graph of a linear equation.

Theorem 9.21: The equation of a line passing through $P(x_1, y_1)$ and $Q(x_2, y_2)$ is $y - y_1 = m(x - x_1)$, where $m = \dfrac{y_2 - y_1}{x_2 - x_1}$ and $x_2 \neq x_1$.

INDEX

1-space (one-dimensional space)
    defined, 168
    Distance Formula, 171
    Midpoint Formula for, 174
2-space (two-dimensional space)
    defined, 169
    Distance Formula, 171–173
    Midpoint Formula for, 174–176

A

AA Theorem for Similarity, 90–91, 97,
    122–123, 124, 188, 228
AAS Theorem, 58, 226
acute angles, 15–16, 213
acute triangles, 45, 213
adjacent angles, 13, 213
alternate exterior angles, 31, 213
alternate interior angles, 31, 213
altitude
    base and, 46–47
    of prisms, 152, 213
    of pyramids, 158, 213
    of triangles, 46–47, 213
angle bisector
    defined, 21, 213
    of triangles, 48
angle subtended by the arc, 111
Angle Sum Theorem, 44, 66, 75, 119,
    224
angles
    about, 11–13
    acute, 15–16, 213
    adjacent, 13, 213
    alternate exterior, 31, 213
    alternate interior, 31, 213
    base, 45–46, 74, 213
    central, 13–14, 214

    classifying triangles by, 44–46
    complementary, 17–18, 214
    consecutive exterior, 31, 214
    consecutive interior, 31, 214
    corresponding, 31, 215
    defined, 11, 213
    exterior, 31, 42–43, 67–68, 214
    inequalities regarding, 51–52
    inscribed, 110–117, 215
    interior, 31, 65–67, 214
    obtuse, 16–17, 216
    right, 15, 218
    sides of, 11, 218
    special, 15–18
    special names for, 45–46
    straight, 11, 219
    supplementary, 18, 219
    vertical, 19–20, 219
    zero, 11
apothem of a regular polygon, 140, 213
arbitrary triangles, 135–137
arcs
    angle subtended by, 111
    of circles, 14, 104–117, 213
    degree measure of a major, 104, 215
    degree measure of a minor, 104, 215
    inscribed angles and, 110–117
    intercepted, 111, 215
    major, 104, 215, 216
    minor, 104, 215, 216
    opposite, 110
area
    about, 127–128
    of circles, 143–147
    defined, 127, 213
    finding for a polygon, 141
    formulas for, 148, 165

area (*cont.*)
    lateral, 152–153, 165, 216
    of parallelograms, 137–138
    of rectangles, 130–134
    of regular polygons, 140–142
    of squares, 130–134
    theorems for, 231
    of trapezoids, 138–140
    of triangles, 134–137
    of unit circle, 143, 213
ASA Theorem, 57–58, 225

B

base angles
    of isosceles triangles, 45–46, 213
    of trapezoids, 74, 213
bases
    altitude and, 46–47
    of isosceles triangles, 45–46, 213
    of prisms, 151, 213
    of trapezoids, 74, 213
    of triangles, 45, 213
basic rigid motions of a plane
    about, 25
    defined, 214
    reflections, 36–37, 214, 218
    rotations, 26–30, 214, 218
    theorems for, 223–224
    translations, 37–38, 214, 219
    transversals, 30–36, 219

C

Cartesian coordinate plane, 169, 190–191
center
    of circles (spheres), 13, 103, 164, 214
    of regular polygons, 140, 214
central angle of a circle, 13–14, 214
centroid of a triangle, 81, 214
chords
    of circles, 104, 214
    defined, 13
    segments of intersecting, 121–125
circles
    about, 13–15
    arcs of, 14, 104–117, 213
    area of, 143–147
    area of unit, 143, 213
    center of, 13, 103, 164, 214
    central angle of, 13–14, 214
    chords of, 104, 214

    circumference of, 143–147
    closed disk of the given, 13
    concyclic points, 117–121, 214
    defined, 13, 214
    degrees of, 14
    diameter of, 13, 104, 215
    equations of, 176–178
    formulas for, 148
    inscribed angles, 110–117, 211, 215
    parts of, 103–104
    quarter, 146
    radius of, 13, 104, 217
    secant line to, 106, 218
    sector of, 14, 218
    segments of intersecting chords and
        tangents, 121–125
    theorems for, 229–230
    unit, 13, 143, 219
circular cones, right, 161–163,
    165, 218
circular cylinders, right, 156–158, 165,
    218
circumcenter of the triangle, 78, 214
circumcircle of the triangle, 78, 214
circumference
    of circles, 143–147
    defined, 127, 214
    formulas for, 148, 165
    of unit circle, 143
clockwise rotation, 26–30
closed disk of the given circle, 13
collinear points, 6, 214
complementary angles, 17–18, 214
concave polygons, 214. *See also* convex
    polygons
concurrence theorems, 78–81
concurrent lines, 78, 214
concyclic points, 117–121, 214
cones, right circular, 161–163, 165, 218
congruence
    defined, 84, 214
    theorems for, 55–63, 224–226
    triangles and, 53–55, 214
consecutive exterior angles, 31, 214
consecutive interior angles, 31, 214
consecutive sides of a polygon, 22–23,
    214
Converse of the Pythagorean Theorem,
    98–99, 214, 228. *See also* Pythagorean
    Theorem

convex polygons. *See also* concave
   polygons
   defined, 214
   exterior angles of, 67–68
convex subset, 11
coordinate, 9, 168, 214
coordinate axes, 169
coordinate geometry
   about, 168–171
   equations of circles, 176–178
   formulas for, 199
   linear equations in *x* and *y*, 190–199,
      216
   lines on a coordinate plane, 178–180
   Midpoint Formula for One-
      Dimensional Space, 174, 234
   Midpoint Formula for Two-
      Dimensional Space, 174–176, 234
   One-Dimensional Distance Formula,
      171, 234
   Slope Theorem, 180–190, 234
   theorems for, 234–235
   Two-Dimensional Distance Formula,
      171–173, 234
coordinate planes. *See also* two-
   dimensional space (2-space)
   defined, 169, 215
   lines on, 178–180
coordinates of a point, 169, 215
corresponding angles, 31, 215
corresponding parts of triangles, 55–63, 215
counterclockwise rotation, 26
Crossbar Postulate, 48, 222
Cross-Multiplication Algorithm, 89,
   91–92, 228
cubes
   defined, 154, 215
   volume of a, 155
cubic inch, 155, 215
cylinders
   defined, 215
   right circular, 156–158, 165, 218

D

decagon
   defined, 215
   as a regular polygon, 69
degree measure of a major arc, 104, 215
degree measure of a minor arc, 104, 215
degree measure of a semicircle, 104, 215

degrees
   of circles, 14
   defined, 215
Descartes, Rene, 169
diagonal of a polygon, 22, 215
diameter of a circle, 13, 104, 215
dilation
   about, 84–85
   diameter of, 215
   of scale factor *r* on area of polygons,
      142

E

edges
   lateral, 152, 158, 216
   of triangles, 21
ending point, 37
equation of a line
   slope-intercept form of, 194, 199, 218
   standard form for the, 194, 199, 219
equations
   of circles, 176–178
   lines, 190–199, 216
equiangular triangle, 45, 215
equilateral triangles, 23–24, 44, 45, 215
exterior angle sum, 67–68, 215
Exterior Angle Theorem, 43, 108,
   112–113, 118, 224
exterior angles
   alternate, 31, 213
   consecutive, 31, 214
   of convex polygons, 67–68
   of a triangle, 42–43, 215

F

faces, lateral, 152, 158, 216
formulas
   area, 148, 165
   circles, 148
   circumference, 148, 165
   coordinate geometry, 199
   geometric solids, 165
   lateral area, 165
   parallelograms, 148
   perimeter, 148, 165
   rectangles, 148
   regular polygons, 148
   regular pyramids, 165
   right circular cones, 165
   right circular cylinders, 165

formulas (*cont.*)
    right prisms, 165
    spheres, 165
    squares, 148
    total area, 165
    trapezoids, 148
    triangles, 148
    volume, 165
FTS (Fundamental Theorem of Similarity), 85–87, 91, 109, 227, 228
Fundamental Fact of Fraction Pairs, 132
Fundamental Theorem of Similarity (FTS), 85–87, 91, 109, 227, 228
fundamentals
    theorems for, 222–223

G

geometric solids
    about, 151
    formulas, 165
    prisms, 151–154, 165, 213, 216, 217, 218, 219
    pyramids, 158–161, 165, 213, 216, 217, 218, 219
    right circular cones, 161–163, 165, 218
    right circular cylinders, 156–158, 165, 218
    right prisms, 152–156, 165, 216, 218
    spheres, 13, 103, 164, 214, 217, 219
    theorems for, 232–234
geometry. *See also* coordinate geometry; *specific topics*
    about, 5
    angles, 11–13, 213
    circles, 13–15, 214
    lines, 6, 216
    midpoint of a line segment, 10–11, 216
    parallel lines, 19, 217
    planes, 6, 7, 217
    points, 6, 217
    polygons, 22, 217
    postulates, 7–9, 217
    quadrilaterals, 21–24, 217
    ray, 11, 217
    segments, 9–10
    sets, 7, 218
    special angles, 15–18
    theorems, 7–9, 219
    triangles, 21–23, 42, 219

H

heptagon
    defined, 215
    as a regular polygon, 69
hexagon
    defined, 22, 215
    as a regular polygon, 69
hexagonal pyramid, regular, 159
HL Theorem, 58–59, 120–121, 125, 226
horizontal lines, 178, 179
hypotenuse
    defined, 215
    of triangles, 46

I

identity transformation, 54
incenter of a triangle, 80, 215
inequalities, regarding sides and angles of triangles, 51–52
inscribed angles
    arcs and, 110–117
    defined, 111, 215
    intercepting the arc, 111
intercepted arc, 111, 215
interior angle sum, 65–67, 215
interior angles
    alternate, 31, 213
    consecutive, 31, 214
interior space, of a solid, 154–156
intersecting lines, 19–20, 215
isosceles right triangle, 216
isosceles trapezoid, 74, 216
isosceles triangles
    about, 23–24, 44, 45
    base angles of, 46, 213
    bases of, 213
    defined, 216
    legs of, 216
    special features of, 48–50
    vertex angle of, 45–46, 219

L

lateral area
    formulas for, 165
    of right prisms, 152–153, 216
lateral edges
    of prisms, 152, 216
    of pyramids, 158, 216

lateral faces
  of prisms, 152, 216
  of pyramids, 158, 216
legs
  of isosceles triangles, 21, 216
  of right triangles, 21, 216
  of trapezoids, 74, 216
  of triangles, 21, 45, 46
length
  about, 127–128
  of line segments, 128–129
  of polygonal curves, 129–130
  rectangles, 130–134
  squares, 130–134
  theorems for, 231
line segments
  about, 9–10
  defined, 216
  length of, 128–129
  midpoint of, 10–11, 216
  perpendicular bisector of, 21, 217
line separation, 27, 216
Line Separation Postulate, 27, 221–222
linear equations in two variables x and y, 190–199, 216
lines
  concurrent, 78, 214
  on coordinate planes, 178–180
  defined, 6, 216
  equation of, 218, 219
  horizontal, 178, 179
  intersecting, 19–20, 215
  number, 168
  parallel, 19, 184–186, 217
  perpendicular, 20, 187–190, 217
  secant, 106, 218
  slope of, 178–179, 218
  slope-intercept form of the equation of, 194, 199, 218
  standard form of the equation of, 194, 199, 219
  straight, 6
  tangent, 106
  vertical, 178, 180

M

major arc
  defined, 104, 216
  degree measure of a, 104, 215

median
  of trapezoids, 216
  of triangles, 47, 216
Midpoint Formula for One-Dimensional Space, 174, 234
Midpoint Formula for Two-Dimensional Space, 174–176, 234
midpoint of a line segment, 10–11, 216
Midpoint Theorem, 77, 99, 100, 227
minor arc
  defined, 104, 216
  degree measure of a, 104, 215

N

nonagon
  defined, 216
  as a regular polygon, 69
noncollinear points, 6, 216
n-sided polygon (n-gon), 22, 216
number line, 168. *See also* one-dimensional space (1-space)

O

oblique prism, 152, 216
obtuse angles, 16–17, 216
obtuse triangle, 45, 216
octagon
  defined, 216
  as a regular polygon, 69
One-Dimensional Distance Formula, 171, 234
one-dimensional space (1-space)
  defined, 168
  Distance Formula, 171
  Midpoint Formula for, 174
opposite arcs, 110
ordered pair, 168–169, 216
origin, 168, 217
orthocenter of a triangle, 79, 217

P

parallel lines
  defined, 19, 217
  slopes of, 184–186
parallel planes
  defined, 217
  of prisms, 151
Parallel Postulate, 19, 221

parallelograms
    about, 70–72
    area of, 137–138
    defined, 23, 217
    formulas for, 148
    rectangles as, 72
    rhombus as, 72–74
pentagon
    defined, 22, 217
    as a regular polygon, 69
perimeter
    defined, 127, 217
    finding for polygons, 141
    formulas for, 148, 165
perpendicular bisector of a line segment,
    21, 217
perpendicular lines
    defined, 20, 217
    slopes of, 187–190
plane separation, 27, 217
Plane Separation Postulate, 27, 222
planes. *See also* basic rigid motions of a
    plane
    Cartesian coordinate, 169, 190–191
    coordinate, 169, 178–180, 215
    defined, 6, 7, 217
    parallel, 151, 217
    parallel lines in a, 19, 184–186, 217
point of tangency, 106, 217
points
    collinear, 6, 214
    concyclic, 117–121, 214
    coordinates of, 169, 215
    defined, 6, 217
    ending, 37
    noncollinear, 6, 216
    starting, 37
    symmetric, 36
point-slope form of the equation of a line,
    195, 199, 217
polygonal curves
    defined, 217
    length of, 129–130
polygons
    apothem of regular, 140, 213
    center of regular, 140, 214
    concave, 214
    concurrence theorems, 78–81
    consecutive sides of, 22–23, 214
    convex, 67–68, 214

    defined, 22, 217
    diagonals of, 22, 215
    dilation of scale factor *r* on area of,
        142
    exterior angles of convex, 67–68
    finding area for, 141
    Midpoint Theorem, 77
    n-sided (*n*-gon), 22, 216
    parallelograms, 23, 70–72, 137–138,
        148, 217
    regular, 69–70, 140–142, 148, 213,
        214, 217, 218
    similar, 218
    theorems for, 226–227
    trapezoids, 23, 74–77, 138–140, 148,
        213, 216, 219
    triangulation of, 65–67, 219
postulates
    about, 7–9
    appendix of, 221–222
    defined, 7, 217
prisms
    altitude of, 152, 213
    bases of, 151, 213
    defined, 151, 217
    lateral edges of, 152, 216
    lateral faces of, 152, 216
    oblique, 152, 216
    parallel planes of, 151
    right, 152–156, 165, 216, 218, 219
Properties of Reflections Postulate, 37,
    222
Properties of Rigid Motions Postulate, 38,
    222
Properties of Rotations Postulate, 27, 222
Properties of Translations Postulate, 38,
    222
proportional parts, of similar triangles,
    97–98
protractor, 14
Protractor Postulate, 14–15, 221
pyramids
    about, 158
    altitude of, 158, 213
    defined, 217
    lateral edges of, 158, 216
    lateral faces of, 158, 216
    regular, 158–161, 165, 218
    regular hexagonal, 159
    regular triangular, 159

slant height of regular, 159, 218
square, 159
vertex of, 158, 219
Pythagorean Theorem, 98–100, 217, 228.
See also Converse of the Pythagorean
Theorem

Q

quadrants, 169, 217
quadrilaterals
about, 21–24
defined, 217
as regular polygons, 69
special, 23–24
quarter circles, 146

R

radius of a circle (sphere), 13, 104,
217
radius of a regular polygon, 140, 217
ray, 11, 217
rectangles
area of, 130–134
defined, 23, 218
formulas for, 148
lengths of, 130–134
as a parallelogram, 72
reflections, 36–37, 214, 218
regular polygons
about, 69–70
apothem of, 140, 213
area of, 140–142
center of, 140, 214
decagons as, 69, 215
defined, 218
formulas for, 148
heptagons as, 69
hexagons as, 69
nonagons as, 69
octagons as, 69
pentagons as, 69
radius of, 217
triangles as, 69
regular pyramids
about, 158–161, 218
formulas for, 165
slant height of, 159, 218
rhombus
defined, 24, 218
as a parallelogram, 72–74

right angles, 15, 218
right circular cones
about, 161–163
defined, 218
formulas for, 165
right circular cylinders
about, 156–158
defined, 218
formulas for, 165
right prisms
defined, 152, 218
formulas for, 165
lateral area of, 152–153, 216
total surface area of a, 153–154,
219
right triangles
about, 45
area of, 134–135
defined, 218
isosceles, 216
legs of, 21, 216
rotations
about, 26
clockwise, 26–30
counterclockwise, 26
defined, 214, 218
Ruler Postulate, 9–10, 221

S

SAS Theorem, 55–57, 225
SAS Theorem for Similarity, 90, 97, 99,
228
scalene triangle, 44, 45, 218
secant line to a circle, 106, 218
secant segments, 121
sector of a circle, 14, 218
Segment Addition Postulate, 10, 221
segments
defined, 9
of intersecting chords and tangents,
121–125
line, 9–11, 128–129, 216, 217
midpoint of a line, 216
secant, 121
tangent, 124
semicircle
defined, 104, 218
degree measures of, 104, 215
septagon, 218
sets, 7, 218

sides
classifying triangles by, 44–46
inequalities regarding, 51–52
special names for, 45–46
of triangles, 21
sides of an angle, 11, 218
similar polygons, 218
similar triangles, 89–92, 97–98
similarity
about, 83
applications of, 92–96
defined, 88–89, 218
dilation, 84–85, 142, 215
Fundamental Theorem of Similarity
(FTS), 85–87, 91, 109, 227, 228
proportional parts of similar triangles,
97–98
Pythagorean Theorem, 98–100, 217,
228
similar triangles, 89–92, 97–98
theorems for, 227–228
slant height of a regular pyramid, 159, 218
slope of a line, 178–179, 218
Slope Theorem, 180–190, 234
slope-intercept form of the equation of a
line, 194, 199, 218
slopes
defined, 178
of parallel lines, 184–186
of perpendicular lines, 187–190
solids
geometric. *See* geometric solids
interior space of, 154–156
solution set, 190
special angles, 15–18
special quadrilaterals, 23–24
special triangles, 23–24
spheres
center of, 13, 103, 164, 214
defined, 164, 219
formulas for, 165
radius of, 13, 104, 217
square pyramid, regular, 159
squares
area of, 130–134
defined, 23, 219
formulas for, 148
lengths of, 130–134
unit, 130, 219
SSS Theorem, 59–60, 138, 144, 226

SSS Theorem for congruence, 114
SSS Theorem for Similarity, 91, 97, 228
standard form for the equation of a line,
194, 199, 219
starting point, 37
straight angles, 11, 219
straight line, 6
subset, 7, 11
supplementary angles, 18, 219
surface area, of a right prisms, 153–154
symmetric points, 36

T

tangency, point of, 106, 217
tangent line, 106
tangent segment, 124
tangents
defined, 106, 219
segments of intersecting, 121–125
theorems. *See also specific theorems*
about, 7–9
appendix of, 222–235
area, 231
basic rigid motions, 223–224
circles, 229–230
concurrence, 78–81
congruence, 55–63, 224–226
coordinate geometry, 234–235
defined, 7, 219
fundamentals, 222–223
geometric solids, 232–234
length, 231
polygons, 226–227
similarity, 227–228
triangles, 224–226
total area, formulas for, 165
total surface area of a right prism,
153–154, 219
translations, 37–38, 214, 219
transversals, 30–36, 219
trapezoids
about, 74–77
area of, 138–140
base angles of, 74, 213
bases of, 74, 213
defined, 23, 219
formulas for, 148
isosceles, 74, 216
legs of, 74, 216
median of, 216

Triangle Inequality Theorem, 52–53, 225
triangles
    about, 21–23, 42
    acute, 45, 213
    altitude of, 46–47, 213
    angle bisector of, 48
    angle sum of, 44
    arbitrary, 135–137
    area of, 134–137
    base angles of, 45–46 , 213
    bases of, 45, 213
    centroid of, 81, 214
    circumcenter of, 78, 214
    circumcircle of, 78, 214
    classifying by sides or angles, 44–46
    congruence theorems of, 55–63,
      224–226
    congruent, 53–55, 214
    corresponding parts of, 55–63, 215
    defined, 21, 42, 219
    edges of, 21
    equiangular, 45, 215
    equilateral, 23–24, 44, 45, 215
    exterior angles of, 42–43, 215
    formulas for, 148
    hypotenuse of, 46, 215
    incenter of, 80, 215
    inequalities regarding sides and angles,
      51–52
    isosceles, 23–24, 44, 45, 48–50, 213,
      216, 219
    isosceles right, 216
    legs of, 21, 45, 46
    median of, 47, 216
    obtuse, 45, 216
    orthocenter of, 79, 217
    proportional parts of similar, 97–98
    as regular polygons, 69
    right, 45, 134–135, 216, 218
    scalene, 44, 45, 218
    sides of, 21
    similar, 89–92, 97–98
    special, 23–24
    theorems for, 224–226
    Triangle Inequality Theorem, 52–53, 225
    vertices of, 21

triangular pyramid, regular, 159
triangulation of a polygon, 65–67, 219
Two-Dimensional Distance Formula,
    171–173, 234
two-dimensional space (2-space)
    defined, 169
      Distance Formula, 171–173
      Midpoint Formula for, 174–176

U

undefined terms, 6
unit circle, 13, 143, 219
unit squares, 130, 219

V

vector, 37, 219
vertex, 11, 219
vertex angle of an isosceles triangle,
    45–46, 219
vertex of a pyramid, 158, 219
vertical angles, 19–20, 219
vertical lines, 178, 180
vertices, of triangles, 21
volume
    of cubes, 155
    defined, 219
    formulas for, 165

X

x, linear equations in two variables y and,
    190–199, 216
x-axis, 168, 219
x-coordinate (of a point), 169, 219
x-intercept, 184, 220

Y

y, linear equations in two variables x and,
    190–199, 216
y-axis, 168, 220
y-coordinate (of a point), 169, 220
y-intercept, 184, 220

Z

zero angles, 11